D1478216

Eagle in the New World

EAGLE IN THE NEW WORLD

German Immigration to Texas and America

Edited and with an Introduction by
THEODORE GISH *and* RICHARD SPULER

Foreword by RICHARD THOMA

Published for the Texas Committee for the Humanities
by Texas A&M University Press
College Station

Library of Congress Cataloging-in-Publication Data

Eagle in the New World.

   Revised ed. of papers presented at a symposium held at the University of Houston in September, 1983.
   "Published for the Texas Committee for the Humanities."
   Includes index.
   1. German Americans—Texas—History—Congresses. 2. German Americans—History—Congresses. 3. Texas—History—Congresses. I. Gish, Theodore G.
II. Spuler, Richard.   III. Texas Committee for the Humanities.
F395.G3E24 1986   976.4'00431   86-5797
ISBN 0-89096-260-X

Manufactured in the United States of America
FIRST EDITION

Contents

Foreword

IN talking about German immigration to America, it is natural to think of New York and Philadelphia rather than the South, not to mention Texas. Who realizes that the Hanseatic city of Bremen maintained a consulate in Galveston for many years, or that San Antonio for a time was more German than Mexican, or that Hoffmann von Fallersleben, author of the German national anthem, was so impressed with the Republic of Texas that he wrote a collection of patriotic poems, *Texanische Lieder (Texas Songs)*, as well? Many of the German settlers who came to Texas were also enthusiastic about their new homeland and wrote glowing letters back home, such as the one by the legendary immigrant from Oldenburg, Friedrich Ernst, often called the father of German immigration to Texas. In February, 1832, Ernst wrote: "Climate like that of Sicily. The soil needs no fertilizer. No winter, almost like March in Germany." Town names like New Braunfels, Fredericksburg, Boerne, New Ulm, Schulenburg, and Weimar bear witness to this wave of immigration.

It is no surprise that the idea of developing a symposium dealing with the many aspects of the German settlement of the United States was one of the first matters brought up at the new Goethe Institute in Houston. The Department of German of the University of Houston—University Park, particularly Theodore Gish and Richard Spuler, actively participated in the planning phase of the project, and the University of Houston—University Park was co-host of the ensuing symposium, "Lone Star and Eagle: German Immigration to America, German Immigration to Texas." The administrative headquarters of the Goethe Institute in Munich supported the project by awarding a grant that enabled four German scholars to journey to Houston for the symposium, while the College of Humanities and Fine Arts of the University of Houston—University Park supported the participation of a number of Texas scholars. The fundamental objective was to permit the exchange of informed opinions among German and American scholars. The German participants were asked to address the issue of German immigration to all areas of America in their own particular field, while the Texas participants, representing the same disciplines, were to concentrate on the topics as they pertain to the Lone Star State.

It is gratifying that the papers presented at the symposium can be published and thus made available to a larger audience. I would also like to express my thanks to Professors Gish and Spuler as well as to the Texas Committee for the Humanities and the Institute of Texan Cultures. I sincerely hope that this publication will be another contribution to the mutual understanding of our two peoples.

RICHARD THOMA

Goethe Institute
Houston

Introduction

THROUGHOUT 1983 numerous commemorative activities, both in the United States and in the Federal Republic of Germany, celebrated the three hundredth anniversary of the immigration of the first German colonists to America and the establishment here of the first German settlement, Deutschstadt (present-day Germantown, Pennsylvania), as part of William Penn's colony. The governments of both countries established public commissions to assist in these commemorative events, both countries issued commemorative postage stamps (each displaying the *Concordia*, the German *Mayflower*), and major German and American public officials visited each other's country to participate in the public celebrations.

Understandably, the tricentennial activities varied greatly in scope and content. In Krefeld, on the Lower Rhine, from which thirteen Mennonite families, under the leadership of their pastor, Francis Daniel Pastorius, left in the summer of 1683 on their long voyage to the New World, there were several months of activities during the city's "Philadelphiade" (which were marred only slightly by occasional demonstrations against the American military presence in West Germany). Public events elsewhere in the Federal Republic were understandably not as numerous as those in the United States, but there was considerable television, radio, and especially newspaper coverage of the tricentennial and of the "German element" in America. It was this climate of interest, no doubt, that also stimulated German scholars of history, literature, sociology, anthropology, and folklore—many of whom up to that time had not been involved in American studies—to undertake innovative research projects dealing with German immigration to America.

In the United States, where nearly a third of the population, according to a census study of 1980, is of at least partial German descent, the commemorative activities ranged from the development of a

German-American Friendship Garden on the grounds of the Washington Monument in the nation's capital to the programs of a metropolitan German-American club or of the *Gesangverein* (choral society) of a rural German-American community.

There were also many academic presentations and symposia, but such topics as "German Business Opportunities," on the one hand, and "Nazism and Postwar Germany," on the other, demonstrated the occasional deviation from the historical content. A number of scholarly gatherings did, of course, deal with the substance of the commemorative act itself: the immigration of Germans to America and, in one form or another, the consequences of "German-Americanism." The primary academic meeting, the Tricentennial Conference of German-American History, Politics, and Culture, was held in Philadelphia under the auspices of the University of Pennsylvania in October, 1983 (the colonists had arrived on October 6, 1683). In terms of both its unusual scope and its participants, the symposium "Lone Star and Eagle: German Immigration to America, German Immigration to Texas," sponsored jointly by the University of Houston and the Goethe Institute and held on the University of Houston—University Park campus on September 22–24, 1983, was, by all reckoning, the most significant conference during the tricentennial year at the state or regional level. This symposium was the central academic event of two months of tricentennial activities in Houston jointly sponsored by the Institute for International Education, the offices of the German consulate-general, and the Goethe Institute. The chapters in the present volume were delivered in their original form as papers at this symposium.

Texas, despite its "southwestern" and "Mexican-American" images, is one of four states (Pennsylvania, Missouri, and Wisconsin are the others) with significant concentrations of German immigration and communities even today showing relatively strong German-American ethnicity. At times in the nineteenth century, as much as 40 percent of the population of the cities of Galveston, Houston (the earliest settlement of which was known popularly as "Germantown"), and San Antonio was estimated to be German. Current estimates suggest that at least fifty thousand Houston residents speak German, while "Texas German" is still spoken widely not only in New Braunfels and Fredericksburg but in dozens of communities scattered throughout the state. Reflecting the resurgence of interest in German-Americanism in the

United States during the last decade in Texas, several academic conferences have dealt with German immigration to Texas. But the symposium "Lone Star and Eagle" was the first to bring together outside—that is, "German"—experts and those from Texas and to view systematically the process of immigration from the standpoints of history, folklore, literature, visual arts, gender roles, and language. Finally, the symposium was able to consider this process of immigration and its consequences from both the German-American and the Texas-German points of view.

The authors of these chapters represent a rich and creative variety of scholarly experience. They are acknowledged experts on their particular topics. Most of the German visitors had not traveled to Texas before, and this enterprise alone, in a scholarly-peripatetic sense, was immensely rewarding. The scholars were grouped according to topics and thus had the opportunity to compare and evaluate the others' views, German-American, on the one hand, and Texas-German, on the other. As might be expected, these pairs diverged in one way or another in their approaches. Only the chapters on the visual arts by Anneliese Harding and James Patrick McGuire exhibit a similarity, perhaps because their subject matter is more similar than that of the other pairings and because both art historians are working in the United States. The broadest methodological differences obtain between the traditional German historical scholarship of Günter Moltmann in his "Roots in Germany: Immigration and Acculturation of German-Americans" and the scholarship of Glen E. Lich in his "Rural Hill Country: Man, Nature, and the Ecological Perspective," which reflects the regional traditions developed by historian-folklorists such as J. Frank Dobie and naturalists such as John Graves. In the chapters by Hans Galinsky and Hubert P. Heinen it is the scope rather than the methodological approach that differs so greatly. Galinsky's account of literary views of the "German in America," spanning centuries, continents, and ideologies, is panoramic, while Heinen, in his investigation of the "literary consciousness of being German" in Texas, focuses upon a territory of the heart and the mind, which, of necessity, is more uniform than Galinsky's ethnic terrain. The folklore topics of Lutz Röhrich and Gilbert Jordan are complementary: acts of *emigration* motivated the folk songs which Röhrich discusses, while the oral and written German Texana described by Jordan is a consequence of *immigration*. Despite the differences, all of these paired essays also exhibit similarly instructive complementary aspects. Moltmann's comments, for example, concerning the German-American enclaves in the urban eastern United States illuminate Lich's remarks about the evolution of the rural Texas-German Hill Country, while Galinsky's discussion of the novella *Uhland in Texas*, which describes a Texas-German community but was written by a nineteenth-century German-American who had never visited the Lone Star State, sheds a unique light on Heinen's examination of similar kinds of prose literature written in Texas in the nineteenth century.

A minor stylistic point: obvious linguistic differences appear in the essays. The scholars of this collection generally prefer the term "immigration." Yet, for the most part, the general literature seems to employ the terms "immigration" and "emigration" interchangeably. Because of this, Lich argues for the single designation "migration" (see his note 6). A similar situation occurs with the choice of "Texas-German" or "German-Texan." In general vernacular practice some speakers regard the terms as more or less synonymous, while others vigorously insist on one of the two choices. The editors of this volume believed, consequently, that this was not a subject for editorial decision. Rather than forcing a uniformity, we deemed it prudent to leave the decision to the individual author.

The ten chapters appear in their order of presentation as papers at the symposium. The sequence—history, folklore, literature, and the visual arts—reflects an increasing "refinement" of the consequences of the event of immigration. Only time constraints on the symposium caused other subject areas, such as religion, politics, and education, to be omitted. Arguably, in the sense of the biblical Genesis at least ("In the beginning was the Word"), Joseph Wilson's presentation on the Texas-German language could have initiated the conference. But since there is no such thing as an *American*-German language as such, Wilson was the only speaker on the topic of language per se. Consequently, a dialogue does not obtain, as in the pairings already discussed, even though Wilson engages successfully on his own in a "dialogue" with the de facto detractors of Texas German as a language. His chapter also provides a linguistic epilogue for the other chapters. The tandem presentation on gender roles, "Tales of the Grandmothers: Women as Purveyors of German-Texan Culture," represents the ongoing research of Dona Reeves-Marquardt and Ingeborg McCoy. These two scholars, coincidentally, also represent their own pairing in the ethnic sense of the conference, since one of them is a native-born American and the other a native-born German. As Reeves-Marquardt indicates in her section of the chapter, this sort of research, moreover, has not found much reception in Germany. This situation has also positioned the chapter near the end of the collection, not as an epilogue of sorts but rather as a sign, perhaps, of things to come.

Günter Moltmann is the preeminent German historian of German immigration to America. He designed the Federal Republic of Germany's exhibit, "Germans to America: 300 Years of Immigration, 1683–1983," which traveled throughout the United States during the tricentennial year. Moltmann also wrote the descriptive catalog that accompanied the exhibit. In his chapter, "Roots in Germany: Immigration and Acculturation of German-Americans," Moltmann appropriately sets the stage for the succeeding chapters by highlighting the broad historical contexts in which the different waves of German immigration to America took place. Statistics, of course, tell only part of the story, and, as Moltmann correctly observes, "Such figures . . . say little . . . about the dangers of traveling to America in earlier centuries, and about the various problems of acculturation. Going to America was not just a numbers game; it was a personal experience for everyone engaged in the venture of leaving home, crossing the Atlantic, and settling in the New World."

Moltmann proceeds to discuss some of the historical sources that indicate the range and intensity, as well as the authenticity, of these personal experiences. He anticipates the contribution from Lutz Röhrich by alluding first to songs as significant vehicles of expression, although Moltmann advises us not to forget that "songs usually reflect not experience but rather feelings of hope and wishful thinking. People probably sang . . . to encourage themselves and to overcome hardships and stresses." As a counterpoint Moltmann draws attention to the travel reports of emigrants, in which descriptions of the harsh sea journey are particularly striking. In the face, then, of a promise of not only adventure and possible gain but also—and more likely—harrowing experiences, Moltmann asks, "What kinds of people left their familiar homeland to seek their fortune in a distant land?" Effectively using firsthand accounts, Moltmann enumerates some of the emigrant "types" and then considers their varying motives: "religious, political, social, economic, and psychological personally oriented ones." Of particular note here is Moltmann's discussion of emigration as an alternative to political revolution.

Moltmann goes on to discuss the various "pull factors" that worked in conjunction with the assortment of hardships experienced at home in Germany to encourage emigration. While addressing the question of "Little Germanys" in America, Moltmann also broaches the problem of acculturation—both the acceptance of Germans by Americans and the degree to which Germans have formed a distinct ethnic group in the United States. ". . . it is difficult," he writes, "to speak of a distinct German ethnic group in the United States today," and thus he raises a final, and intriguing, question: "What is the meaning of three hundred years of German settlement in North America for us today?" Moltmann notes how, in spite of recent periods of intense enmity, American-German relations have quickly evolved again, a phenomenon that is nearly without parallel "in international relations of modern times" and one that further admonishes us to learn from history.

Glen Lich, whose *The German Texans* is the most comprehensive account to date, is himself a German-Texan who has spent much of his life in the Hill Country. In his "Rural Hill Country: Man, Nature, and the Ecological Perspective," Lich traces the settlement of Germans in Texas from the arrival in 1831 of Friedrich Ernst, the "father of German immigration," to the present situation in the "German" Hill Country, where, because of recent real-estate and recreational developments, as Lich says, "everywhere, the German heritage is packaged for sale." In examining the process of settlement, from the beginnings at Ernst's community, Industry, to the further taming of the frontier with the arrival of the Adelsverein (Society for the Protection of German Immigrants in Texas), the windmill, the railroad, and the automobile farm-to-market road, Lich observes the constant interaction between the German settler and the Texas land. Far too few interpreters of the German-Texans have considered this "ecological perspective," and Lich's description of it is masterful. Lich also sees how the social status of the immigrants (that is, peasant, artisan, or aristocratic) was a factor in this process. Lich describes, furthermore, the limited extent to which the colonial and utopian plans of the Adelsverein were part of this settlement process.

Just as he sees the settling of Texas by the Germans as an interrelationship between individuals and nature, so too he regards the actual physical settlement itself (brought about largely by the Adelsverein) as an accommodation not only to the environment but also to the architecture of the older Mexican and Anglo neighbors. In conclusion Lich describes the agricultural and social changes wrought in the Hill Country by the arrival of the windmill and the railroad and, in recent years, by the development of a new economy based on tourism and recreation. Lich does not regard the recent economic upswing as necessarily negative: museums can now be maintained, old homes and buildings can be refurbished and preserved, and a pioneer town like Comfort can become a National Historic District. And Lich believes that the German-Texans, who have "zigzagged into modernity, one eye toward the future and the other fixed on the past," will continue to live in this fashion, even though nowadays "ethnicity is big business" in the Hill Country.

Lutz Röhrich, the leading authority on German folklore, is the author of the *Handbuch des deutschen Volksliedes* (*Guide to German Folk Songs*) and the *Handbuch des deutschen Spruches* (*Guide to German Proverbs*), both of which are in every public library in Germany. His contribution at the symposium had a unique aspect that cannot be duplicated in the printed version, since Röhrich also sang—to the participants' instruction and delight—selections of the song texts reproduced here. There was, then, in a tangible sense a kind of reencounter with these rich historical texts. As Röhrich points out:

> Folk songs are the statements of many, even if a nameless many. In them we hear the voice of the people, a voice that no statistics, no regulations can replace as a source. As such they are not simply economic, political, or religious documents but firsthand accounts from the emigrant's point of view. They are subjective documents, much like autobiographies, diaries, letters, travel journals. . . . Emigrant songs indicate the reasons and motivations for emigration. . . . The songs function as a psychological safety valve. In part they look forward, and in part they look back. They not only describe the experiences and fates of emigrants but also tell us something about the relationship between those who stayed at home and those who left.

The cross section of songs that Röhrich presents is fascinating, indeed, and reveals the variety and range of motivations and experiences behind the German immigration. Especially interesting is Röhrich's presentation and discussion of several broadside, or broadsheet, ballads, which served (and serve) the important function of reminding us just how disastrous emigration could be, in terms of not only physical danger but also "moral corruption." Thus the well-known motifs of Schlaraffenland (Land of the Cockaigne), Utopia, and Shangri-la find also their negative counterparts.

Too, songs not only recorded actual experiences but also served as instruments of propaganda both to deter and to promote emigration. Röhrich provides illustrative examples of what he terms "this stay-at-home ideology." Röhrich concludes that "songs can provide us with a typology of emigration, but it is not always clear in these texts which historical wave of emigration they refer to." What the songs may lack in precise historical determinability, however, they make up for with an immediacy that is, as Röhrich notes, "moving, precisely because they deal with the human and the everyday."

A native Texan, Gilbert Jordan grew up in a Methodist German family in the small farming community of Plehweville, near Mason, Texas. While he taught German for many years at Southern Methodist University and Sam Houston State University, Jordan never abandoned the folkways he learned firsthand as a child. Throughout his life, both as a hobbyist and as a researcher, Jordan has collected German Texana, which he calls the "software" of our folk heritage, as opposed to the material culture (the "hardware"). Incidentally, Jordan's son and daughter have also followed in their father's footsteps. Terry G. Jordan is a well-known cultural geographer of German Texas, while Janice Jordan Shefelman has recently published an appealing children's story about the settlement period. Jordan's essay incorporates material from two of his own publications, *Yesterday in the Texas Hill Country* (1979), which describes growing up in Plehweville, and *German Texana* (1980), a richly illustrated compendium of oral and written folk materials. In his chapter in this book Jordan describes various kinds of German Texana: verses from autograph albums, religious songs, prayers and table blessings, nursery rhymes and children's verses, Christmas and New Year's songs and verses, cemetery inscriptions, songs of the German singing societies, humorous and light verse and nonsensical ditties, proverbs and riddles, and anecdotes. (From the last category it is reassuring to know that the German-Texans have a locally well-known anecdotal figure in the person of Sheriff Klaener, of Fredericksburg.) Of the many examples of vernacular folk material provided by Jordan in this book, perhaps the following, with what Jordan calls its "good Texas flavor," deserves to be quoted here:

> Durch einen Ochsenstoss
> Flog ich in Abrahams Schoss;
> Ich ging zur ewigen Ruh
> Durch dich, du Rindvieh du.
>
> [By a wild ox I was gored,
> So to Abraham's bosom I soared;
> To eternal rest I flew
> Through you, dumb ox, through you.]

Missing from Jordan's chapter, as from Röhrich's, is the author's own unique verbal presentation of these materials as a lifelong speaker of Texas German and a living storehouse of German Texana. This notwithstanding, the chapter provides the reader with a broad spectrum of the sorts of German Texana that were once and to some extent still are part of the folk idiom.

Hans Galinsky, "dean" of American Studies in the Federal Republic of Germany, has his own "Texas-German" connection in a son who teaches at the University of Texas. His chapter, "Three Literary Perspectives on the German in America: Immigrant, Homeland, and American Views," is encyclopedic in scope. The immigrant writers are represented by Francis Daniel Pastorius and by Mathilde Anneke, the nineteenth-century journalist, fiction writer, abolitionist, and feminist. Goethe and the poet and prose writer Günter Kunert, a former resident of East Germany (and American visitor), represent the homeland view. The American view is provided by the physician-writer William Carlos Williams, whose father-in-law was a German immigrant.

In Pastorius's writing, the "German in America" appears not only in his promotional tracts for Germantown and his letters back home but especially in his autobiographical, didactic, and religious verse, written in both German and English. Anneke's views are found particularly in her novella *Uhland in Texas*, mentioned earlier, and in her occasional poetry and her political speeches. Of timely interest are her views on German immigrant women that appear in her correspondence. In a careful analysis of the two novels that constitute Goethe's *Wilhelm Meister*, Galinsky describes the elaborate way in which the various sorts of "Germans in America" in the *Lehrjahre* and the *Wanderjahre* not only provided a vehicle for Goethe's views on the New World but as immigrants or at least travelers to America, fit into the overall symbolic and ideological structures of *Wilhelm Meister*. Günter Kunert provides a multifaceted homeland view. Not only is he an emigrant from the German Democratic Republic who settled in the West, but he also visited America in 1972, when his base of operations was the University of Texas at Austin. Finally, Kunert's great-grandfather and his family were short-term immigrants to Tennessee. Galinsky describes Kunert's views, which appear in the account of his visit to the United States, published in 1975 as *Der andere Planet: Ansichten von Amerika* (*The Other Planet: Views of America*). Given Kunert's experiences, it is not surprising that his view of German-Americans is somewhat ambivalent.

The "fullest view of the German in America has emerged," Galinsky believes, in the writing of William Carlos Williams. Because of Williams's German-American wife; because he grew up, resided in, and wrote about ethnically rich New Jersey; and because he himself came from a multiethnic background, Williams was able to portray the German-American from Albert Einstein or the evangelist Klaus Ehrens (see Williams's poem *Paterson*) to the skilled industrial worker (of *White Mule*), both divergently and sympathetically. In each of the five accounts, along with the individual writers' intrinsic views, Galinsky points out their many similarities (such as the proverbial "uncle from America" in the writings of Anneke, Goethe, and Kunert). All of this makes his study both far-reaching and extremely stimulating.

Like Lich and Jordan, Hubert P. Heinen is also a German-Texan. In his chapter, "The Consciousness of Being German: Regional Literature in German Texas," Heinen proposes to "date the beginning of regional literature in German Texas to a song by Prince Carl von Solms-Braunfels from 1845," even though such a date—not to mention the authorship of the text in question—is controversial, as Heinen himself admits. Controversy notwithstanding, it provides a convenient and illuminating point of departure for Heinen's discussion of those clichéd realities that go toward creating a "consciousness of being German on Texas soil." German wine, German song, German loved ones, and the German view of Indians are among the requisite features of this literary landscape. In addition Heinen identifies common references to "industry, the establishment of homesteads, the perpetuation of German customs and morality." With thorough familiarity of the material, sensitivity, and a refined wit, Heinen draws on a variety of sources and authors to present the kind of "inscape" with which he is concerned in his chapter.

Heinen pays special attention to the question of German loyalty, in particular as it became a heated issue with the onset of World War I. It is interesting that, as he says, the "events of World War I evoked a number of poems, though not, to my knowledge, any stories." While the reactions to the war registered in the poetry are in no way uniform—jingoism also had its share of detractors—one can only speculate why prose per se should be conspicuously absent. Also, but perhaps more readily understandable, it is interesting to note, for example, in the postwar work of Hedwig Klappenbach Schroeter a "lack of contemporaneity [that] is part of the conscious message of the author."

As Heinen extends his survey to the present, he draws the important conclusion that "the consciousness of being German is certainly not lost among those native Germans now living in Texas, but it is lost as a theme of regional literature in German." Here it is clear that Heinen bases his understanding of a "German-Texan literature" not only on the aspect of literary production but on the perhaps equally significant dimension of literary reception; he hesitates to identify Lisa Kahn, for example, as "a German-Texan poet" because "her audience, to the extent that it is not a general German one, comprises not an ethnic but rather an intellectual community."

Anneliese Harding's chapter, "German-American Contributions to Eighteenth- and Nineteenth-Century Art," reveals that "what is often considered typical American art is actually the work of a German immigrant." Harding explains that not all German immigrant artists arrived in America as artists, or, if they did, they did not always remain artists, some choosing instead at times to abandon art "to turn to more profitable occupations." Generally speaking, however, as Harding points out, "in America most immigrant artists felt less inhibited, for no glorious artworks of the past overshadowed their own achievements."

Harding begins her survey with Justus Engelhardt Kühn, the first professionally trained painter to come to America from the German-speaking territories of Europe. She then proceeds to highlight various artists (for example, Jeremiah Theus, John Valentine Haidt, and John

Eckstein), their distinguishing traits, and their special accomplishments. Particular attention is given to John Lewis Krimmel, who came to America in 1809. His untimely death at the age of thirty-six cut short a promising career as an artist, for although "Krimmel had painted for only eleven years, . . . the rapid development of his talent had enabled him to leave behind a body of work that not only pointedly illustrates American life of this period but itself became a lasting fiber in the fabric of American art."

Harding notes also that, as was common in the nineteenth century, when German scholarship and art were viewed as exemplary on so many fronts, many American painters in turn ventured to Germany to pursue their art studies in Düsseldorf. There the central figure in the American artist community was Emanuel Gottlieb Leutze, most noted, perhaps, for his large-canvas work *Washington Crossing the Delaware*. The training they received in Düsseldorf provided painters with a new dramatic flair, and painters like Albert Bierstadt first introduced to the American public the full splendor of the western panorama. Along with Bierstadt, Charles Christian Nahl made an important contribution to American painting and illustrating. By the time of Nahl's death in 1878, American painters were looking toward Munich, which in the 1880s became the major German art center. The Munich experience of several American artists, such as Joseph Decker and Ignatz Gaugengigl, provided new creative energies for highly original paintings. All in all, Harding concludes, "the romantic realism" that these immigrant artists "brought from Germany to America was precisely right for the United States in the nineteenth century."

James Patrick McGuire is research associate for the University of Texas Institute of Texan Cultures, in San Antonio. McGuire has published widely on the German painters in Texas, including Carl G. von Iwonski, Julius Stockfleth, and Hermann Lungkwitz. The publication of his book on Lungkwitz, in fact, coincided with an exhibit of the painter's works that was prepared by McGuire and the Institute of Texan Cultures as part of the tricentennial commemoration in Texas and shown in San Antonio, Houston, and Austin. McGuire's "Observations on German Artists in Nineteenth-Century Texas" focuses on the major painters—Iwonski, Lungkwitz, and Lungkwitz's brother-in-law Richard Petri. Iwonski came to New Braunfels from Silesia with his parents while he was still a youngster, and he learned to paint in Texas. After he had achieved some local renown as a painter and political cartoonist and had worked for a time with Lungkwitz in San Antonio as a photographer, Iwonski went back to Silesia with his widowed mother and did not return to Texas. Both Lungkwitz and Petri were educated at the Academy of Fine Arts in Dresden, and both immigrated to America in part for political reasons. The two friends farmed together near Fredericksburg, where Petri, always in ill health, died prematurely in a drowning accident in the Pedernales River. Near the end of the Civil War, Lungkwitz moved with his large family to San Antonio, and after his wife's death he spent the remainder of his years primarily in Austin. While neither Petri nor Lungkwitz achieved fame or wealth with his painting in his lifetime, both left a considerable legacy—Petri in intimate character studies of Texas-Germans and Texas Indians (whom he, unlike many of his contemporaries, painted sympathetically) and Lungkwitz, with romantic landscapes of the Hill Country.

In his chapter McGuire also discusses many of the lesser-known German artists in Texas, in particular the north German seascapist Julius Stockfleth, who painted in Galveston, and the San Antonio portrait painter Louise Heuser Wueste, from Gummersbach. Summing up the efforts of the German painters in Texas, McGuire writes: ". . . they employed little of the usual iconography of America's westward expansion." Theirs was "a more personal interpretation of Texas with its German colonies, landscapes and social activities," forming an "intimate insight into the artists' own experiences." As he comments, "Their contributions to Texas, however, prove solid, providing for a pioneering region the foundation of a tradition in the fine arts."

The two-part chapter by Dona Reeves-Marquardt and by Ingeborg McCoy, "Tales of the Grandmothers: Women as Purveyors of German-Texan Culture," is the result of cooperative research. Reeves sets the initial context by addressing the state of German-Texan "historiography," which has to date exhibited a predominant concern for historical "firsts" as recorded by mostly male chroniclers and thus told from a distinctly male perspective. As Reeves-Marquardt notes:

> Scholarly attention devoted to this in no way unique but nevertheless neglected aspect of German-American and German-Texan literature and culture has approximately paralleled the attention devoted to German-

American studies in general: it has progressed from the slightly illegitimate through the back door of ethnic and sociolinguistic studies into a
marginally acceptable area of our discipline.

Still, as Reeves-Marquardt correctly observes, ". . . we have cause to
wonder about the validity of frontier images of women molded and nurtured by male writers."

As Reeves-Marquardt notes, and as McCoy later shows, "A strong
case can be made for approaching the subject of ethnic women through
language." Such a study "may lead to fruitful insights and better understanding of the so-called immigrant experience." Reeves-Marquardt
goes on to describe those textual sources that were crucial for their research, a project that began in 1981 with the video documentation of
"authentic, natural, present-day German-Texan culture as it remains in
the first German settlements in Texas."

Following the general methodological introduction by Reeves-
Marquardt, McCoy illustrates the application of their method in a
close analysis of a selection from Ottilie Fuchs Goeth's autobiography,
Was Grossmutter Erzählt (*What Grandmother Tells*). She focuses on
the textual as well as sociocultural significance of quilting. The quilt,
through the passage by Goeth, becomes for McCoy a metaphor: it
"equates the ordering of old and new bits of cloth into an artistic pattern with the quilters' ability to function as *bricoleurs* who collect and
retain elements and signs of traditional culture to recombine them with
newly encountered cultural facets, thus constantly fashioning their own
order of cultural experience." Consistent with the reordering of narrative perspective and role priorities advocated by Reeves-Marquardt,
McCoy suggests that "the women in the German settlements in Texas
in the nineteenth century were the true purveyors of German culture."

McCoy applies both a linguistic and a structural analysis to the
"grandmothers' tales." She isolates several recurrent thematic threads
running through these narratives, so common as to function as narrative formulas: that is, they "convey the values of traditional belief
systems." Viewed in this light, the didactic dimension of Goeth's text
becomes clear: "to persuade her descendants to continue the traditions
of the German culture, including the use of the German language, and
to realize that such continuity of *Deutschtum* evolves from the con-

tinued existence of a close family." McCoy pursues the problem further by examining the (symbolic) status of nature and culture in Goeth's work. McCoy concludes that "time and again the tales contain the textual configurations of how the women structured the similarities and differences in both the natural and the cultural realms, respectively: how they established connections between these two orders; and how this ordering happened by means of objects that . . . are not just objects but, in effect, messages."

Joseph Wilson is the foremost expert on the Texas-German language in the state. In a sense Wilson "married" into this interest, for his wife is a Wendish-German who grew up in Lee County. Wilson's chapter, "Texas German and Other American Immigrant Languages: Problems and Prospects," is a forceful and yet thoughtful plea for a better understanding of Texas German as a bona fide language, important both culturally and historically. Wilson begins by comparing Texas German to Gothic in the linguistic singularity of its importance as a historical document of the Germans in Texas. Wilson indicates that, although Wendish has essentially died out, there is still time to study Texas German. Denying a validity to the question of whether Texas German is "good" or "bad" German, Wilson states that it is not a dialect but a form of standard German. Wilson describes the language in some detail, especially its grammar and its use of anglicisms. In discussing the past importance of Texas German in the individual and community affairs of many people, Wilson compares that situation with the present status of Texas Spanish. This comprehensive defense of Texas German concludes with a report of what is now available and what is needed for the continued study and preservation of the language.

Support for the development of this book has come from many quarters. The symposium "Lone Star and Eagle: German Immigration to America, German Immigration to Texas" was a joint undertaking of the Goethe Institute of Houston and the College of Humanities and Fine Arts of the University of Houston—University Park and its Department of German. The preparation of the volume was made possible by a stipend from the Texas Committee for the Humanities and a grant from the Publications Committee of the University of Houston— University Park.

The editors of this volume hope that it will provide both a definition of the best of Texas-German and German-American scholarship and, now that the euphoria of the tricentennial has abated, will also point to new and valid ways of looking at this area of research, which, despite a tricentennial anniversary, is still only in its early stages.

Eagle in the New World

GÜNTER MOLTMANN

Roots in Germany: Immigration and Acculturation of German-Americans

AMONG the letters from America that reach the Department of History of the University of Hamburg, requests like this are not rare:

> I have been doing considerable research on my family's history, and I am trying to determine why my great-grandfather . . . left the area of Laufen am Kocher, Württemberg, in 1854 with his brother and sister to immigrate to America. Circa 1858 his wife and two sons joined him in Chicago, Illinois. . . . I have studied several books on that subject . . . with some conclusions, but little about that specific area in Württemberg. Can you tell me the conditions that existed there at this time that might have prompted their emigration?[1]

Other universities receive similar inquiries, and community, town, and city archives in Germany are busy searching for genealogical information for Americans who are interested in their German roots. Obviously many people in the United States invest quite a bit of energy tracing ancestors in the Old World. Sometimes they can be helped, sometimes not. Sources for the study of the great migratory movement from Germany to North America from the seventeenth to the twentieth centuries are abundant, but they do not unveil the history of every family. Too many of them left no discernible traces.

On the other side of the Atlantic many Germans are looking for descendants of their own, deceased relatives who, decades ago, left their fatherland for good and settled in the New World, initially wrote some letters, but grew silent after years of residence in America. The intensified interest in tracing family roots is a common phenomenon in America as well as Germany. People in both countries want to know something of their past; they want to reestablish contacts. Nothing is

---

[1] Letter of April 1, 1983, files of the Department of History, University of Hamburg.

better proof that history means something to people and that there is an awareness that the great migration to America was an exciting development worth being remembered and studied.

How many Germans, in the course of the centuries, have immigrated to British North America and the United States, respectively? This question is not an easy one to answer. For an understanding of the movement it is necessary to know the scope of the whole process. Few statistics exist for early times, and later figures are often not reliable. Lists of arrivals in American ports are available for the years from 1821 on, but they do not tell the complete story. Overland migration through Canada was not recorded for a long time. Often no distinctions were made between Germans, Austrians, German-speaking Swiss, and immigrants from Alsace-Lorraine. Return migration from the United States, which at times was not small, was not recorded until 1908.[2]

Nevertheless, estimates are possible. During the colonial period about 65,000 to 75,000 and possibly as many as 100,000 Germans immigrated. At the time of the American Revolution there were approximately 225,000 people of German descent in America, equaling about 8 to 9 percent of the total population of the rebellious colonies.[3] During the following four decades, until the War of 1812 and the Congress of Vienna, immigration was relatively low, apart from a few years at the turn of the nineteenth century.

From 1815 to 1914, during the period of German mass immigration, about 5.5 million Germans came to the United States, and from World War I to the present some 1.5 million more came. Altogether the number of Germans who departed for America can be set at more than 7 million (an estimate that does not take into consideration return migration).[4]

[2]Günter Moltmann, "American-German Return Migration in the Nineteenth and Early Twentieth Centuries," Central Europe History 13 (1980): 378–392. For statistics on immigration to the United States see U.S. Bureau of the Census, Historical Statistics of the United States (Washington, D.C.: U.S. Government Printing Office, 1971), pp. 56–57.

[3]See Albert Bernhardt Faust, The German Element in the United States, with Special Reference to Its Political, Moral, Social, and Educational Institutions (New York: Steuben Society of America, 1927), I, 282–85; Stephan Thernstrom, ed., Harvard Encyclopedia of American Ethnic Groups (Cambridge, Mass.: Harvard University Press, 1981), p. 407.

[4]U.S. Bureau of the Census, Historical Statistics of the United States: Colonial Times to 1970 (Washington, D.C.: U.S. Government Printing Office, 1971), pp. 105–106.

The exodus of German people to North America was only one component of a larger transatlantic movement in which English and Irish settlers as well as Scandinavians; Dutch; Swiss; and eastern, southeastern, and southern Europeans also participated. Immigrants came to North America from all countries of the world. Total immigration to the United States from 1820 to the present is over 46 million. The Germans' share was numerically the largest but made up only about 15 percent. In peak years, however, up to a quarter million Germans arrived (in 1854, 215,000; in 1882, 250,000). In the second half of the nineteenth century, Americans born in Germany made up more than 30 percent of all Americans born abroad and between 4 and 5 percent of the total U.S. population.[5]

Such figures give an idea of the large volume of people involved in the migratory process. They say little if anything, however, about the hopes and feelings of the persons involved, about the dangers of traveling to America in earlier centuries, and about the various problems of acculturation. Going to America was not just a numbers game; it was a personal experience for everyone engaged in the venture of leaving home, crossing the Atlantic, and settling in the New World.

People liked to give expressions to their feelings by singing songs. One of many such songs goes as follows:

> Jetzt ist die Zeit und Stunde da,
> wir reisen nach Amerika;
> der Wagen steht schon vor der Tür,
> mit Sack und Pack marschieren wir.
>
> Ihr Freunde wohl und anverwandt,
> reicht mir zum letztenmal die Hand.
> Ihr Freunde, weinet nicht so sehr,
> Wir sehn uns nun und nimmermehr.
>
> Und wenn das Schiff am Ufer steht,
> so wird ein Liedchen angestimmt.
> Wir fürchten keinen Wasserfall,
> wir denken, Gott ist überall.
>
> Und sind wir dann in Baltimore,
> so heben wir die Händ' empor
> und rufen dann "Viktoria,"
> jetzt sind wir in Amerika.

[5]Thernstrom, ed., *Harvard Encyclopedia of American Ethnic Groups*, p. 406.

In Amerika, da ist es fein,
da fliesst der Wein zum Fenster rein.
Wir trinken eine Flasche Wein
und lassen Deutschland Deutschland sein.

Und woll'n wir nun spazieren gehn
im grünen Wald, wo Blumen stehn,
da fand ich eine, die das spricht:
"Blaublümelein, Vergissmeinnicht!"

[*The Time Has Come*

The time has come for us to go,
We're leaving for America;
The wagon's waiting at the door,
With bags in hand we're marching forth.

O true and steadfast friends,
One last time will we shake hands.
Dear friends, do not shed a tear,
Though we meet for the last time here.

And when the ship is on the sea,
Then we shall sing a melody.
We know no fear of water,
We think of God, our Father.

And when we land in Baltimore,
Then we shall raise our hands before
Us, crying out "Victoria,"
At last we're in America.

In America life is fine,
With an abundance of good wine.
We'll put a bottle of wine away,
And let Germany stay where it will stay.

And should we want to stroll around
In the forest green, where flowers abound,
Then I would find one that could talk:
"O, little blue flower, forget me not!"][6]

This immigrant song was probably the most popular one in existence. The author was Samuel Friedrich Sautter, from southwestern

---

[6] For another version of this song, see Röhrich's chapter. See also George Korson, ed., *Pennsylvania Songs and Legends* (Philadelphia: University of Pennsylvania Press, 1949), pp. 66–68. For another of many different German versions of "Jetzt ist die Zeit

Germany, who first published the text in 1845. There are still people today, in Germany as well as in the United States, who can sing it. It is a song of optimism and happiness. Emigrants say farewell to Germany with sorrow, they have strong feelings about the journey across the ocean, they are assured that in America everything is better, and they trust in God. One must not forget, however, that songs usually reflect not experience but rather feelings of hope and wishful thinking. People probably sang the song to encourage themselves and to overcome hardships and stresses.

Travel reports of emigrants often give a different picture. Transportation across the sea in the eighteenth century was quite an adventure. Francis Daniel Pastorius, the founder of Germantown, Pennsylvania, sailed from Rotterdam to England, where he had to wait until enough passengers had assembled to fill a ship going to America. His vessel left England on June 6, 1683, and reached Philadelphia on August 20. His journey across the ocean lasted seventy-four days (seven and a half weeks). The Crefelders, who arrived later and settled in Germantown, made the trip in forty-four days. They were more fortunate. Passengers of early times received basic foodstuffs and beverages on board but had to provide any extra refreshments and do the cooking themselves. They were usually crowded into poorly lighted tween decks but could go on deck when weather permitted. Medical care was not available,. except that the captain would help in cases of emergency—if he had the know-how.[7]

There was not much change during the eighteenth century. In times of great demand captains took more immigrants on board, and vessels were overcrowded. Contemporary accounts sometimes speak of brutal treatment of passengers by the crew, the officers, and the captain. Disease sometimes broke out, causing heavy loss of life. Disasters from gales, running aground, collisions, and fire occurred from time to time. Pirates occasionally seized immigrant ships, which were easy, though not very rewarding, prey.[8]

---

und Stunde da," see Wolfgang Steinitz, *Deutsche Volkslieder demokratischen Charakters aus sechs Jahrhunderten*, 2 vols. (Berlin: Akademie-Verlag, 1954–62), I, 122.

[7] For a critical account of emigrant travel during the eighteenth century, see Gottlieb Mittelberger, *Reise nach Pennsylvanien im Jahr 1750 und Rückreise nach Teutschland im Jahr 1754* (Stuttgart: n.p., 1756), pp. 18–19.

[8] See Günter Moltmann, "Das Risiko der Seereise: Auswanderungsbedingungen

The interior of the emigrant ship *Samuel Hop*. Courtesy Institut für
Auslandsbeziehungen, Stuttgart.

Technological innovations and the Industrial Revolution changed
traffic conditions considerably during the nineteenth century. Steam
navigation on rivers and the construction of the railway system improved transportation from the old homes to the seaports in Germany
and from the landing places in America to the new homes. The introduction of packet lines with fixed routes and timetables for departures
and arrivals made ocean transportation easier: it particularly shortened
the waiting time in the ports. Ocean steamers, which replaced sailing
vessels after the middle of the nineteenth century, meant greater comfort and faster traveling. Instead of seven weeks immigrants could
reach this side of the Atlantic in two weeks.

Although the mortality rate on board fell remarkably, disasters
still occurred. In 1858 a fire on the immigrant steamer *Austria* destroyed the ship and took the lives of 453 people; only 89 were saved.
The outbreak of typhoid fever on the Hamburg ship *Leibniz* during the
winter crossing in 1867–68 resulted in the deaths of 108 of the 544 pas-

im Europa-Amerika-Verkehr um die Mitte des 19. Jahrhunderts," in Heinz Duchardt
and Manfred Schlenke, eds., *Festschrift für Eberhard Kessel zum 75. Geburtstag*
(Munich: Fink, 1982), pp. 182–221, esp. pp. 183–86.

Fire on the steamer *Austria*. Courtesy Museum für Hamburgische Geschichte.

sengers. Visitors to the pilgrimage church Vierzehnheiligen, in Upper Franconia, Germany, can still look at a votive tablet of 1845 on which a blazing immigrant ship is shown. A woman and 2 of her daughters thank God for being saved. A prayer to the 14 holy rescuers had, as they believed, helped to extinguish the fire instantly.[9] Only during the last decades of the nineteenth century were ship companies able to guarantee more safety. The twentieth century finally saw the virtual end of dangers and hazards in traveling across the ocean. Going to America on one of the great liners or in a plane became a pleasure rather than an ordeal.

What kinds of people left their familiar homeland to seek their fortunes in a distant land? What were the driving forces behind the 300-year mass exodus? At a high point of the emigration phenomenon, 130 years ago, the German author Friedrich Gerstäcker, a well-known travel writer who himself initially had left Germany with the intent of

[9]Reproduced in Günter Moltmann, ed., *Germans to America: Three Hundred Years of Immigration* (Stuttgart: Institute for Foreign Cultural Relations, 1982), p. 88.

migrating to America, described the types of people whom one could meet in the ports:

> "Nach Amerika," leicht und keck ruft es der Tollkopf, trotzig der ersten schweren, traurigen Stunde entgegen, die sein Kraft prüfen sollte. . . .— "nach Amerika," flüstert der Verzweifelte, der hier am Rand des Verderbens dem Abgrund langsam aber sicher entgegen gerissen wurde — "nach Amerika," sagt still und entscholssen der Arme, der mit männlicher Kraft, und doch immer und immer wieder vergebens gegen die Macht der Verhältnisse ankämpft. . . .—"nach Amerika" lacht der Verbrecher nach glücklich verübtem Raub. . . .—"nach Amerika," jubelt der Idealist, der wirklichen Welt zürnend, . . . und über den Ozean drüben ein Bild erhoffend, das dem in seinem eigenen tollen Hirn erzeugten, gleicht.

> ["To America," cries the madcap gaily and audaciously, defiant against the first sad hour which will put his strength to the test. . . .—"to America," whispers the desperate man who here on the margin of ruin was being pulled, slowly but surely, toward the abyss—"to America," says the poor man, softly and resolutely, who again and again had struggled with manly strength, but futilely, against the power of circumstances. . . .—"to America," laughs the criminal after his successfully perpetrated robbery. . . .—"to America," exults the idealist, spurning the real world, . . . hoping for a world over there across the ocean that matched the one produced in his own frantic brain.] [10]

The idea of going to America, Gerstäcker continues, inspired the farmer who had only a few acres, the craftsman who was hard-pressed by competition, the artist who was harassed by concerns about his livelihood and lack of freedom, and the small businessman troubled about making his accounts balance: "Aus den verschiendenartigsten Verhältnissen und Sphären, aus allen Schichten der menschlichen Gesellschaft sehen wir sie ziehen—Gute und Böse, den Leichtsinnigen und den Spekulanten, den Bauern und Handwerker, den Gelehrten und den Arbeiter, den rechtschaffenen Bürger und den heimlichen Verbrecher, alle dem einen Ziel entgegen" ("From the most diverse of circumstances and spheres, from all the strata of human society, we see them moving—good and bad, the profligate and the speculator, the farmer and the artisan, the scholar and the worker, the upright citizen and the furtive criminal—toward a single goal"). [11]

[10] Friedrich Gerstäcker, *Nach Amerika! Ein Volksbuch*, 6 vols. (Leipzig: Costenoble, 1855), preface.
[11] Ibid.

The emigrant-landing in New York. From *Harper's Weekly*, June 26, 1858. Courtesy Museum of the City of New York.

This list of emigrant types could be extended. Gerstäcker did not mention religious dissidents who escaped from persecution in Germany and headed for a country of religious tolerance. Many such groups went to America during the seventeenth and eighteenth centuries, but one could still see them immigrating during the nineteenth century—Harmonites, Zoarites, Amanists, Old Lutherans, and also Roman Catholics at the time of Bismarck's Kulturkampf.

Political refugees should also be mentioned. After 1815 liberals escaped persecution under the conservative, political "Metternich system" and went to America. The Forty-eighters left their homes in Germany after their attempted revolution of 1848–49 failed and resulted in their persecution. Socialists, harassed during the time of Bismarck's anti-Socialist legislation, found asylum in the United States. The greatest exodus impelled by political persecution occurred during the twentieth century under the Nazi regime. More expulsion than emigration, this last exodus perhaps should not be included in the history of German emigration without some reservations.

Many Germans went to America as adventurers who hoped to become rich without much effort. Around the middle of the nineteenth century not a few Germans left for California, touched by the gold fever. Of a very different nature were industrial workers who left toward the end of the century to find jobs in American industrial plants. At that time there were also many young women looking for jobs as servants or salesclerks—or looking for husbands. In addition there were those who left the country because they could not cope with the society and its demands and regulations: draft evaders, young boys or girls who wanted to marry without the consent of their parents, and transatlantic vagabonds of all kinds.

The driving forces behind the movement were manifold. In 1831 the German poet Heinrich Heine left Germany and settled in France. It was the year after the July Revolution, which had overthrown the reactionary monarchy and created the citizen-kingdom of Louis Philippe. Heine had decided to spend some time at the seashore near Le Havre to rest and think about himself, his fatherland, and his new home country.

One day while he was walking along the highway from Paris to Le Havre, he met a trek of German emigrants heading for their port of embarkation. The wagons were heavily laden, packed full with bags and boxes, and the people themselves looked somewhat melancholic and resigned to their fate. "Why did you leave Germany?" Heine asked them, and they answered that they "could not stand it any longer." They complained about the authorities who had put too much pressure on them, about high taxes and the arrogant behavior of the privileged class of nobles who had made them suffer. "What should we have done?" they asked. "Should we have started a revolution?"[12] Heine felt sympathetic toward them and sad. When he later described the incident, however, he added some stinging remarks:

> Ich schwöre es bei allen Göttern des Himmels und der Erde, der zehnte Teil von dem, was jene Leute in Deutschland erduldet haben, hätte in Frankreich sechsunddreissig Revolutionen hervorgebracht und sechsunddreissig Königen die Krone mitsamt dem Kopf gekostet. . . . wenn den Franzosen die landesherrlichen Plackereien so ganz unerträglich werden oder auch nur etwas allzustark beschwerlich fallen, dann kommt ihnen doch nie in den Sinn, die Flucht zu ergreifen, sondern sie geben vielmehr ihren Drängern den Laufpass, sie werfen sie zum Lande hinaus und bleiben hübsch selber im Lande, mit einem Wort, sie fangen eine Revolution an.

[12]"'Und warum habt ihr denn Deutschland verlassen? Das Land ist gut, und wären gern dageblieben,' antworteten sie, 'aber wir konnten's nicht länger aushalten—Was sollten wir thun? Sollten wir eine Revolution anfangen?'" Heinrich Heine, preface to "Der Salon," in Heine, *Sämliche Werke*, ed. Ernst Elster (Leipzig: Bibliographisches Institut, n.d.), IV, 16–17.

Emigrants in Hamburg. *Hamburg-Altonaer Illustrirte Zeitung*, 1886.
Courtesy Staatsarchiv, Hamburg.

[I swear it by all gods in heaven and on earth, just one-tenth of what those
people in Germany had suffered would have caused thirty-six revolutions
in France, and thirty-six kings would have lost their crowns, and their
heads right with it. . . . When the French feel that the pressure of the
sovereigns becomes unbearable or puts just a little too much of a burden
on them, then they never get the idea of escaping; rather they give walking papers to their oppressors and throw them out of the country—in
other words, start a revolution.][13]

This little story and commentary raise the question whether German emigration during the nineteenth century can be considered a

[13]Ibid., II, 17–18.

substitute for revolution. In raising this issue, I forgo the question which is better, engaging in a forceful revolution—perhaps leading to bloodshed and failure—or leaving an oppressive political and social system and escaping to freedom.

The German immigration to America in the nineteenth century—comparable to other migratory movements from European countries to the New World—is often interpreted as an escape from imminent poverty or from unbearable living conditions. Different motives were intermingled: religious, political, social, economic, and psychological personally oriented ones. There are many studies about motives, and we are well aware of the various push-and-pull factors behind the mobility. Generally speaking, emigration was a result of tensions between the emigrant and a complex of forces impossible to cope with and from which escape offered the easiest solution.

One emigrant may have left his native country and society in resignation, accepting his departure as inevitable, and said farewell to his environment without any inner break with it. Another emigrant may have left, aware that he lacked the ability to coexist with his society. He believed that he had failed. He escaped from an environment whose norms oppressed him personally and drove him out. Finally, there were emigrants who left their fatherland out of protest and rejected the social system in which they had lived. In this instance a definite break resulted with the environment that could not offer adequate living space or tolerable living conditions.

Only the third kind of emigrant could be considered a potential revolutionary. This emigrant, perhaps, would have stood up against the authorities if circumstances had permitted. Since it was difficult to do this—that is, organize opposition in the country and rally forces against the political and social system in Germany—these people preferred escape to revolution. Thus emigration was a substitute for revolution for some Germans. Others who went to America were perhaps not potential revolutionaries but would have sympathized with a revolution if it had erupted. During the uprisings of 1848–49, many German-Americans rejoiced in seeing things changing in their former country, and they were disappointed when the uprisings failed.

Historians of emigration have sometimes claimed that the Germans, particularly the Swabians, were born with an inherent wanderlust and for this reason ventured abroad. They overlooked, however, the fact that migrations have taken place among many peoples and have often been no smaller than those from Germany. Some interpreters say that there are sedentary and mobile types among people and that this alone explains why some remain at home while others emigrate.[14] This thesis, too, is untenable. No doubt external circumstances such as economic crises, inadequate social-welfare provisions, and labor-market problems virtually created emigrants at certain times. Individual predispositions and external circumstances usually interacted when the decision to emigrate was made. Simple explanations do not give the truth.

Of no little importance were pull factors working from the country of destination. Every emigrant expects something better than conditions at home. A specific image of the new country develops that, whether right or wrong, lures the emigrant away. What was the German image of North America and the United States? What were the attractive features? In 1903 the German banker Ludwig Max Goldberger published a book whose title immediately became a standard phrase: *Das Land der unbegrenzten Möglichkeiten* (*The Land of Unlimited Opportunities*). In his preface he said:

> Die Vereinigten Staaten sind "*das Land der unbegrenzten Möglichkeiten.*" Die wirtschaftliche Entdeckung Amerikas, heute in Texas und Kansas, morgen in Idaho und Californien, macht von Tag zu Tag neue und ungeahnte Fortschritte. Die Schätze, die der Boden erzeugt, und die Schätze, die unter der Erde gehoben werden, sind märchenhaft. Die maschinelltechnische Ausrüstung der Industrien scheint unübertrefflich.

> [The United States is the country of "unlimited opportunities." The economic discovery of America, today in Texas and Kansas, tomorrow in Idaho and California, marches on, day after day in new, unthought-of directions. The wealth produced by the soil and the wealth lifted from underground are fabulous. The equipment of the factories, machines, and technology seem to be unsurpassable.][15]

Although in his book Goldberger described specific innovations and implied economic possibilities in the early twentieth century, the

---

[14] Cf. Gert Raeithel, "Freundliche Weiten: Die europäische Auswanderung und der amerikanische Nationalcharakter," *Merkur* 33 (1979): 1078–87.

[15] Ludwig Max Goldberger, *Das Land der unbegrenzten Möglichkeiten: Beobachtungen über das Wirtschaftsleben der Vereinigten Staaten von Amerika* (Berlin: F. Fontane, 1903), p. 12.

title of the book became a catchphrase. As vague and probably incorrect as it was, it expressed an image of America that was shared by many Germans and seemed to correspond with what Germans always had thought of the New World and that would apply in the future too.

It is true that Germans always cherished the idea that, to a certain degree, America was paradise, that it offered happiness and wealth to everybody. If one takes a closer look at the image of America in different periods, one can discover certain changes in accentuation. In colonial times the New World meant freedom of religion, hard but rewarding labor, and the absence of serfdom and social barriers. After the American Revolution, American became the land of freedom, justice, and equality. During the late nineteenth century it was the country of unlimited progress, of the "self-made man," of upward mobility from ditchdiggers to wealthy industrialists. In the twentieth century the United States was regarded as a country of power and generosity, continued technical progress, and an informal life-style.

Praise was accompanied by criticism, and there were always certain negative aspects that darkened the picture in the eyes of some Germans: America—the country without culture and manners, the country of selfish Yankees and money-minded businessmen, the country of ruthlessness and gangsterism. But images are strange things. Individuals pick out aspects that correspond to their wishes. Germans who thought of emigrating looked only at good things and believed in them. They felt that they had to justify their decision. Even later, after they had settled in the new country, they preferred to report positive aspects rather than bad experiences.

People who remained at home were often skeptical about the emigrants' adventurism and their dreamlike image of America. There were many warnings against emigration. Political authorities warned, the church warned, and friends and relatives tried to talk people out of their intention to leave the country. Economists warned of the loss of the labor force, the loss of public money put into the education of emigrants, and the loss of property and even wealth. The poet Friedrich Rückert published a poem in 1817 with the following verses:

> Bleibet im Lande und nähret euch redlich,
> Rücket zusammen und füget euch fein.
> Machte nur keiner zu breit sich und schädlich,
> Wäre das Land nicht für alle zu klein.
> Aber wo alle sich drängen und reiben,

The Modern Ship of the Plains, from *Harper's Weekly*, November 13, 1886.

Da ist für Menschen im Land nicht zu bleiben,
Flösse das Land auch von Milch und von Wein.

[Remain in the country and work honestly,
Draw near to each other and behave well.
Do not take much space and injure others,
Then there will be enough room for everybody.
Please do not jostle each other and rub yourselves,
Then all people can remain in the country,
And theirs will be milk and honey in affluence.][16]

Rückert was not very successful with this poem. The years 1816 and 1817 saw the first big nineteenth-century wave of immigration to America. Words like his could hardly dissuade desperate people from going away. But what they expressed was common to many Germans at that time. The words "Remain in the country and work honestly" were taken from the Bible,[17] and the church was, for a long time, particularly critical of emigration. The decision to leave the community, go out into

[16] Friedrich Rückert, "Zeitgeschichte in zwei Büchern (1814–1817)," bk. 2, in Rückert, *Werke*, ed. Conrad Beyer (Leipzig: Hesse, n.d.), II, 514–15.
[17] Psalm 37:3, Luther translation.

the world, and be without the protection of the church seemed an ungodly undertaking. The words implied that emigrants were unable to work honestly. Behind this was the fear that they would not be able or willing to join the church in their new communities.

Such an attitude was widespread in the first half of the nineteenth century. When more and more people left the homeland for America, however, it became impossible to blame all of them for godless behavior and dangerous adventurism. Quite obviously a movement was in progress that had some justification, and turning their backs on those who left was arrogant and even inhuman. The exodus of so many people thus came to be a consequence of overpopulation and a natural way to alleviate a socially difficult situation.

Thus from the 1840s charity organizations sprang up in Germany to try to help the emigrants. State authorities removed barriers and abolished special taxes for emigrants. The revolutionary National Assembly at Frankfurt in 1848–49 worked on a law regulating and protecting emigration. During the second half of the nineteenth century the churches also became more friendly. They felt responsible for the well-being of the travelers and founded special charity institutions in the major German ports.

Not only did charity develop, but an organizational network came into being, making it easier for people to go abroad. Improved transportation conditions have already been mentioned. Business made strong efforts to channel the movement. Emigration agents helped people move and, of course, profited from the activity. Emigration societies that experimented with group migration and settlement emerged, achieving various degrees of success. The most famous of these societies was the Texas Adelsverein, in which different efforts were combined: assistance and protection for immigrants, the founding of a colony of German settlers in America, elimination of a dangerous potential for unrest and revolution, new activity for members of the nobility who had lost their sovereign rights in early nineteenth-century political reforms, and financial profit for the members of the society.

Such a venture could be undertaken only because emigration had become an accepted fact. German state authorities did not do much to protect emigration, but there were no longer any obstacles from their side. It is safe to say that from the middle of the nineteenth century, every German who had sufficient financial means to go away and settle in a distant country was free to do so, provided he had fulfilled his obligation toward the home society and the home country. He had to pay his debts before leaving, and he was not allowed to evade military service.

The attitude of the receiving society toward immigration was not a simple one either. How did Americans react to the hosts of incoming Germans? At times they were very divided in their judgments. America was an asylum for "your tired, your poor, / your huddled masses yearning to breathe free, the wretched refuse of your teeming shore," as Emma Lazarus said to the Old World in her sonnet on the Statue of Liberty, in New York.

But at times Americans were afraid of too many immigrants flocking to their land. Nativist tendencies emerged. Immigration restrictions of the twentieth century and quota regulations of the 1920s were not the beginnings of such trends. They were not directed against Germans in the first instance in any event, but against eastern, southeastern, and southern Europeans, against the so-called New Immigration. Nativist, anti-German sentiments had already been expressed during colonial times, when Benjamin Franklin expressed the fear that Pennsylvania, with its strong German-American component, might become germanized and lose its English character.[18] The influx of migrants into America was welcomed as long as labor was needed and acculturation without difficulties seemed possible.

What most Americans expected from immigrants was expressed by John Quincy Adams, secretary of state, in a letter to a German in 1819:

> Neither the general government of the Union, nor those of the individual states, are ignorant or unobservant of the additional strength and wealth, which accrues to the nation, by the accession of a mass of healthy, industrious, and frugal laborers, nor are they in any manner insensible to the great benefits which this country has derived, and continues to derive, from the influx of such adoptive children from Germany. But there is one principle which pervades all the institutions of this country, and which must always operate as an obstacle to the granting of favors to newcomers. This is a land, not of *privileges*, but of *equal rights*. . . . They come to a life of independence, but to a life of labor—and, if they cannot accommo-

[18] Benjamin Franklin, "Observations concerning the Increase of Mankind" (essay written in 1751), in *The Papers of Benjamin Franklin*, ed. Leonard W. Labaree (New Haven, Conn.: Yale University Press, 1961), IV, 225–34, esp. p. 234. Cf. Glenn Weaver, "Benjamin Franklin and the Pennsylvania Germans," *William and Mary Quarterly*, 3rd ser., 14 (1957): 536–59.

date themselves to the character, moral, political, and physical, of this country, with all its compensating balances of good and evil, the Atlantic is always open to them, to return to the land of nativity and their fathers. To one thing they must make up their minds, or they will be disappointed in every expectation of happiness as Americans. They must cast off European skin, never to resume it.[19]

German-Americans, like members of other ethnic groups, had to solve the problem of adjustment, that is, the coexistence of the heritage of their native land and the life-style of their new environment. American society did not usually put direct pressure on them to adjust. Acculturation was something they had to accomplish by themselves. But if they wanted to be successful in their lives, they had to pick up the language, the customs, and the life-style of Americans.

At certain periods, however, Americans did become impatient and expected Germans to adjust more quickly and willingly. This was the case after the arrival of the Forty-eighters. These immigrants came not to stay forever but rather to wait for the next revolution in Germany. They had fixed ideas about how to reform a political system and how to improve social conditions. Finding that the American system did not match all their illusory expectations, they began to criticize their hosts and tried to teach them how to improve their system. This was not appreciated very much by Americans.

Criticism of the behavior of German-Americans in the United States also was to be heard during the later decades of the nineteenth century and before World War I. It was a time of nationalism everywhere in the Western world. Germans in America had greeted the unification of Germany with some enthusiasm. They were proud of their origin and pointed to the cultural achievements of the German nation. This was all right as long as no expression of superiority was involved. But one or the other German-American occasionally would say that it was the Germans who brought culture and ingenuity to America—a statement which Americans understandably resented.

Later German immigration to America decreased drastically: 250,000 had come in 1882; 120,000 came in 1892. Afterward figures went down to an average of about 30,000 a year. This ebbing of the German influx threatened the continuing existence of a strong and self-

---

[19] *Niles' Weekly Register*, April 29, 1820; reprinted in Günter Moltmann, ed., *Aufbruch nach Amerika: Friedrich List und die Auswanderung aus Baden und Württemberg 1816/17* (Tübingen: Wunderlich, 1979), pp. 243–46, esp. p. 244.

assured German ethnic group in the United States. To compensate for weakening German-Americanism, nationalist sentiments became stronger. In 1901 the German-American National Alliance was founded to combine all forces of German-Americans in defense of their position in the country. This did not result in open clashes, but it probably helped stimulate oppression of German-Americans during World War I because doubts sprang up about Germans' loyalty at a time of war between the United States and Germany. The great majority of German-Americans were absolutely loyal, but some apprehension was provoked, and emotional reaction followed.

The decrease of German immigration and the repression of German-American culture during the war hastened the decline of German-American quarters in American cities. Beginning with the mass immigration of the 1830s, "Little Germanys" had sprung up. In New York Germans preferred to live on the lower East Side for many decades until they moved north and founded a new quarter in Yorkville. The Bowery, today one of the most unpleasant streets in New York, was once the center of German life. The *Atlantic Monthly* reported in 1867:

> That very heterogeneous and perplexing jumble of things foreign and domestic may be likened to an immense chain of German sausages, interlinked here and there with material properly American. All along the Bowery, the principal German theatres and Lager-bier "gardens" are interspersed at short intervals. . . .
>
> On a far greater scale than the beerhouses . . . are the German places of entertainment where music is provided for the gratification of the customers. The largest of these halls—some of which are capable of accommodating from two to three thousand people at a time—are situated in the Bowery. Many are roofed with glass and fitted with fixed tables which extend, in rows, from end to end of the room. Common wooden benches, instead of chairs, are provided for the customers. From the afternoon until a late hour at night, musicians ply their art industriously in a gallery high overhead. . . . It is common to see a table in these places occupied by one family, the smallest baby of which comes in for its share of Lager-bier.[20]

Germans were famous for their love of beer. Perhaps they still are. But Little Germanys consisted of more than theaters and beer gar-

[20] Charles Dawson Shanly, "Germany in New York," *Atlantic Monthly* 19 (1868): 555–64, esp. pp. 555, 558–59.

dens. There were German shops in which German food and other German goods were sold. The German language could be heard everywhere. German churches and schools existed here, as well as German libraries and clubs of all kinds. Mutual-aid societies, voluntary fire and police organizations, and German institutions for various other purposes were also typical of the Little Germanys.

There was a Bohne-Viertel in Brooklyn, a quarter called Over-the-Rhine in Cincinnati, the North Side in Milwaukee, and a Little Saxony in New Orleans. These German enclaves in American cities helped preserve the German heritage. Nativists sometimes criticized them because of their foreignness.

The role of the Little Germanys was not, however, limited to the conservation of traditions. Such neighborhoods and homogeneous German quarters provided protection and support for members of a minority group during the time of their adjustment. There they could learn how to cope with the problems of a strange environment, learn the English language, and prepare themselves for the future. The German quarters functioned like buffers or "decompression chambers."

Today these Little Germanys have all but disappeared. Only a few traces can be found here and there, as in a house inscription in German or a German restaurant. In Yorkville there still exists the Heidelberg restaurant—"famous for German-Viennese cooking"—and a German drugstore. Poor Americans from the Appalachian Mountains have moved into Cincinnati's Over-the-Rhine. Milwaukee's North Side is mainly inhabited by black Americans, as is Germantown, Pennsylvania. In all of this one thing must not be overlooked: the purpose of the Little Germanys was a transitory one. The more the Germans became Americanized, the more these quarters became unnecessary. Though interesting from the historian's point of view, they were not erected for eternity.

Like other ethnic groups in the United States, German-Americans preferred to live in certain regions. They went to places where earlier German immigrants had settled. During colonial times it was Pennsylvania where many of them built their new homes. Later the Old Northwest was a favored region of German settlers. At the beginning of this century Albert Bernhardt Faust, the historian of the German element in the United States, wrote, "The last Census Report [1900] shows that the German population is not only widespread, but is more

The interior of a German restaurant in New York. Source unknown.
Courtesy Museum für Hamburgische Geschichte.

equally distributed over the territory of the United States than any
other foreign element." [21]

Nevertheless, in the twentieth century there were certain regions
where Germans preferred to live. From New York through Pennsylvania, Ohio, Indiana, and Illinois the so-called German Belt existed,
with extensions into Michigan, Wisconsin, Minnesota, Iowa, Nebraska,
Missouri, and Kansas. Obviously this was a region which appealed
most to German immigrants. The scenery and the climate correspond
more closely to Germany than anywhere else in the United States.

There were other "dispersed" centers of German settlements as
well: in Louisiana, Colorado, Utah, California, Oregon, Washington,
Montana, and especially Texas. Historical reasons can be given for the
existence of many such centers. There was the attractiveness of New
Orleans as one of the major ports where Germans arrived in the New
World. German settlements in Texas initially came into being because—
as Mexican territory, as the Lone Star Republic, and as one of the

[21] Faust, *German Element* I, 574.

United States—it was particularly inviting for tough pioneers and settlers even from distant Europe. Land was cheap and tax-free in Texas, and people did not know how poor it was. California, on the other hand, had a strong influx of Germans because of the gold rush.

Today Germans can be found in every state. They participated and are still participating in the special mobility of Americans. There are even new centers of Germans in the country in places where they were scarcely to be found in earlier times, for example, in Atlanta and in Houston, where German industries have established branches.

Despite this widespread German element it is difficult to speak of a distinct German ethnic group in the United States today. Kathleen N. Conzen, historian at the University of Chicago, recently wrote in her excellent article on the Germans in the *Harvard Encyclopedia of American Ethnic Groups*:

> . . . the Germans in the 1970s were among the least visible of American ethnic groups. Theirs was the first immigrant tide to ebb, with a sharp drop in numbers of annual arrivals (relative to the total immigration) in the 1890s. By 1972 most American residents calling themselves German were of third or subsequent generations. They differed little from national norms demographically or economically. Only their slightly greater tendencies toward marriage, male-headed households, higher education, lower unemployment, and greater than average proportions of farmers in their ranks suggested the last remnants of historically distinctive values and behavior.[22]

This leads us to a final question: What is the meaning of three hundred years of German settlement in North America today? Germans have become Americans. They sometimes look back to Germany, but from the perspective of those who have parted with it to become citizens of the United States. They are interested in the fate of their ancestors' fatherland, much as Germans of today are interested in the development of the country to which many of their relatives moved. Is this interest only for nostalgic reasons?

There is probably more to it. Centuries of migration, mainly from east to west, but to a certain degree from west to east also, have resulted in closer ties between the two nations. There is an affinity between Germany and America that can be attributed to the migratory

<hr>

[22]Thernstrom, ed., *Harvard Encyclopedia of American Ethnic Groups*, p. 406.

process. Immigrants and people who stayed at home kept in touch with each other or reestablished connections after long periods of silence. Genealogical research across the ocean reflects this affinity.

Close relationships, however, did not prevent periods of enmity and hate. In two world wars Americans and Germans have fought against each other, and bitter feelings replaced an atmosphere of friendship and cooperation. There is no room here for an analysis of these events, but one remarkable thing should be mentioned: after two life-and-death struggles American-German relations quickly returned to normal. As a historian I am puzzled about that, and I can find few parallels for the phenomenon in international relations of modern times. Perhaps three hundred years of migration between Germany and America have helped bring this about. History has its effects on the present and, we hope, on the future too. Therefore, it pays to keep alive the past and remember that it can teach us lessons for survival.

Rural Hill Country: Man, Nature, and the Ecological Perspective

To an extraterrestrial visitor circling the earth at a low altitude in search of a hospitable landing place, Texas would reveal broken terrain, shallow and stony soils, and relatively sparse vegetation. Such a visitor would doubtless select one of the gardens of the earth, one of the cradles of civilization, for his landing. Only later, distant centuries later, when his descendants had filled the gardens and pushed north-ward and southward from the gentle climates, would some son of this visitor find his way into a place like Texas. Then, especially if he were possessed of a romantic imagination, he might find this land beautiful after a fashion. This descendant would survive in this semiarid landscape, but he would see his romanticism tamed and his body toughened.

Coming

Such a son was Friedrich Ernst, who came to Texas in 1831 some-what by accident. He knew nothing about building cabins, hated guns, and brought none of the necessary goods for clothing his family on the frontier. Still he loved his new country, and he expressed his feelings in an at times eloquent letter to a friend in Oldenburg, urging him to come to Texas at once. The friend turned the letter over to a news-paper, and it was widely published. In this way Germans learned of a hilly land similar to Sicily, alternately forested and covered with grassy prairies. The constant breezes, almost always from the east, were gentle, and the climate was mild, like springtime in Germany. The soil needed no fertilizer. Wine grapes thrived, honey could be found in hollow trees, and "wild prey such as deer, bears, raccoons, wild tur-keys, geese, and partridges" filled the woodlands. Even the meadows

A German map of the state of Texas after 1850. German settlement was concentrated in the counties of Fayette, Colorado, and Washington in the east and in the Hill Country counties of Comal, Bexar, Guadalupe, and Gillespie in what was then "west" Texas. After the Civil War, Germans dispersed throughout the state. Courtesy Barker Texas History Center, University of Texas at Austin.

were carpeted with "the most charming flowers." Of course, there were panthers and leopards and rattlesnakes, but every planter knew "safe means against them." Besides that, passports were unnecessary.[1]

Every dream is nourished by myths and legends. The dream of Texas as a great, golden land is no exception. One myth started with Karl Anton Postl, who may have visited Texas under the assumed name of Charles Sealsfield. His novel of 1841 about life in Texas, *Das Ka-*

[1] Friedrich Ernst, letter written February 1, 1832, from Mill Creek, Texas, quoted in G. G. Benjamin, *The Germans in Texas: A Study in Immigration* (1910; reprint, Austin: Jenkins, 1974), pp. 17–19. Del Weniger discusses the term "prairie" in "Nature, the Settler, and the Ecological Perspective in Rural Texas," in *Texas Country: The Changing Rural Scene*, ed. Glen E. Lich and Dona B. Reeves-Marquardt (College Station: Texas A&M University Press, 1986).

An original engraving of Captain Murky's "cabin," a bizarre plantation
house that gave its name to Charles Sealsfield's early Texas classic *The
Cabin Book* (translation of *Das Kajütenbuch*, 1841; reprint, Austin:
Eakin, 1985). Sealsfield's Texas was loud and flamboyant, a golden land
where sensitive plants grew six feet tall and the oaks were the tallest
on earth. Sealsfield compared winning the West with taming spirited
horses: westering Americans pursued something they had lost, something that had run away from them, something that promised to take
them far into the future. Courtesy Eakin Press, Austin.

jütenbuch (*The Cabin Book*),[2] became a best-seller throughout Europe. Texas for Sealsfield was a "boundless sea of . . . green," an unspoiled Garden of Eden in "God's world immaculate." It was part of an
immeasurably beautiful and rich land that stood for "the progress of all
civilization."[3]

[2]Charles Sealsfield, *Das Kajütenbuch* (1841; reprint, Stuttgart: Philipp Reclam,
1982, with an introduction by Alexander Ritter), had numerous printings and editions in
German and English. See also Charles Sealsfield, *The Cabin Book* (New York: St. John
and Coffin, 1871; reprint, with foreword by Glen E. Lich and afterword by Alexander
Ritter, Austin, Tex.: Eakin, 1985).

[3]Charles Sealsfield is quoted in A. Leslie Willson, "Another Planet: Texas in German Literature," in Joseph Wilson, ed., "Texas and Germany: Crosscurrents," *Rice University Studies*, 63, no. 3 (1977): 102. Compare Henry David Thoreau's essay "Walking."

In politically, economically, and agriculturally depressed Germany, Texas was generally known as a fabulous and wild land. With the intent of alleviating this depression, the Texas Adelsverein, a league of five sovereign German princes and sixteen nobles, assembled in 1842 to lay long-range plans for a massive transplantation of German farmers and artisans to the New World.[4] The next year four objectives were formulated by the Adelsverein:

> To improve the lot of the working class who are without employment, thus controlling their increasing impoverishment;
> To unite the emigrants by giving them protection through this Association in order to ease their burden through mutual assistance;
> To maintain contacts between Germany and the emigrants, and to develop maritime trade by establishing business connections;
> To find a market for German craft in these settlements, and to provide a market in Germany for the products of these colonies.[5]

This venture, which combined ethical idealism, directed economy, and mercantilism to effect controlled social evolution, was not unusual in the context of the 1840s, the inchoate years of communitarianism, Darwinism, and Marxism.

Nearly ten thousand colonists came to Texas under the auspices of the society in the first two years, but overhead was high, and the investment showed little promise of repaying stockholders. The nobles lost interest in the colonization of Texas after its annexation by the United States. In 1847, after the establishment of seven colonies in the Hill Country, the directors of the Adelsverein declared bankruptcy, leaving the colonists to develop on their own in accordance with the free-enterprise and political institutions of their Anglo-American neighbors in Texas. The migration continued, however, and by 1850 Texas counted as many as thirty thousand Germans, 20 percent of the total white population. This migration was sustained by the social and psychological phenomena of cluster migration, the cult of "trailblazer" personality, and New World letters until well into the 1870s.[6]

[4] Rudolph L. Biesele, *The History of the German Settlements in Texas: 1831–1861* (Austin: Von Boeckmann-Jones, 1930), pp. 66–67. See also Otto W. Tetzlaff, trans. and ed., *The Immigrant to Texas: A Handbook and Guide* (Burnet, Tex.: Eakin, 1979).

[5] Ibid., p. 69.

[6] The words "emigration" and "immigration" are misleading and artificial, especially, as is frequently the case, when they are used synonymously. Historically, furthermore, the terms have shifted since the Adelsverein was founded, and today the distinc-

I would feel uncomfortable continuing beyond this point if I did not advance first some speculations about the context and meaning of this migration. A rumor, for example, persisted in the Hill Country through at least the second and third generations that the Adelsverein was an agent for certain British designs to effect a pincer action from an independent and pliable Republic of Texas in the Southeast (keep in mind the pre-1850 map of Texas) to a British-contested Oregon Territory in the Northwest, the effect of which ideally would have been to contain American westward expansion in the Mississippi-Missouri basin and to deny the United States access to the Pacific. Texas-German scholars from R. L. Biesele to Minetta Goyne have alluded to this rumor, but apart from several striking parallels in the ebb and flow of American and British diplomatic negotiations during the period 1842–46, I am aware of no foundation to this story other than its apparently widespread currency in the Hill Country at least until after World War II. The annexation of Texas in 1845 and the discovery of gold in California in 1849 squelched these schemes, if indeed they ever existed.[7]

We must, moreover, be mindful that the migration to Texas represents only a small percentage of the overall German migration to North America in the nineteenth century and that after the Civil War the percentage of Germans in the state's population was likewise quite small. The significance of the Adelsverein rests therefore in its mission, and the seeming cultural preeminence of the Germans in parts of the state results from this minority's isolation from other, far larger ethnic groups and from the advantages that accrued to educated Germans who moved into positions of leadership during Reconstruction. The dominant climate of opinion among these people confirms their qualitative rather than quantitative approach to life. They saw themselves as experimenters. Using a simple yet amazingly neglected approach to

---

tion suggests some uncanny ability to catch the migrant(s) precisely at midpoint—in the Atlantic—when the *e* changes to *im*—and suddenly the experience is different. To speak of "migrants" and "migration" embraces the entire process, including the sea voyage.

[7] See Biesele, *The History of the German Settlements in Texas*, pp. 75, 109; Minetta Goyne, *Lone Star and Double Eagle* (Fort Worth: Texas Christian University Press, 1982), p. ii. See also Ephraim D. Adams, *British Diplomatic Correspondence concerning the Republic of Texas, 1838–1846*; Hunter Miller, *Treaties and Other International Acts of the United States of America*, Vol. V, *1846–1852*. Cf. Seymour V. Connor, *Adventure in Glory*, Saga of Texas Series (Austin: Steck-Vaughn, 1965), pp. 235–53.

the study of history—through the lives of individuals as recorded in their diaries and journals, art and architecture—one catches frequent glimpses of their belief that they were part of progress. Their struggle for existence on their own terms is a simple but admirable story. One might, in fact, consider them characters in search of a new history. They were, in varying degrees, aware of a kind of social engineering that went into their planned communities, admittedly as much through personal affinity as through design, and I suspect further that some of them may have seen society as an organism subject to genetic laws. They knew not to eat but to save their best seeds for next year's crops. And I am sure that in so believing they were not essentially different from the Massachusetts Colony with its metaphor of a City on the Hill. They differed from previous "countercultures" like the Naj Hamadi, the Anabaptists, and the New England settlement in that their corporate experiment was social in a political and economic rather than religious way and that their social protest was based on a secular or this-worldly teleology. Their favored metaphors might easily have pictured the frontier vintner grafting highly developed vines from the Old World onto the healthy rootstock of the New World or old Europe riding into the future on the wild mustang that is Texas.

What continues to startle one in reencountering this history is the striking difference in Texas in the way that the peasants ascended and the intellectuals descended in society and in the rapidity with which a formerly liberal and educated group became archconservative and ignorant of the world as their parents and grandparents knew it.[8] It may have been that in Texas, as the weather stunted and gnarled plants, so too the political climate contorted the experiment. At any rate, German culture in Texas can hardly be said to have flowered, though it did indeed grow.

For many colonists the migration may have satisfied an often unconscious need to reconcile social myth and reality. Migration, like science fiction, affords an unusual opportunity to alternate on reality while preserving a deteriorating status quo—a solution at once radical and reactionary. Born of social, political, and economic protest, the mi-

[8] See also Ferdinand von Roemer, *Texas: With Particular Reference to German Immigration and the Physical Appearance of the Country,* trans. Oswald Mueller (1935; reprint, Waco: Texian, 1967, 1983), p. 100.

gration abruptly modernized these people. As their old sacred order
gave way to modern secular values, hardly any part of their lives remained unshaken. The sociology of the family, the psychology of behavior, and the rules of the marketplace as they knew them were frac-
tured by their very act of leaving. It was a moral dilemma. With her
soul thus inhabiting two worlds, one young German girl spoke for all
the migrants:

> Well do I remember my apprehensions as we boarded this fearsome crate
> that was to carry us into the new world. Our former and happy childhood
> now lay behind us, soon to be followed by more serious times. Yet we
> were cheerful. There was no lack of singing, everyone attempting to en-
> courage the other, with probably many a secret tear falling into the
> waves. We hurried towards the sinking sun, the magic West beckoning, as
> we wondered what the future held in store.[9]

Encounter

From the Gulf Coast the colonists moved inland up the Guadalupe
River valley beginning in 1845. The land struck them with wonder and
fear, fulfilling the expectations of a young woman writer: ". . . that recently opened paradise, the eternally blue sky, the radiant sun about
the great uncultivated uninhabited land, tempting tropical fruits, Indians and wild animals, too, to break the monotony of existence, and
above all else, golden freedom."[10]

Following, in part, the prejudices of some of the officers of the
Adelsverein, they distrusted the damp, populated coast; but the interior they invested with the qualities of abundance and promise. As
they pushed into the forbidden wilderness, they felt themselves transformed. Writing home, one of them described a strange landscape in
which fear of the unknown mingled with the temptation to see what lay
ahead: "Everybody tries to stop you, to hold you, by painting the next
succeeding region as horrifying, but up to now as far as we have come,
the land has become more and more beautiful." She continued: "I find

[9] Ottilie Fuchs Goeth, *Memoirs of a Texas Pioneer Grandmother (Was Grossmutter Erzählt: 1805–1915)*, trans. Irma Goeth Guenther (Austin: n.p., 1969; reprint, trans.
and ed. Irma Goeth Guenther, Austin: Eakin, 1982), p. 17.
[10] Emma Murck Altgelt is quoted in Crystal Sasse Ragsdale, *The Golden Free
Land: The Reminiscences and Letters of Women on an American Frontier* (Austin: Landmark, 1976), p. 134.

that as soon as one is here, one is overcome with an amazing change; the farther one comes, the more civilization ceases, but one transforms with the changes and begins to think it must be so, and is astonished when noticing something European." [11]

The first wagonloads advanced inland through the coastal plain (described by Sealsfield in *The Cabin Book*), the post-oak belt (which Friedrich Ernst described in his letter), and the blackland prairie to the rocky Hill Country: an eroded fault-line scarp where the Great Plains come to a halt above the coastal plain of the Gulf of Mexico. [12] There, at the edge of the Balcones Escarpment, the colonists made their first permanent settlement, naming it New Braunfels in honor of the first commissioner-general of the Adelsverein.

The Germans reached New Braunfels on Good Friday, 1845, thus encountering their new homeland in the spring, its most pleasant season, and they innocently believed that it was as pleasant throughout the year. Not only did they arrive just before a Texas summer, but they also arrived in the last years of a rainy cycle before the start of a drought.

The climate of this transitional countryside, they soon learned, was characterized by irregularity, wide extremes, and rapid changes. With the northeastern end of the Hill Country straddling a line dividing the humid and subhumid regions of the southern United States and the southwestern tip bordering the arid and semiarid Southwest, the Hill Country climate of sharp contrasts was an abrupt change for these forest people from northern Europe.

The Hill Country, which rises from five hundred to three thousand feet above sea level, consists basically of three parts: the narrow edge of the blackland prairie that borders the Balcones Escarpment; the fertile river and creek valleys, which became avenues of dispersal into the hinterland; and finally the hills and broken pieces of upland called the "divide," where the Hill Country scarpland changes into the Edwards Plateau. The vegetation and wildlife of the region, like its climate and terrain, are varied.

[11] Ida Kappell Kapp, letter written on January 15, 1850, from Comaltown, Texas.

[12] For a useful nontechnical description of the geology of this region, see Paul A. Johnsgard, "The Grassy Heartland," in *Our Continent: A Natural History of North America*, ed. Edwin H. Colbert (Washington, D.C.: National Geographic Society, 1976), esp. p. 257.

The springtime was a pleasant introduction. Men and women wrote eloquently of the unspoiled Hill Country, describing the six-thousand-square-mile region drained by the Guadalupe, bordered on the northeast by the Colorado and on the southwest by the Nueces, as a "true paradise":

> The hilly plots could be justly called a natural park; in the mountains there were lovely far-stretching valleys and romantic rock structures. Silver-clear streams flowed everywhere. But the whole district comprising an area out of which several small kingdoms could be cut was still in possession of the Indians who extended their roving expeditions down to the coast. When the German immigrants took possession of western Texas the main force of the Comanches, the most feared Indian tribe, was already broken; they were, however, still strong enough to keep control of the mountains, the pastures and the buffaloes. Apart from them there were living in Texas the Lipans, a powerful tribe, the Kiowas, the Tonkawas, the Wacos, the Apaches and Mescaleros who, like all Indians, led a nomadic life and settled sometimes here and sometimes there for a shorter or longer period.[13]

Just as they encountered the land, with naive wonder and fear, the Germans encountered the Indians. Later, their view of these native inhabitants of their new homeland became more ambiguous. Still later, after Anglo-Americans had joined them in the Hill Country and during the time of the last raids and depredations, their attitude toward the Indians came to be more like that of their Anglo-American neighbors. To the present, however, their descendants in the Hill Country retain a curious myth of the Indians, a view that overlooks occasional hostile contacts and remembers some early state of peaceful coexistence and noninterference. Certainly the early German colonists could have also learned much from the Indians, but there are no legends of local Squantos or Sacajaweas who helped the settlers during their initial encounter with the land.

Adaptation

Although the Balcones Escarpment is not rugged where it rises from the gently rolling blackland prairie, this wall of hills had been a

[13]August Siemering, "Texas, Her Past, Her Present, Her Future," translated from *Texas Vorwärts* (newspaper, Austin), 1894.

barrier to European advance. Settlement had twice been made at the edge of the Hill Country: once in 1718 at San Antonio, where the San Pedro springs bubble from the Balcones Escarpment; and again, over a hundred years later, at the San Marcos springs, fifty miles northeast of San Antonio. But these springs were the sources of rivers that began in the blackland below the escarpment. At their backs were no river valleys that afforded the enticement of natural passages into the rocky hinterland.

Such a passage existed only at New Braunfels, situated between San Antonio and San Marcos. Here, moving through a majestic rock-walled canyon above the town, the Guadalupe River dropped from the hills and divide of the Hill Country down into the rolling prairie that sloped downward for two hundred miles to the coast. The small spring-fed Comal River, lined with lush flora, also flowed into the Guadalupe near the German township, thus producing a verdant plain where this mother colony for European settlement of the Hill Country took root.[14]

Guided to this valley by botanist Ferdinand Lindheimer, who for two years had combed the wooded Brazos, Colorado, and Guadalupe valleys collecting and classifying the flora of Texas, the commissioner-general of the Adelsverein laid out New Braunfels in the form of a traditional northern European farm village. Such agglomerated rural settlements had evolved over centuries in populous farming regions of the world because such villages conserved land, preserved traditional social patterns, promoted economic stability, and afforded mutual protection for the townspeople. Fields and pastures radiated outward on all sides from a centrally located cluster of multistory dwellings, barns, shops, and church. Daily the farmers—men and women—walked to their fields during the growing season, and daily the herdsmen circled the village with their charges of sheep, cattle, goats, geese, and swine until snow again covered the ground. Crops were harvested by entire extended families. Produce was stored in barns and cellars under the

---

[14] Until the arrival of the German colonists European civilization had hardly penetrated the hilly scarpland of the southeastern Edwards Plateau. Occasional reconnaissance from 1709 to 1831 had passed near the Hill Country region, but if any passed directly through it, they are obscured in history. The presence of Europeans in central and southwest Texas had left the landscape largely unaltered; their contribution, other than diseases and dissensions that hastened the decline of the native Indian cultures, had been minimal because their numbers had been small.

same roof where the family lived with its livestock when the herds and flocks were brought in and fed through the cold months.

In Texas several factors contributed to an alteration of this traditional farm village. First, space to expand was readily available, and towns were often laid out with fifty-foot-wide streets, in sharp contrast to the narrow, crooked streets of nineteenth-century European villages. Furthermore, town lots were large, and there was no need to put houses and outbuildings under one roof or to build them more than one and a half stories high. Besides, the heat of summer suggested low, open town plans that allowed cooling breezes to pass through the towns. The fourth, and possibly most significant, reason was that farms had to be larger in a semiarid climate to produce satisfactory yields of grains, vegetables, fruits, and livestock. The result, then, was that the Germans spread out, induced perhaps by a fifth, more subtle, reason, namely, the no doubt unconscious desire to make their towns *look* like the Anglo and Mexican towns through which they passed on their trek inland.

For the most part an assimilation-prone ethnic group, the Germans also adapted their traditional building methods to Anglo and Mexican plans. Although they had settled, in the exaggerated words of an early pioneer, in a "complete 'terra incognita,' one hundred miles from all white settlement," they learned quickly from their distant neighbors to modify their architecture with the materials and climate of the Hill Country.[15] Log cabins were sometimes erected, either single-room or dogtrot structures, but they were usually converted to barns or cribs after more substantial family quarters could be erected. Otherwise, a two-room, one- or one-and-a-half-story structure, outwardly resembling the lowland houses common from Georgia to Texas, was built, and to this basic plan was added a porch in front and later a one-story ell or shed on the back. The walls of these homes were sometimes made of limestone (especially if the building was to have a full two stories), but more often they were of traditional German half timber with casement windows—the characteristics that distinguished these immigrant homes from the homes of their Anglo-American neighbors, for otherwise the plans, porches, and roof lines were quite similar. In Texas roofs of shingles cut from abundant stands of cypress along

---

[15] Siemering, "Texas, Her Past, Her Present, Her Future."

the Guadalupe and its tributaries replaced the traditional thatch, slate, and tile roofs of Germany. Later, when milling—the first major German industry in the Hill Country—became more advanced, lumber was cut into siding. Frequently, then, the old German construction methods were hidden under grooved weatherboards and shiplap. In the end their buildings could not be readily distinguished from the low-land southern frame structures that they already resembled in shape.[16]

In sum, land, climate, and cultural exchange hastened not only the demise of the Adelsverein and its communal patterns of organization but also the modification of much material culture imported from Europe. In these respects most of the German colonists seemed willing to let their new environment dictate solutions and to learn from their non-German neighbors. Many of their buildings were changed or camouflaged to look like prosperous Anglo-American homes, barns, stores, churches, and public buildings. Their far-flung farmsteads dotted the countryside for miles around the towns. Within a generation the only landscape feature vaguely resembling a German farm village was the extended farm complex that developed when two or three offspring built homes adjacent to those of their parents and then divided their inherited landholdings so that each new farmstead connected to a slice of the original farm or ranch. In general this assimilatory pattern was characteristic of the way in which these Germans adapted their agriculture and way of life as they took charge of the Hill Country and became increasingly self-sufficient.[17]

By and large the settlers could be divided into two unequal groups: first, the majority, who were small-town people of sufficient means to emigrate, predominantly from the peasant and artisan classes, and, second, a small minority of nobles and middle-class intellectuals who

[16] See Terry G. Jordan, "German Folk Houses in the Texas Hill Country," in *German Culture in Texas: A Free Earth*, ed. Glen E. Lich and Dona B. Reeves (Boston: Twayne, 1980), pp. 103–20. See also Terry G. Jordan, *Texas Log Buildings: A Folk Architecture* (Austin: University of Texas Press, 1978); and "A Russian-German Folk House in North Texas," in *Built in Texas*, ed. Francis E. Abernethy (Waco: E.-Heart Press, 1979), pp. 137–38. See also Glen E. Lich and Lera Tyler, "When the Creeks Run Dry: Water Milling in the German Hill Country," in *Built in Texas*, pp. 237–45; Glen E. Lich, "The Kammlah House: A German Family Residence and Store Complex," *Perspective* 11, no. 2 (December, 1982): 2–6.

[17] See Terry G. Jordan, *German Seed in Texas Soil: Immigrant Farmers in Nineteenth-Century Texas* (Austin: University of Texas Press, 1966).

were Old World refugees from the revolutions of 1830 and 1848. Although these two groups had divergent mind-sets, they shared several fundamental beliefs. They were dissatisfied—economically, politically, or culturally—with the German future, and they looked to the glowing promise of the New World, although, of course, they defined the promise of their new future differently.[18] Their confidence in this future was not shaken, even by the hardships they endured throughout the first decade. They shared a belief that such hardship was of a passing nature, that it was a test that they could overcome through perseverance and hard work.

At no time was this faith challenged more severely than when the second increment of settlers landed on the coast in the winter of 1845. The outbreak of war between the United States and Mexico left them stranded on the shore when freighters and teams were commandeered for the American army. Four thousand immigrants spent a rainy, cold winter in dugouts with inadequate provisions. A fourth of them died of petechial fever (*Blutfleckenkrankheit*), or cerebrospinal meningitis, accompanied by scurvy and dysentery.[19] This catastrophic experience led to a shared distrust of the sickness-infested coastal areas and port cities that were peopled with exploitive manipulators and "drifters," as Germans called the Anglo-Americans who were continually following the lure of easy gains.

Both groups also shared the feeling that to learn from their neighboring cultures made good sense but that the loss of a distinctive German cultural identity should be avoided. The Mexican War, their experiences on the coast and in the port cities, and later their trial by fire during the Civil War confirmed a defensive posture that was reinforced by their low regard for certain Anglo-American deficiencies bred of generations on the frontier, such as the use of tobacco by women, illiteracy, primitive and evangelistic religion, political nativism, and rootlessness, which the Germans equated with shiftlessness.

The Germans—nobles, intellectuals, artisans, and peasants alike— remained rooted to the land on which they established themselves in the New World. That characteristic, in the words of social historian Os-

[18]See Glen E. Lich, "Goethe on the Guadalupe," in *German Culture in Texas: A Free Earth*, ed. Glen E. Lich and Dona B. Reeves (Boston: Twayne, 1980), pp. 29–71.
[19]Biesele, *The History of the German Settlements in Texas*, pp. 130–31.

car Handlin, harked back to "an ancient way of life" that "yielded only slowly to forces of time." These people shared a sense of community that transmuted into a strong sense of place—they were "part of a community and the community was held in the land as a whole. . . . This was the fixed point" by which they knew their "relationship with all humanity."[20]

Not only did they identify the land with themselves by giving it their own names and the nostalgic names of their old homeland, but they learned how to extract from it the cures for their physical, political, and spiritual illnesses. After the epidemic on the coast, which was then carried inland to the colonies of New Braunfels and Fredericksburg (founded by the second commissioner-general in 1846), they boiled medicinal teas from native herbs, trusting that the land would produce the necessary remedies for its own peculiar diseases.

Others looked to the land for other cures. The philosopher Ernst Kapp (1808–96), originally a Hegelian, formulated in the hills above New Braunfels a new philosophy of environmental rather than historical determinism based on a comparative cultural geography that he completed in Texas. Kapp theorized, a century ahead of his time, that not only was humanity shaped by its surroundings, but the future— even in this virginal wilderness in the 1850s and 1860s—was threatened by pollution and dehumanization resulting from man's headlong search for bigger and better machines.[21]

Like Kapp, others also expected miracles to spring from the land. Ottomar von Behr (1810–56), son of the prime minister of Anhalt and Köthen and an acquaintance of Alexander von Humboldt, experimented with agricultural reform, wrote a guide for German immigrants, and developed a new breed of sheep especially adapted to the climate of the Southwest. In 1847, with a similar intent, Ferdinand von Herff—friend of Humboldt, of Prince Albert of Great Britain, of Prince Frederick of Prussia, and of Czarina Maria Alexandra of Russia—led a small fraternity of "communistic" freethinkers to Texas, where they es-

[20] Oscar Handlin, *The Uprooted: The Epic Story of the Great Migrations That Made the American People*, 2nd ed. (Boston: Little, Brown, 1973), p. 8.

[21] For a summarized treatment see Lich, "Goethe on the Guadalupe," in *German Culture in Texas*. For a more comprehensive explication of major tenets in Kapp's two studies, see Hans-Martin Sass, "Man and His Environment: Ernst Kapp's Pioneering Experience and His Philosophy of Technology and Environment," in ibid., pp. 82–99.

tablished the seventh and last Adelsverein colony, naming it Bettina (for the well-known Bettina Brentano von Arnim). Within less than a year the commune "went to pieces like a bubble,"[22] but Herff, wiser from his experiences, persisted and in 1850 published a treatise, *The Regulated Emigration of the German Proletariat with Special Reference to Texas*, on the incremental transplantation of workers by a heavily financed national organization. This scheme called for a directed economy, controlled production and distribution, and curtailed personal liberty so that the lower classes could rise by their own efforts to become decent and worthy citizens of their new fatherland.[23]

Like Kapp, Behr, and Herff, most of the settlers believed that the new land would willingly yield them its riches if they learned enough and remained flexible enough to prevail. In this vein the second commissioner-general (who had come to Texas also to study the patterns of nature to discern mankind's destiny)[24] rode with a small escort into the Lipan-Apache and Comanche hunting grounds to conclude a treaty with the assembled chiefs that allowed Germans to move freely up the fertile river and creek valleys of the Hill Country. They looked to nature to yield answers to other problems. A story is told that settlers seriously considered abandoning the second colony of Fredericksburg after several years of severe drought. Among the German colonists, however, one scientist discovered a clue that gave others some hope: Jakob Kuechler noted in the tree rings of an old oak felled for building that short periods of drought alternated in cycles with longer periods of adequate rainfall. Kuechler predicted that the drought would end soon. His projection of the past onto the future was right, and the lean years were indeed followed by years of plenty.

In the end it was probably as much their curiosity for exploration as their trust in the land and a growing understanding for its capacities that drew the Germans in family clusters up the valleys and hillsides

[22] Louis Reinhardt, "The Communist Colony of Bettina," *Texas State Historical Association Quarterly* 3 (1899): 39.

[23] For a fuller treatment, see Arthur L. Finck's translation of Herff's work (master's thesis, University of Texas, 1949), pp. 24–29. Finck's translation, with an introduction, was published as *The Regulated Emigration of the German Proletariat with Special Reference to Texas, Being Also a Guide for German Emigrants* (San Antonio: Trinity University Press, 1978).

[24] Irene Marschall King, *John O. Meusebach: German Colonizer in Texas* (Austin: University of Texas Press, 1967), p. 32.

Artist Hermann Lungkwitz's Hill Country was a mythic and monu-
mental idyll that conveyed qualities of the supernatural, along with
mystery and wonder. Courtesy James Patrick McGuire.

during their dispersal from the original farm villages and their filials.
Letters to Germany speak of "the beautiful blue of the skies, and the
clear atmosphere so peculiar to this country," of roaming about the
countryside, looking at its "strange grasses, shrubs, flowers, cacti, and
palms."[25] They speak of "mountains . . . rich in minerals . . . still waiting for exploration."[26] They record impressions of "mysterious crystal-
clear water spouts from the depths of the Comal springs."[27] These
letters assured distant readers that these adventurers were no longer
fearful of "the occasional howling of the wolves from the hills, the
sneaking steps of a panther, or the suspicious 'huhuhu' of the owl."[28]
They sing of untapped abundance, of "twenty bee-trees, of which the
best one had thirty bottles of honey."[29] They record the view toward

[25] Emma Murck Altgelt, quoted in Ragsdale, *The Golden Free Land*, p. 136.
[26] Siemering, "Texas, Her Past, Her Present, Her Future."
[27] Julius Dresel, MS in translation, Dresel file, San Antonio Public Library.
[28] Ibid.
[29] Franz Kettner, "Letters of a German Pioneer in Texas," *Southwestern Historical*

the magic West that beckoned onward—from "a high hill . . . looking down into a large and gorgeous valley through which a silvery clear stream flows, gushing from rocks impetuously, meandering until it vanishes from sight!"[30]

Domestication

During the late 1840s and 1850s scientific agriculture became increasingly widespread as German agricultural societies were formed to translate and disseminate information of interest to farmers. The limited availability of water curtailed a great deal of expansion, keeping farmsteads near streams with year-round water. An improving network of roads facilitated communication over relatively large distances between settlements, and this improvement stimulated economic development both within the towns and villages and between them and San Antonio, the trade center of the Hill Country. Germans dominated the teamster industry, and their wagon trains plied a weekly circuit from the hinterland, carrying lumber, shingles, and produce to the city and back again with loads of goods that could not be raised or manufactured at home. Later the development of various cottage industries sent some manufactures to the city too, but by then trucks and cars had supplanted the ox-drawn wagons, and the whole economic system had broadened.

During the 1850s and 1860s the farms and isolated communities of the hinterland maintained a precarious self-sufficiency. And as Anglo-Americans moved into the area and the German population increased as well, conflicts with renegade Indians became commonplace. Local volunteer militias and Texas Rangers detailed to the frontier were inadequate to safeguard citizens, especially during the Civil War.

A generation passed before the land was domesticated and the culture firmly rooted. Once that point was reached (roughly around 1875), the frontier had passed: transformed, and with it the people transformed. The geologist Ferdinand Roemer, dispatched to Texas by Alexander von Humboldt and the Berlin Academy of Science, had al-

---

Quarterly 69 (1965): 463–72, trans. Terry G. Jordan and Marlis Anderson Jordan, letter written on April 2, 1856, from Fredericksburg, Texas.

[30] Siemering, "Texas, Her Past, Her Present, Her Future."

ready foretold a class shift among these New World Germans when he departed in 1847. He wrote in *Texas*, published in 1849, that in this "romantic" environment the upper classes would decline to an ascendant peasant and worker class:

> The colonist who has not farmed in the old country must have an unusual amount of endurance and will-power. I have seen quite a few German peasants and laborers, who had come here without any funds, come into possession of little farms through their industry. These supplied them with the necessities of life and even gave promise of future affluence and comfortable living. On the other hand, I have hardly seen ten people of the higher class, supplied with moderate funds, who within a year were able to acquire a house with a fenced-in field and of whom one could hope that they would be able to sustain themselves through their own efforts.[31]

Then he added, almost echoing Sealsfield, "I had grown to love the beautiful land of meadows, to which belongs a great future. . . . May its broad, green prairies become the habitation of a great and happy people."[32]

Farm to Market

By 1875, a generation after their arrival, the Germans had completed the domestication of this frontier. Several innovations that coincided with the end of this process led, then, to the third and last stage of dispersal—the advance from river and creek valleys onto the upland divide and the subsequent transition from farming to ranching in large parts of the Hill Country. Generally speaking, the year 1875 marked the cessation of Indian raids into Texas. Shortly thereafter the sale of railroad lands financed the laying of new tracks, stimulated the economy, and promoted settlement of the divide and higher regions of the Edwards Plateau. Approximately thirty-two million acres in western Texas (an area the size of Alabama) were sold in this way. The farther west this sale of land continued, the more Anglo-Americans equaled and then outnumbered the Germans, so that, by the time these vast holdings were completely disposed of, the Germans had been boxed into the eastern fifth of the Edwards Plateau. During the 1880s wind-

[31] Roemer, *Texas*, p. 100.
[32] Samuel W. Geiser, *Naturalists of the Frontier* (Dallas: Southern Methodist University Press, 1948), p. 171.

mills began to appear in this higher country, and together with barbed-wire fences they changed the ecological landscape by making large-scale cattle, sheep, and goat ranching possible.

From the 1880s through the agricultural boom years of the 1940s this tamed landscape was changed only by a continual pattern of agricultural growth. Then, after the forties, when there was no more land to be had for agriculture and the region sustained its maximum capacity to produce without radical innovations, the people who had shaped that land, and been shaped by it, began during the drought years of the fifties to develop a new economy based on tourism and recreation. Along with the marketing of a wholesome climate and scenic landscape, the selling of the region's distinctive ethnic heritge became a major source of income to this "unspoiled" land lacking both oil and industry. Then the German-Texans were no longer "an unsightly thorn in the countryside," as Larry McMurtry had called a north Texas German enclave because they farmed in an area dominated by ranchers,[33] but rather they found themselves sitting on a statewide monopoly in *Fachwerk*, or half-timbered, houses.

The gnarled and brushy live oaks, broken landscape, and sun-drenched summers attracted first a regional and then a national market. *Partnerstadt*, or sister-city, arrangements with European towns, coupled with massive promotion of the "Wild West" starting in 1980 and of the German tricentennial in 1983, promise to move the Texas Hill Country into international tourism. Artificial lakes, white-tailed deer, and exotic game may now run second to the New Braunfels Wurstfest, the "Night in Old Fredericksburg," and the Kerrville music and art festivals. Everywhere, the German heritage is packaged for sale: at Das Peach Haus, at Das Kinder Haus, and at Das Zahn House (general dentistry). What we have now can hardly be called the "generation that forgets." They are remembering things that they never knew. People who grew up with a *Fachwerk* room in the center of their home but who never knew the name of the construction method either in English or in German until the Hill Country was "discovered" now know the insurance and real-estate value of half timbers, all about mar-

[33] Larry McMurtry, *In a Narrow Grave: Essays on Texas* (Austin: Encino, 1968), pp. 146–47.

The Fritz Stieler ranch house near Comfort. "German houses stand for
something we all want today," observed one Anglo traveler through
Texas in the 1980s. "They represent solidity, stability, surety. They are
close to nature. These are things we have forgotten today." Courtesy
University of Texas Institute of Texan Cultures, San Antonio.

keting primitive antiques, and quite a lot about federal and state
matching funds and tax benefits for historic preservation. Ethnicity is
big business, certainly not the private thing of a generation ago. On
the other hand, some charming town museums are being maintained;
well over five hundred old buildings will be or have been saved rather
than torn down, and Comfort, the freethinker town, is now protected
almost entirely by its National Historic District designation. There is
in that, and in *Newsweek*'s choice in 1981 of Comfort as one of the ten
best small towns in America,[34] a seemingly clear recognition of stasis.
But appearances may deceive. The Hill Country's isolation from the

[34] *Newsweek*, July 6, 1981, p. 32.

rest of Texas—first geographic, then political, and eventually economic—fostered a spirit of backward progress[35] in the region, an attitude that one first sees in the radical-reactionary posture of the migrant forebears. All along the way since then, the region and the
people have zigzagged into modernity, one eye toward the future and
the other fixed on the past. In the Hill Country the style is called
"primitive refurbished."

[35] John Graves, *Hard Scrabble: Observations on a Patch of Land* (New York: Alfred
A. Knopf, 1974), pp. 59, 263–67.

LUTZ RÖHRICH

German Emigrant Songs

FOLK songs are the statements of many, even if a nameless many. In them we hear the voice of the people, a voice that no statistics, no regulations can replace as a source. As such they are not simply economic, political, or religious documents but firsthand accounts from the emigrant's point of view. They are subjective documents, much like autobiographies, diaries, letters, travel journals, reports of bad news, and firsthand accounts of the new home. Emigrant songs indicate the reasons and motivations for emigration, the hopes and fears, the disappointment, the longing and desire to escape from the restrictions and lack of freedom in Europe. The songs function as a psychological safety valve. In part they look forward, and in part they look back. They not only describe the experiences and fates of emigrants but also tell us something about the relationship between those who stayed at home and those who left.

For these and other reasons I have chosen to discuss emigrant songs here. They provide us with models and patterns of orientation with which the emigrants themselves strongly identified. Above all, these songs clearly illustrate how diverse were the motivations for crossing the Big Pond: love of adventure, the desire to make money, political or religious oppression, dissatisfaction with the political situation after the failed Revolution of 1848, the mid-nineteenth-century gold rush, bad harvests and famine at home, economic crisis in the wake of the Industrial Revolution—all played a role in one way or another.

In the German Folk Song Archive in Freiburg, West Germany, one finds many such texts, often in the form of handwritten songbooks.[1] Handwritten material like this often expresses very personal,

[1] Editorial note: All translations of German song texts in this chapter are by Richard Spuler.

even private feelings, such as homesickness or fears and anxieties about the unknown. Many cannot suppress their feelings at the thought, or realization, that they will never again see their loved ones or their birthplace.

In the following pages I consider several songs that can be seen to function as a kind of psychological safety valve in response to a lack or need behind emigration. The songs I consider typify several such "pressure situations":

Auf der Reise nach Amerika

Endlich ihr Brüder wills der Himmel,
Die längst gewünschte Stunde naht,
Endlich aus Europas Volksgetümmel,
Geh'n wir in's Land Amerika.

Mit Kummer, Sorgen und viel Plagen,
Sind krumm geworden wir bald schier,
Drum wollen wir es weiter wagen,
Mit Weib und Kindern ziehen wir.

Ist einer, der nicht hat den Muth
Oder hält das Heimweh ihn,
Der bedenke nur, wie schön und gut,
Amerika wird sorgen für ihn.

Ja man hat bei der schwersten Arbeit
Klein Verdienst und wenig Brod,
Tag und Nacht viel Herzeleid,
Und in Amerika leid't man keine Noth. . . .

[On the Trip to America

Finally, brothers, heaven wills it,
The long-awaited hour nears,
Finally from Europe's mass of peoples
We come to find America here.

Trouble, worry, and great plight
Burden our backs to the point of breaking,
Thus shall we wager this great flight,
Women and children shall we be taking.

If one finds he lacks the courage
Or longs for home day after day,
He should now dispel his worry,
America will show the way.

Yes, even for the hardest labor
But a pittance, a piece of bread,
Misery here's what day and night are made for,
So in America we seek our trade. . . .]

The following song belongs to the same category, one that can be described as a complaint about the dire predicament in which the people find themselves. I quote here only a few lines:

Aus der Heimat in die Ferne
nicht aus Wohllust, auch nicht gerne,
nur aus Zwang in Armutsstand
ziehen wir aus unserem Land. . . .
Ach wie muss der Mensch sich plagen
hier in dieser Jammer-Welt,
bis in höchste Alters Tage
immerfort ums Geld.
Darum müssen wir auch fort
verlassen jetzt den Heimatort.

[From our home to far away,
Not for adventure, not for play,
Only from our poverty's need
Do we of our own land take leave. . . .
Oh, all of this suffering,
Living in this vale of tears,
Until life's final years
And always just for money.
Thus we too must go forth now,
Leaving here our dear hometown.]

The next text, written by Heinrich Schacht as part of his sailor songbook, strikes a more pathetic note. The expectations expressed here are certainly not high; the general tenor is, "It can't be any worse over there than it is here":

Die deutschen Auswanderer

Ein stolzes Schiff streicht langsam durch die Wellen,
Es führt uns unsre deutschen Brüder fort;
Die Flagge weht, die weissen Segel schwellen,
Amerika ist der Bestimmungsort.

Dort zieh'n sie hin, wer wagt es, noch zu fragen,
"Warum verlassen sie ihr Vaterland?"

O, altes Deutschland, kannst du es ertragen,
Dass deine Völker werden so verbannt?

Schaut her, ihr Volksbeglücker,
Schaut her, ihr Unterdrücker,
Seht eure besten Arbeitskräfte flieh'n,
Seht, wie sie über's grosse Weltmeer zieh'n.

Wir stehen hier am heimatlichen Strande
Und blicken unsern deutschen Brüdern nach.
Nicht Hochmuth treibt sie aus dem Vaterlande,
Nein, Nahrungslosigkeit und Noth and Schmach.

Was hier nicht war zu finden,
Woll'n sie sich dort begründen;
Sie segeln von dem deutschen Boden ab,
Und suchen in Amerika ein Grab.

Dort ziehn sie hin auf wilden Meereswogen,
Arm kommen sie im fernen Welttheil an,
Und unter'm fremden, weiten Himmelsbogen
Erwartet sie ein neues Schicksal dann:

Elend, Armuth und Kummer
Wiegt sie gar oft in Schlummer.
O, altes Deutschland, kannst du ohne Grau'n
Die Flucht der armen Landeskinder schau'n?

[The German Immigrants

A proud ship sails slowly through the waves,
Taking away our German brothers' voice;
The white sails swell, the flag does wave,
America is the port of our choice.

There shall they go, who dares to ask,
"Why do they leave their fatherland?"
O aged Germany, will it break your back
That your people shall be thus banned?

Look here, you crowd pleasers,
Look here, you oppressors,
See your best workers on the run,
See how they cross the ocean with the sun.

We stand here upon the shores of home
And look where our German brothers have gone.
Arrogance does not cause us to roam,
No, 'tis hunger and need and shame to the bone.

What here could not be found,
There they hope to turn new ground.
They're sailing from the German soil,
And in America will end their toil.

They journey there on stormy, wild seas,
Arrive in distant corners poor,
And under strange, wide, unfamiliar skies
A new fate will await them on the shore:

Misery, worry, and need
Rocks them now into their sleep.
O aged Germany, can you bear the sight
Of your poor children taking flight?]

A quite different type of immigrant is the gold panner. He is more of an adventurer and not so concerned with working for his daily bread. He does not suffer at leaving his native country, does not even feel particularly close to it (unusual for a Swiss). In 1848 the California gold rush began. This is the context for the following song, attributed to a Swiss emigrant:

Ich habe hier kein Glück gefunden
In meinem alten Heimatland,
Des Bittern hab' ich viel empfunden,
Drum zieht's mich in ein neues Land.
Es zieht mich nach Amerika,
Ins Goldland California . . .

Und muss ich hier die Alpen missen,
Verlassen Berg und Wald und Strom,
Ist doch ein Trost für mich zu wissen,
Ich bleib' auch dort Helvetiens Sohn.
Mich zieht's fort nach Amerika,
Ins Goldland California . . .

So leb' denn wohl, du Schweizererde,
Ich will mir dort die Heimat bau'n.
Leb' wohl, du Quell, du frohe Herde,
Auch dort lässt sich's in Frieden ruh'n.
Mich zieht's halt nach Amerika,
Drum lebet wohl, ihr Alpen da!

[Here I've found no luck at all
In my old home and country,
Hard knocks are all I can recall,

So I'm leaving for the land of plenty.
America is calling me,
To the California gold land. . . .

And if the Alps here I must miss,
Leave forest, river, and mountain,
It helps at least to know this,
There too I'll be Helvetia's son.
America is calling me,
To the California gold land. . . .

Fare thee well, then, you Swiss earth,
O'er there shall I build my home.
Farewell, you spring, you happy hearth,
There one too in peace can roam.
America's now calling me thither,
So farewell, you Alpine treasures!]

As stated earlier, political as well as economic motivations find a voice in these songs, especially after the failure of the Revolution of 1848. The best-known song in this connection is the "Columbus Song," popular especially among southwest Germans. In this song the figure of Christopher Columbus becomes almost a kind of saint, a patron of pilgrimage, so to speak:

Heil dir, Columbus, sei gepriesen,
Sei hoch geehrt in Ewigkeit!
Du hast mir einen Weg gewiesen,
Der mich von harter Dienstbarkeit
Errettet hat, wenn man es wagt
Und seinem Vaterland entsagt.

Hier ist der Mensch an nichts gebunden,
Was er erwirbt, gehört auch sein,
Die Steuern sind noch nicht erfunden,
Die unser Leben machen zur Pein.
Wer redlich schafft, der hat sein Brot,
Er leid't kein Mangel und kein' Not. . . .

Hier in Amerikas freiem Lande,
Da haben wir kein' Adelsstand,
Da ist der Mensch von jedem Stande
Als Mensch auch wahrhaft anerkannt.
Hier gilt der Graf und der Baron
Nicht mehr als wie der Bauernsohn. . . .

Nun will ich dieses Lied beschliessen,
Will Deutschland sagen gute Nacht,
Und sollt' es jemand besser wissen,
So steht's in seiner eigenen Macht.
Ich aber denk, 's ist gut gedacht,
Drum sag' ich Deutschland gute Nacht!

[Hail to thee, Columbus, praise!
Be honored all eternity!
For you have shown me the way
And led me from servility,
Away, if one will dare
To leave his home for over there.

Nothing holds a person here,
What you earn is yours to keep.
Taxes we don't need to fear,
That hold our lives in dire need.
For honest work you'll get your bread,
Will suffer not from lack or dread. . . .

Here in America's spaces free
We have no nobility.
Here the man from every class
As a man is judged to pass.
Here the earl and the baron
Count no more than the farmer's son. . . .

Now I wish to close this song,
Wish to bid Deutschland a warm good night,
And should someone smarter come along,
Then let him do what's in his might.
I for my part, though, I'd say it's right
To bid this Deutschland a last good night!]

The next song is also from southwest Germany. Today we would call the topic with which it deals "the problem of family reunification." One emigrant follows the other:

Lied der Auswanderer

Auf, ihr Brüder, lass uns reisen
Fröhlich nach Amerika,
Unsre Brüder sind schon alle
In Amerika, la, la, la.

Denn die Freiheit ist verloren
In dem ganzen Europa
Darum, Brüder, lass uns reisen
Nach Amerika, la, la, la. . . .

Heut zum letzten Mal, ihr Brüder
Sehen wir einander nah;
Ach, wann sehen wir uns wieder?
In Amerika, la, la, la. . . .

[*Song of the Emigrants*

Rise, ye brothers, let us wander
Gladly to America.
All our brothers, they're all yonder,
In America, la, la, la.

For freedom's gone lost
In all of Europe,
So, brothers, let's be off
To America, la, la, la. . . .

Today, brothers, for the last time
We say our last hurrahs;
Oh, when shall your eyes next meet mine?
In America, la, la, la. . . .]

In retrospect the immigrants viewed Germany as a country without liberty:

Deutscher Nationalreichtum

Haleluja, haleluja,
Wir wandern aus nach Amerika.
Was nehmen wir mit ins neue Vaterland?
So allerlei, so allerhand. . . .

Steuer-, Zoll-, Tauf-, Trau-, und Totenscheine,
Päss' und Wanderbücher, gross' und kleine,
viele tausend Zensurinstruktionen,
Polizeimandate, drei Millionen.
Weil es in der neuen Welt
Sonst dem Deutschen nicht gefällt. . . .

Was nehmen wir mit ins neue Vaterland?
So allerlei, so allerhand:
Schlendrian, Bocksbeutel und Perücken,
Privilegien, Sorgenstühl' und Krücken,
Hofratstitel und Konduitenlisten

neunundneunzighunderttausend Kisten.
Weil es in der Neuen Welt
sonst dem Deutschen nicht gefällt.

[*German National Riches*

Hallelujah, hallelujah,
We're leaving for America.
What shall we take upon our trip?
Some of that, some of this. . . .

Taxes, customs, birth and death cards,
Passports, papers, small and large,
Censorship everywhere you look,
Not to mention police black books,
Because without such German stuff
The New World wouldn't be German enough. . . .

What shall we take upon our trip?
Some of that, some of this:
Old habits, pouches, and old wigs,
Easy chairs, crutches, and privileges,
Councillor's titles and conduct lists,
Nine hundred ninety thousand boxes of this.
Because without such German stuff
The New World wouldn't be German enough.]

This ironic and humorous song, mocking German bureaucracy in
the civil service and the army, comes to us from Hoffman von Fallersleben, the author not only of the German national anthem but of a
number of popular songs as well.[2] Here are some samples:

Heimweh

. . . Lebt wohl! uns treibt es fort.
Was hier das arme Herz nicht fand,
Ein freies, glücklich Vaterland,
Lebt wohl! wir suchen's dort.

[*Homesick*

. . . Farewell! It calls us forth.
What here our poor hearts did not find,

[2] For example, "Winter ade" ("Farewell, Winter") and "Alle Voegel sind schon da"
("All the birds have now arrived"). In the middle of the nineteenth century several "pro-
gressive" authors wrote political emigrant songs. A great many of them are attributed to
Hoffmann von Fallersleben.

A free and happy fatherland,
Farewell! We seek it there!]

Auswanderungslied

Deutsche Freiheit lebet nur im Liede,
Deutsches Recht, es ist ein Märchen nur.
Deutschlands Wolhfahrt ist ein langer Friede—
Voll von lauter Willkür und Zensur.

Darum ziehen wir aus dem Vaterlande,
Kehren nun und nimmermehr zurück,
Suchen Freiheit uns am fremden Strande—
Freiheit ist nur Leben, ist nur Glück.

[Song of the Emigrant

German freedom lives but in the song,
German justice, a fairy tale at best.
On Germany's trip of peace you take along
Censorship and despotism, nothing less.

Thus we go forth from the fatherland,
Turn back not now or evermore,
Seek freedom in the foreign land—
Freedom's life and fortune, nothing more.]

Ein Guadalupelied
(Aus den "Texanischen Liedern")

. . . In dem Tal der Guadalupe
Fragt mich nie ein Polizist,
Was ich denke, was ich schreibe,
Ob ich dies, ob jenes treibe,
Ob ich bin ein guter Christ. . . .

[A Song of Guadalupe
(From "Songs of Texas")

. . . In the land of Guadalupe
No officer will ever ask me
What I think or what I write,
What I do to pass my time,
If I respect Christianity. . . .]

Lied vom Mississippi

. . . Adel, Ordenskram,
Titel, Räng, und Stände

Und solch dummes Zeug
Hat allhie ein Ende.
Hier darf nie ein Pfaff
Mit der Höll uns plagen,
Nie ein Jesuit
Uns die Ruh verjagen
Hier am Mississippi. . . .

Michel, baue nicht
Ferner deine Saaten
Fürs Beamtenheer
Und die Herrn Soldaten!
Michel, fass ein Herz,
Endlich auszuwandern:
Hier gehörst Du dir,
Dort nur stets den andern.

[*Song of the Mississippi*

. . . Nobility, stuff of honor,
Title, position, and class,
And all such prima donnas
Belong here to the past.
Here you won't find a preacher
Preaching fire and brimstone,
Never a Jesuit teacher
Not leaving you alone,
Here on the Mississippi. . . .

Michael, do not grow
Your crops there any more
For such bureaucracy
And the soldiers of war!
Michael, take heart,
Emigrate now too:
There you but play their part,
But here you belong to you.]

In all these songs we find certain key words repeated, words expressing the pressure of the Old World: poverty, taxation, serfdom, lack of liberty, bureaucracy, aristocracy, police control, religion. All these are counterbalanced by the corresponding positive values associated with the new.[3]

[3] I should mention here that Fallersleben never emigrated (though he thought about it). The hopes he expresses in these texts are thus not based on firsthand experience.

In addition to the economic and political motives, the religious overtones in the songs cannot be ignored. A good example of this aspect is a Saxony emigrant song, published in Leipzig in 1841. In this song Abraham calls the emigrants to follow God's command and go to the Promised Land. America was hailed as the New Canaan:

Auf Brüder, auf zur Reise,
Hin nach Amerika!
Gott, der allgut und weise
Er ist ja stets uns nah;
Er führt auf seinen Händen
Uns durch des Meer's Gefahr,
Lässt unser Leid sich enden
Dort in Amerika. . . .

Gott selbst hat uns berufen,
Wie käm's uns sonst zu Sinn?
So glauben wir, und wandern
Auf sein Geheiss dorthin.
Vertraun, wie Juda's Vater,
Fest auf des Herren Wort,
Und ziehen froh und heiter
Nach fremdem Erdtheil fort. . . .

Und jetzt nach langem Segeln,
Nach monatlanger Bahn,
Ensteigt ein Strand dem Meer,
's ist unser Kanaan,
Es ist das Land des Segens,
Das land des Glücks, der Ruh,
Auf, Freunde, auf, und eilet
Dem Segenlande zu. . . .
Amerika, ihr Brüder
ist gar ein schönes Land,
Gott gab's dem Vater Abraham
Zu einem Unterpfand.

[Rise, brothers, rise to travel
Forth to America!
God, the good one and the wisest,
Will ever be beside us.
He'll take us in his hands
Across the sea's adversity
To the American land,
Where will end our misery. . . .

God himself has called us,
How else should we proceed?
Thus we believe, and go forth,
His words shall we heed.
Trusting, as Judah's father,
Fast in the word of the Lord,
And leave with nary a bother
About the foreign land before us. . . .

And now after sailing long,
After months of rugged journey,
A shore arises from the sea,
Our Canaan shall it be.
It is the land of plenty,
The land of fortune and peace,
Rise, friends, rise and hurry,
This land of plenty now to greet. . . .

America, oh, brothers,
Is such a wondrous land,
God gave it Father Abraham
Entrusting it unto his hand.]

One kind of song of particular prominence in the mid-nineteenth century was the broadside (so called because of its appearance: a narrative/pictorial depiction prepared for circulation on folio sheets), also known as the broadsheet. The first text we considered, *Auf der Reise nach Amerika*, is a broadside song, or broadside ballad. The important values in these broadsides are one's home country and property. Living in a foreign country is synonymous with danger and misery, lack of security, and, generally speaking, a hard life. On the voyage to America the emigrants go through terrible ordeals; some even meet their death. In one such text a passenger, thought to be a friend, even murders a fellow emigrant.

Broadside ballads are both entertaining and didactic, and this in a conservative sense. They are designed to satisfy those who stayed at home, who were perhaps envious of those who left but who could later say, "We told you so." The antiemigration propaganda used the mass media of the time, namely, pamphlets and broadside ballads. The ordeal of the voyage is described: heat, thirst, hunger, seasickness, and death. Death in a foreign country became an especially prominent

theme of broadside ballads. In this way the "land of milk and honey"
motif finds its antithesis.

Broadsides with "warnings" use stock figures, such as that of the
goldseeker. Time and again the mottoes are: "Adventuring does not
pay"; "Easy come, easy go"; "Greed will be punished," and so on. The
songs usually end with the emigrant despairing, "If only we had stayed
at home!" The broadside ballads reflect especially the negative aspects
of emigration. Usually they deal with descriptions of sad events and
catastrophes, as can be seen in the following titles:

"John and Mary, or the Two Deserted Children among the Negroes"
"The Experiences of German Settlers in America"
"In the Wild West"
"A Robbery on the Pacific Railway Line"
"Sad Experiences of a Young German in America"
"The Terrible Sinking of an Ocean Steamer"
"A Flood Catastrophe in North America"

Almost always the fate of many emigrants is presented through
the description of the plight of individual immigrants. Warning examples show those at home how disaster befell the newcomers soon
after arrival. Broadsides say little about the successes and concentrate
on all kinds of problems the immigrants have: language problems,
crime, the need for support and aid, as well as the problems of integra-
tion and acculturation.[4]

Other broadsides make it clear that people who expect to make
their fortune in America become more and more gold-hungry and
eventually come to an evil end. Terrible shipwrecks are a popular
theme in broadside ballads. One can point to songs like "The Fire on
the Steamship *Austria*, 1858," or "The Collision of the Emigrant Ship
Cimbria, 1883." Songs treating catastrophes at sea usually involve emigrant ships. What is important here, when one is understanding the
songs as indicators of psychological moments, is that in disasters like
these the shipwreck is a symbol of the wrecked future that awaits the
emigrants.

In one broadsheet song from the mid-nineteenth century, by
Christian Hansern, a folksinger from Hamburg, the emigrant is well

[4]Interesting in this context is the broadside ballad entitled "Traurige Erlebnisse
sieben armer, verlassener Waisenkinder in Amerika" ("The Sad Experiences of Seven
Poor Deserted Orphans in America").

aware of the dangers he faces during his journey and in the new country, but his emigrant's pluck and faith prevail. He is certain that he will find a new home in the new country, which will then become an earthly paradise:

Lied der Auswanderer bei ihrer Abreise nach Amerika

Ade, du theures Vaterland,
Es winkt zum Abschied unsre Hand;
Zwar trübet sich nun unser Blick,
Doch lächelt uns der Zukunft Glück;
Im Vaterland nur Angst und Noth,
Typhus, Jammer, Hungerstod;
Drum suchen neue Heimat wir
Amerika, bei dir, bei dir. . . .

Drum treten wir die Reise an
Voll Muth, und das ist wohlgethan;
Besteigen kühn das stolze Schiff
Und trotzen Sandbank, Felsenriff,
Und wenn uns in der Flut auch dann
Der Zahn des Haifischs grimmig droht,
So blicken hoffend wir auf Gott,
Der lässt uns werden nicht zum Spott.

Was ist des Lebens höchstes Gut,
Die Freiheit ist's, drum Gut and Blut
Das setzt daran der deutsche Mann,
Dass er sie kühn erringen kann.
Sich satt zu essen, zweitens ist
Auch ein Grund, wie ihr wohl wisst;
Drum weil man eng uns eingezwängt,
Den Brodkorb immer höher hängt.

Dort lächelt mild der Sonnenstrahl,
Wenn auch kein sanftes Freudenthal;
Dort giebt's auch Arbeit, Schweiss und Müh',
Umsonst gab die Natur noch nie:
Doch was erzielt die fleiss'ge Hand,
Gehört auch in dem neuen Land,
Wer's redlich fleissig sich erwirbt,
Der sparsam ist, der nicht verdirbt.

An des Ohios Blüthenstrand,
Da bauen wir mit reger Hand,
Die neue Heimat uns, die schöne
Wird wie ein Paradies da stehn,
Die Heimath, die uns selbst gehört,

Wo man's Sattessen nicht verwehrt,
Wo das, was unserm Fleiss gelingt,
Auch für uns selbst den Nutzen bringt.

[*Song of the Emigrants upon Their Departure for America*

Farewell, O you dear fatherland,
To fare thee well we raise our hand;
Our gaze does grow sad, of course,
But fortune's eyes do smile upon us;
At home, just fear and poverty,
Typhus, starvation, and misery;
Thus a new home do we seek,
America, we turn to thee. . . .

Thus we set out on our journey,
Courageous of heart and full of merry;
Step bravely onto the proud ship
And defy the journey's hardships.
And if out on the waters a shark
Should threaten us to leave his mark,
Then shall we turn to God with hope,
Who'll lower us his saving rope.

What is the greatest good of life,
Freedom, that's it, thus health and strife
Will risk for it the German man,
To get of it now what he can.
To fill your belly is the second thing,
The second reason why we sing;
For even while they fence us in here,
They slice our hard-earned bread still thinner.

Warmly smiles there the sun,
Although, of course, it's not all fun;
There's work there too, sweat and labor,
For nature is reluctant to bestow her favor.
But what with industrious hand be sought
Is in the new land not for naught,
For him who does a good day's work,
Who saves his money and doesn't shirk.

On the Ohio's flowery banks
With busy hands we lay the planks
Of our new home, so beautiful,
As in a paradise bountiful,
Our home, which now belongs to us,
Where one can finally eat enough,

Where that with which our industry succeeds
Meets for us all of our needs.]

Songs of farewell express very private feelings, especially when the
sweetheart is left behind. A young girl from the Swiss canton of Glarus
describes the situation of the deserted bride in these simple words:

Mi Schatz isch gu Amerika
Wit über ds' Meer.
Und wän i dra tängge
So wird's mer so schwär,
Er hät gseit, er well mer schribe
Doch d'Tinte isch z tür,
Drum lat er's halt blibe,
Emal für hür.

[My darlin's to America
Way far across the sea.
An' when I starts to think on him,
Then it ain't easy bein' me.
He said he'd write, ya know,
But the ink's so darn expensive,
That he'll just have to let it go
This year with the love I sends him.]

Some songs take the form of a dialogue between husband and
wife. In keeping with their conventional roles, the husband is keen to
emigrate, while the wife clings more to the familiar surroundings
of home:

Mann:

O Frau, wie viele' schöne Sachen
kommen aus Amerika.
Was woll'n wir hier noch länger machen,
wie herrlich hätten wir es da.
Hier hat man täglich seine Noth
und kaum das Bisschen liebe Brot.
Wie schön könnten wir nicht leben da,
wenn wir wären in Amerika. . . .

Frau:

O Mann, wie kannst du daran denken,
schlag dir dies aus dem Sinn,
sonst thust du mich damit kränken,
ich ziehe nicht mit dir dahin.

Soll ich von meinen Freunden gehn
und sie nimmer wiedersehn,
so gräm ich mich zu Tode da,
was hilft mir dann Amerika. . . .

Frau:

Mein lieber Mann, du musst mich hören,
verbleibe nur an dienem Ort;
wir können uns hier auch noch nähren,
was kostet nicht der Seetransport?
Das Unsrige müssen wir verkaufen,
verarmt in jener Welt rum laufen,
und wohl auch Hunger leiden da,
ei bleib doch aus Amerika. . . .

But, of course, the man has the last word:

Mann:

Ich lass mir nicht davon abrathen
weil man dort herrlich leben kann,
man hat ja täglich Fleisch und Braten,
das hat hier nur der reiche Mann.
Alle, die dorthin gekommen,
haben wenig Geld nur mitgenommen,
so können wir, wie die auch, ja
hinkommen nach Amerika.

[Husband:

O wife, how many pretty wares
Come from there, America!
Why should we any longer tarry,
So good could we two have it there.
Here's nothing but trouble, day after day,
And not enough bread to make it pay.
How wonderful our life would be there,
If we were in America. . . .

Wife:

O husband, how can you think that?
I want you to forget it now,
Or if you don't I'll feel so bad,
'Cause I'm not goin', no way, no how.
Now if I were to leave my friends
And never ever see them again,

I'd die a troubled death, I would,
So what good's America, tell me, what good? . . .

Wife:

Husband dear, now hear me right,
You just stay put where you've a roof.
Here we'll manage things all right,
Just think how much it'd cost, this move!
What we've got we'd have to sell,
Run around there poor as hell,
And likely die of hunger there.
Oh, stay away from America. . . .

Husband:

Leave off now, you won't change my mind,
Because the good life's over there.
Meat and 'taters, a daily find,
Are only rich men's dishes here.
Everybody who has gone
Took only little money along,
So, like them, we too can get there,
Get there to America.]

By far the best-known and most-loved emigrant song is "Jetzt ist
die Zeit und Stunde da" ("The Time Has Come"). It was written in
1830 by the Swabian teacher Samuel Friedrich Sautter. About one
hundred different oral versions of this song have come down to us, and
it is still as well known today throughout Germany and in America (especially in Pennsylvania and Texas) as it was then.

Jetzt ist die Zeit und Stunde da

Yetzt ist de obshets stunde da,
Ich risa noch America,
Der wagen shtadt shon fore der deer,
Ferlossen mus ich eich all here.

Der wagen shtade shon for de deer,
Mit wibe und kinder stigen mere,
Mit wibe und kinder stigen mere,
Der wagen shtade shon for de deer.

Und wan das shif in mere schwimmed,
So wert das liedlein an gestimpt,
Ich ferichta keine wasserfal,
Und danka Gott sie eber all.

Nun lande mehr in Baltimore,
Und strecke unsera hande for,
Und strecka unsera hande for.
Und grisha oup "Victoria."

Nun gehen mehr zum watshouse nein,
Und drinka eine flasha wine,
Und drinka eine flasha wine,
Und lassen Deutschland, Deutschland sein.

[*The Time Has Come*

The time has come for me to go,
I'm leaving for America.
The wagon's waiting at the door,
And I shall see you nevermore.

The wagon's waiting at the door,
With wife and child I climb aboard,
With wife and child I climb aboard,
The wagon's waiting at the door.

And when the ship is on the sea,
Then we shall sing a melody.
I'll keep the tears down with a smile,
Thanking God then all the while.

Now we land in Baltimore
And extend our hands before
Us, and extend our hands before
Us, and cry out "Victoria."

It's to the tavern straightaway,
To put a bottle of wine away,
To put a bottle of wine away,
And let Germany stay where it will stay.]

This song has been considerably altered and expanded to suit the needs and emotions of prospective emigrants. The variants emphasize only the positive aspects of leaving. On the whole the song expresses a naive expectation of the New World:

In Amerika, da ist es fein
da fliesst der Wein zum Fenster rein.
Da wächst der Klee drei Ellen hoch,
da gibt es Butter und Fleisch genug.

Die grössten Fische, wie bekannt,
die fängt man dort mit blosser Hand.

Die Karpfen sind, bei meiner Ehr,
oft bis zum halben Zentner schwer.

Kartoffeln gibt's wie Marzipan,
an jedem Stock drei Scheffel dran.
Wir ziehen ins Land, wo Immergrün
und selbst im Winter die Rosen blühn.

Allda, dort blühet schon die Flur,
von Herrlichkeit ja die Natur.
Wo hier nur Vogelkirschen blühn,
Wächst dort der Kaffee wunderschön.

Die Schokolade wächst zugleich
selbst Zuckkerrohr an jedem Teich.
Es ist fürwahr zu glauben kaum,
die Wolle wächst auf jedem Baum.

[In America things are great,
The wine flows there right through your gate.
The clover there grows three feet tall,
There's butter and meat enough for all.

The largest fish, knows every man,
Can be caught there with bare hand.
The carp—on this you have my word,
Are larger than you've ever heard.

Potatoes grow thick as a flock,
Three bushels near on every stock.
We leave for the land where the evergreen
And even the roses in winter can be seen.

All over the meadows there are ablossom,
Majestic is nature, top to bottom.
Where here but wild cherries grow,
There coffee, rich and dark, does flow.

Chocolate grows there, take your pick,
As sugar candy on a stick.
I know it's real hard to believe,
But cotton grows on every tree.]

All will immediately recognize the well-known motifs of Schlaraffenland (Land of the Cockaigne), Utopia, and Shangri-la. The song became part of the extremely pro-American, pro-emigration propaganda, a clear advertisement for the land of unlimited opportunities.

Clearly no attempt is made to describe America realistically.

Everything negative in the Old Country is transformed into its opposite in the new one. The exaggerated expectations of the emigrants were thus bound to be disappointed. The first disappointments came during the voyage. A Swiss emigrant of the 1880s is said to have written the following:

Havre ist ein schönes Städtchen,
so es an dem Meere liegt,
Drin verspricht man uns viel Schönes,
aber halten tut's man nicht.

Und ein Schiff, das heisst "la France,"
Führt uns nach Amerika.
Drinnen gibt es schlechtes Fressen
Und eine Schweinerei ist da!

Wer viel frisst, der muss viel kotzen,
Kotzt bei Tage und bei Nacht.
Drum sind all schon unsre Kammern
Nun zum Schweinestall gemacht.

Morgens gibt es braune Brühe
Die zum Spott man Kaffee heisst,
Mittags Fleisch so zäh wie Leder,
dass man sich die Zähn ausbeisst.

Auch der Wein ist wenig nütze,
Bette, die sind ziemlich hart,
Das hat ja schon manchen Schweizer
Bei seiner Wasserreis geplagt.

Den Herrn Doktor sieht man selten,
Selten auch den Kapitän,
Weil die Herren Offiziere,
Gar kein Wörtchen deutsch verstehn.

Wenn euch nun die Leute fragen:
"Wer hat dieses Lied erdacht?"
"Ei, so sollt ihr denen sagen:
"Ein Passagier hat es gemacht."

[Havre is a pretty city,
Lying there upon the sea,
And such promises! A pity,
That their word they never keep.

And a ship, by name *La France*,
Takes us to America.
The food, it gives off quite a stench,
And what a mess there is, oh God!

You eat a lot, you puke a lot,
Puke by day and puke by night.
That's why all our sleeping spots
Have, every one of 'em, gone to pot.

Mornings you can eat brown broth,
They call it coffee for a joke.
Afternoons there's meat like leather,
And if you're lucky you won't choke.

Wine's of little use here either,
All the beds are pretty hard.
More than one Schweizer will admit
That's caused great misery on the trip.

A rare sight is the doctor chap,
Likewise with the captain,
And the officers, to a man,
No German do they understand.

And so when the people ask you,
"Heh, who made up this here song?"
You should turn to them and say,
"One of them who rode along."]

To be sure, the circumstances on the overcrowded ships must have been grim. Pilfering and theft were rife, and sea voyages were often dangerous undertakings (most emigrants thought it best to prepare their last will and testament beforehand). Shipwrecks, pirates, and infectious diseases were all risks to be reckoned with, and the captain and crew were not necessarily enamored of their passengers. On arrival the situation in the harbors was often scandalous and shocking. Some did not survive the voyage; others returned home, despondent and in tatters.

One America song, in Alemannic dialect, is a vivid and impressive account of the voyage across the ocean, the arrival in the New World, and the later settling on a farm:

Get Acht, i will ech öppis zelle
vom neue Land Amerika;
i ha das ietz scho lang geng welle,
u ha's de näue geng la ga.
es ist ietz de es Jar gli scho,
dass mir von öch hei Abschid g'no.

Wo mir von ech eweg si 'gange,
do het's is wê 'ta nit e chli;

mer si vor Herzwê fast vergange,
bis mer es Mal si von ech g'si;
dana si mer bi Paris für
und über's Mêr dur d's Wasser für. . . .

Fast all, die uf 'em Mêr wei rite,
die werde chrank die ersti Stun;
das Wagle spürt me scho bi Zite
u chotze muess me wie ne Hun;
mi selber het es tüchtig g'no,
i ha mi Teil fast übercho.

Me färt g'schwin ihi zu der Lucke,
wo d's Mêr da numme chlis me ist:
Da bist am Lan, du Chetzers Trucke!
ma packt si drus, was hest was gist.
Da steit me uf der neue Wel
u seit scho englisch: Very well!

Me geit u g'schauet afe d'Gegni
un öppe d'Städt u lost o d'Lüt.
Da "Help your self!" so seit der Yankee
u "Hilf dir selber!" deicht der Dütsch.
Wer gnue Geld het, ist obe druff;
wer keis mê het, ist hie o uff.

I chan ech wäger nit recht rate
u säge: chömit, oder nit;
denn üsers Lebe ist e Schatte,
bis dass mer ga i d' Ewigkeit:
dert finne mer enannere scho,
will's Gott doch, öppe frisch und fro.

[Listen up, I want to tell you now
Of the new land called America.
I've wanted to for some time, you know,
But till now I've let it go.
And now a year's gone by already
That I did say farewell to you.

As I said farewell to you,
It hurt me more than just a might.
My heart, it nearly broke in two
Before we got clean outa sight.
Then on to Paris is where we gone,
An' 'cross the ocean, and beyond. . . .

'Bout all who're ridin' on the sea,
Near all got sick afore too long.

That rockin' back 'n forth, it be
What make 'em sick just like a dog;
It got me good too, sure 'nough,
Made me lose near most all my stuff.

We traveled fast on toward the spot
Where the ocean just plain runs out:
You're on land, you roustabout!
Unpack your things, all that you got.
Then you stand ashore the New World
A'talkin' English: "Very well!"

We gone an' looked about a bit,
First off the town and then the townfolk.
"Help yourself" 's the way the Yankees say it.
That's "Hilf dir selber" for the German folk.
If you got lotsa money, yer ridin' high;
And them's got none, why, they'll get by.

I can't give y'all no advice
'n tell ya if you should come here with me,
'Cause but a shadow's what we call life,
Until we end up in eternity.
We'll find each other there, sure 'nough,
All happy n' all, just like now.]

Quite a few found acculturation too difficult and returned home. They
ran out of money:

Als wir kamen an das Meer,
Da waren unsere Säckel leer!
Das Geld war mir jetzt aus der Hand
und ich bin in einem fremden Land.
Ach Bruder, es sieht nicht gut aus,
bleibe du im Vaterhaus.

[When we finally put to sea,
Our sacks were empty as could be!
Money have I got no more,
Standing on this foreign shore.
Oh, brother, it don't look too good,
Stay home with papa, where you should.]

Accounts of negative experiences were, of course, also part of an antiemigration propaganda:

Auf diesem Schiff bin ich gekommen
in die Stadt Philadelphia,

mein Geld ist mir abgenommen,
was soll ich doch fangen an?

Amerika, du verrücktes Land!
Einen Finger gäb ich aus meiner Hand,
einen Finger gäb ich aus meiner Hand,
wenn ich wär wieder in meinem Vaterland.

Ach Gott wie spottschlecht geht es uns hier.
Hier gibt's weder Knackwurst noch Waldschlösschen-Bier.
Hier kommen wir ganz sicherlich noch untern Schlitten.
Und was haben wir alles auf der Reise erlitten!

[It was on this ship I came
To the town of Philadelphia.
No more money to my name.
What now, then, for heaven's sake?

America, you land gone mad,
I'll give you a finger off my hand,
A finger off my right hand,
To be again in my fatherland.

Oh, God, how miserable things are here,
You can't find sausage, you can't find beer.
Here we'll surely meet our end,
And after all we had to spend!]

Admittedly poverty was one reason for emigration, but, to emigrate, some capital was necessary. Those who had nothing in Germany would find starting anew all the more difficult:

Wer nichts hat, der soll nicht kommen.
Wer kommt mit Geld und Gut
Ist angenehm bei jedermann.

Das Geld regiert die ganze Welt.
Wer nichts hat in Europa
Der soll nicht nach Amerika.

Wer kommt hinein und ist auch arm
Die Steine sind hart, die Sonne scheint warm.
Wer kommt hinein mit Gut und Geld
Ist angenehm bei jedermann.

[If you've got nothing, don't bother to come.
He who comes with money and wealth
Will find everyone drinking to his good health.

Money, 'tis true, rules all the world.
He who has nothing in Europe
Should not come to America.

He who comes and is poor to boot
Will sleep on hard stones with the sky for his roof.
He who comes with money and wealth
Will find everyone drinking to his good health.]

A humorous song in the dialect of Hesse reflects immigrant difficulties, especially from the viewpoint of housewives:

Die Fraue, die herüberkomme,
Net mehr ganz jung, vom Vaterland,
Sind gege alles eingenomme
Und schimpfe als, es is e Schand.

Die Wäsch verdirbt von dere Seife,
Die Blume hätte kein Geruch,
Die Vögel könnte hier net pfeife,
Und Dienstmägd wärn e wahrer Fluch.

Zu wässrig wärn die Brunnekresse,
Zu locker sin die Kappesköpp,
Und Quetsche kräg mer kein zu esse,
Un die Kartoffle hätte Knöpp.

Es wär kein Land zum Einzemache,
Die Pisching dehte üwegehn,
Die Zwiwelcher, die thun net krache,
Und auch die Gurke sind net scheen.

Die Kälwar hawe Oschseknoche,
Die gäns die hätte thranig Fett;
In dene Heerd kann mer net koche,
Wann mer nur deutsche Dippe hätt!

Se thun auch bitter sich beklage,
Und komme in e wahre Raasch,
Sich mit me ganze Haus zu plage,
Daheim—ha hat mer sein Etaasch!

Noch letzt hat mer e Dam' verzählt,
Sie lebt erst hier seit eme Jahr,
Ein' die mit eme Haus sich quält,
Wie's drüwe bei ihr'm Vater war.

Da konnt ich freilich net viel sage,
Und mir liegt auch en Deuwel dran-

Wem's hier in gar nix will behage,
Dem rath ich ebe's Heimgehn an.

[The women who come from the fatherland,
Not as young as once they were,
There's nothin' meets their eye that's right,
They curse the land by day and night.

The soap wears holes in the underwear,
The flowers have no scent,
The birds can't even whistle here,
And the maids are devil-sent.

Too watery is the watercress,
And the carrots are too dry,
And plums here you just can't get,
And the potatoes are full of eyes.

This is no land for canning,
The cherries have gone sour,
The onions are no good for skinning,
And the cucumbers make me scour.

The calves are tough and sinewy,
The geese are full of fat.
You can't cook 'em in your cookery,
If only a German pot we had!

They complain till they're blue in the face,
And work themselves into a rage,
Taking care of so large a house,
Back home the one room was large enough.

Just recently a woman told me
She's been here now just shy a year,
How the house is such a headache,
Not like back home with father dear.

Well, there wasn't much that I could say,
Lord knows I've got some bones to pick.
If here you just can't make your way,
Then I suggest you go home, quick.]

Another antiemigration propaganda song is a dialogue between Saxon madames Rappel and Rippel, who are in America now:

"Nun Frau Gevatter sind wir da
In dem gelobten Lande,

Nun sind wir in Amerika,
Worauf mein Mann so brannte;
Nun, wie gefällt es Ihnen hier?"
"Ach Gott gar nicht gefällt es mir,
In dieser Mördergrube!

"Ach wären wir zu Hause noch
In unserm lieben Sachsen;
Dort war's doch schön, man sah dort doch
Auch Baum und Kräuter wachsen. . . .

"Ach Gott, wie gern führ' ich zurück
Mit meinen Kindern, denn das Glück
Hier will ich jedem gönnen."

["Now dear cousin, we're there
In the land so praised,
Here we are in America.
Well, how do you like it here?"
"Dear God, not at all do I like it here,
In this den of murderers!

"Oh if only we were home
In our dear Saxony;
There 'twas beautiful and where'er you'd roam
Grew trees and grass in plenty. . . .

"Oh, God, I wish I could return
With my child dear, and leave the fortune
Here to any who is willing."]

Some emigrants were able to adapt; others were not. The stereo-
type of those tired of Europe is now contrasted with those tired of
America. Alongside the disappointed emigrant in songs we also find
the successful, new, and nouveau-riche American. These songs can be
classified as boastful "lying songs."

Songs focusing on the future stand alongside songs focusing on the
past. These retrospective songs are full of nostalgia and usually revolve
around personal ties to the old country left behind. The values of
friendship, family closeness, and ties to kith and kin are all-important.

Such feelings of genuine homesickness are, not surprisingly, delib-
erately exploited in several songs. The purpose of the songs is to warn
people against emigrating. A prime example of such songs praising the
fatherland is the "Schweizer Buergerbrieflied" ("Song of the Swiss

Certificate of Citizenship"). This song attempts to deter emigrants by
frightening them with the prospect of bitter homesickness:

An einen Auswanderer

Und willst due hier nicht länger weilen,
im grünen Tal, am blauen See?
Du willst der Heimat Los nicht teilen,
nicht deines Volkes Wohl und Weh?
So wandre nach Amerika,
ich bleib' im Land der Alpen da,
so wandre nach Amerika,
ich bleib' im Land der Alpen da.

Die Schweiz, die dich mit Mutterhänden,
Als Kind gepflegt so treu, so gut,
Ihr kannst du kalt den Rücken wenden,
Durchwallt dein Herz kein Schweizerblut?
So wandre. . . .

Du willst den Bürgerbrief zerreissen,
Den die das freie Hochland gab?
Du willst nicht länger Schweizer heissen,
Schwörst unserm Bund auf ewig ab?
So wandre. . . .

Die Väter, die in Unglückstagen,
Nie feig aus ihrer Heimat floh'n,
Die Tell und Winkelriede klagen
Um dich, um den verlor'nen Sohn.
So wandre. . . .

So wähl' ein Grab im gold'nen Sande,
Verschmacht' am Sakramento nun!
Im schönen, freien Schweizerlande,
Bei meinen Vätern will ich ruh'n.
Fahr' hin, fahr' nach Amerika,
Als Schweizer leb' und sterb' ich da!

[To an Emigrant

And is it not your wish to stay
In this green land, by this blue lake?
You wish to part with your homeland's way,
No part of woe nor plenty will you take?
So leave, then, for America,
I'll stay in the land of the Alps, by God.
Leave, then, for America.
I'll stay in the land of the Alps, by God.

Switzerland, with a mother's hand,
Did raise you, child, true and good.
Would'st turn your back now on this land?
Runs through your heart then no Swiss blood?
Leave, then. . . .

You would deny the citizenry
Which this great land did give to thee?
A Swiss will you no longer be,
Swear off our bond for eternity?
Leave, then. . . .

Our fathers, who in times of need
Did never think to run,
Now cry out, Tell and Winkelried,
For you, their long-lost son.
Leave, then. . . .

Choose, then, your grave in the golden sand,
Waste away in Sacramento.
In beautiful, free Switzerland,
To rest with my fathers shall I go.
    Be off, off to America,
    I'll live and die a true Swiss man.]

This song was so popular that by the 1850s male choirs were singing it.
It belongs to the deliberate propaganda praising the home country.
The national symbols—Swiss confederation, free Switzerland, Tell and
Winkelried, green valley, blue lake—are used without subtlety. In
fact, this song is so very sentimental that it has often been the object of
parody. To wit:

Dich reizen Californiens Felder,
das Gold, das man im Flusse wäscht.
Doch was nützen dir die vielen Gelder,
wenn du das teure Hochland nicht mehr häscht?
Dann kriegst du trotz dem vielen Geld
das Heimweh nach der alten Welt. . . .

Es ist umsonst, er ist dahingezogen,
zerrissen ist der Freundschaft Band,
schon tanzt das Schiff auf salzgen Wogen,
das Nastuch schwenkt noch ferne seine Hand.
Es war halt nichts zu machen da,
es zog ihn nach Amerika. . . .
In dem grossen Staate Minnesota,
da hat er sich verakkordiert.

Von der Sprach verstand er zwar kein Jota,
drum wurde ihm das Leben gar nicht leicht.
's war anders als er sich gedacht,
das Heimweh packte ihn mit Macht.

Und schon bald nach einem halben Jahre
er fort aus diesem Lande reist,
wo der Sioux und der Delaware
dem Bleichgesicht den Skalp vom Kopfe reisst.
Und das noch ohne jeden Grund,
da blieb er länger keine Stund.

Und europawärts er sich verschiffte
auf nächstem Weg nach Baselland,
wo süsse heimatliche Düfte
und manches andre er da wieder fand.
Im grossen Land Amerika
da duftet's nicht so schön wie da.

[California's fields attract you,
The gold one pans for in the river.
But what good will the money do you
When your dear homeland is now thither?
In spite of all the money, then,
You're homesick for your home again. . . .

It's no use, he's on his way,
The bond of friendship now is broken.
His ship does dance upon the waves,
His kerchief signals the final token.
There was nothing we could do,
America was all he knew. . . .

In the great state of Minnesota,
He got himself into a pickle.
The language he knew not one iota,
And life, he thought, was surely fickle.
What he'd imagined, the land was not,
Going home was his only thought.

And following but a half a year
He traveled forth from this strange land,
Where the Sioux and the Delaware
Hunt paleface scalps with knife in hand.
And that without the slightest cause.
So lickety-split, away he was.

And he set sail, now Europe-bound,
Coming home by way of Basel,
Where sweet aromas can be found,
To soothe the soul of this Schlemazel.
In the great land of America
The air is, after all, so blah.]

In contrast to this parody there was, of course, massive antiemigration propaganda. Again the Bible is cited as an authority. Psalm 37:3 recommends:

Hoffe auf den Herrn und thue Gutes;
bleibe im Lande und nähre dich redlich.

[Trust in the Lord, and do good;
so shalt thou dwell in the land and verily thou shalt
be fed.]

These verses also appear as subtitles in broadside ballads.

The next example, from the first half of the nineteenth century, comes from Saxony:

Freunde, bleibet hübsch im Lande,
Und ernährt euch redlich dort,
Im amerikanischen Sande
Kommt ihr noch weit wen'ger fort.
Sonne auf den Pelz euch brennt,
Plagen, die ihr hier nicht kennt,
Regnen dort auf euch herab,
Und das Geld ist da auch knapp.

Liess mich leider auch verleiten,
zog mit Weib und Kind dahin,
Tausend Meilen musst' ich schreiten,
That's mit unverdrossnem Sinn;
Hoffte in Amerika
Sei im Vollen Alles da,
Rittergüter klein und gross
Nehme sich nur jeder bloss.

Ach wie soll ich euch noch schildern
Meine Täuschung, meine Noth!
Bei den schön geträumten Bildern
Fehlte mir das liebe Brot.
Kläglich auf der Reise schon
Starb mein lieber kleiner Sohn,

Und mein Weib, erkrankt und matt,
Fühlte sich des Lebens satt.

Als nach Bremen wir gekommen
Waren wir vor Kummer bleich,
Alles was wir mitgenommen
Zahlten für die Fracht wir gleich,
Und die Zahlung an dem Ort
Nahm den letzten Pfennig fort.
Nackte und kahl, wie'n Felsenriff,
Stiegen wir hinein ins Schiff.
Eingepresst im engen Raume
Lagen wir zu Hundert da,
Und behext vom argen Traume
Glaubten wir die Hülfe nah.
Hunger, Durst und Übelkeit,
Ungeziefer wie geschneit
Quälten uns bei Tag und Nacht,
Hätten uns fast umgebracht.

Endlich nach viel trüben Tagen,
Sturm, Verzweiflung, Ungemach,
schien die Rettungsstund' zu schlagen,
Nahte der Erlösungstag.
Fröhlich jauchzend hiess es da:
Wir sind in Amerika!
Und die eingepresste Brust
Hob sich voll erneuter Lust.

Statt uns freundlich zu empfangen,
Wie wir thöricht uns gedacht,
Wurden mit den bleichen Wangen
Wir noch tapfer ausgelacht. . . .

[Friends, be good and stay at home,
Where you can at least be fed.
If you should to America roam,
You'll get even less instead.
The sun will burn upon your skin,
Diseases that you've never seen
Rain down upon you from the sky,
And money there's in short supply.

Too bad temptation got me too,
With wife and child I went away,
A thousand miles, a pair of shoes,

But from that goal I did not stray.
Hoped that in America
All in plenty would be there.
Estates waiting, small and large,
For someone simply to take charge.

Oh, how shall I even tell you
Of my deception or my need.
While I dreamed that all was well
Still there was no bread to eat.
Already under parting sky
My dearest tiny son did die,
And my wife, now sick and weak,
Had nothing more in life to seek.

As we arrived in Bremen town,
We'd paled from all our worry,
Everything we called our own
We paid the freighter in a hurry,
And the payment at that time
Left us with not one thin dime.
Cold and naked, as in war,
We went forth and got on board.

Elbowed into tiny quarters,
By the hundreds did we lie there,
Still that vicious dream did torture
Us, made us think that help was near.
Illness, thirst, and hunger,
Vermin by the dozen,
Tortured us throughout day and night,
Thought the end was soon in sight.

Finally after endless days,
Storms, despair, adversity,
The hour of salvation came,
Or so it seemed, a certainty,
Deliverance on the way!
Happy jubilation rang out:
We are in America!
And the body, worn and tired,
Stood straight again and was inspired.

But instead of being well received,
As we had wrongly thought,
All of us with hollow cheeks
Were laughed at on the spot.]

Reports of this kind could successfully frighten the timid. It was emphasized that only young, healthy people should run the risk of emigrating and that they had to be willing to work hard and do without.

Even the best-known German folk and children's song, "Hänschen klein," a song of little Hans who went out alone into the big wide world, is integrated into this stay-at-home ideology. In the last stanza Hans returns to his mother, saying:

> Sieh Mama,
> ich bin da,
> Hänschen aus Amerika
> Geh nicht mehr
> fort von dir,
> bleib nun immer hier.

> [Look, Mama,
> Here I am
> Little Hans back from America
> I won't go
> From you, oh, no,
> Will stay here evermore.]

Finally, I would like to emphasize the following points. Songs by and about emigrants belong to many different kinds of texts and genres. They also have different functions. In terms of content they form a group within historicopolitical songs. But many songs can also be classified as "fatherland" or "nostalgia" songs. Others are broadside ballads, and still others are mocking songs, complaints, songs of praise, songs of farewell, or love songs.

Not all were really sung. Some were used as propaganda and were listened to; nevertheless, they all had their effects. In every case it is important to ask: "Who sings these songs and who sang them? How long were they sung traditionally by emigrants themselves or their children and grandchildren or by the people at home in Europe? What can be deduced from the songs about their singers, composers, and distributors?" Emigration was such a highly charged emotional experience that it made a deep and lasting impression. Decades later songs of farewell were still among the most popular and frequently sung folk songs.

It is difficult to say how many people sang these songs. Some of the texts presented here were undoubtedly very short-lived. On the other hand, there are songs from the beginning or the middle of the nineteenth century that are still sung today in Europe as well as in America.

It is not always possible to isolate the reasons for emigration in the songs. No doubt this was also true of the emigrants' situation, in which religious, economic, and political reasons usually intermingled. To be sure, the songs can provide us with a typology of emigration, but it is not always clear in these texts which historical wave of emigration they refer to.

Most of the songs are clearly for or against emigration. Like all other folk literature the songs simplify and schematize. America and Europe are juxtaposed in relatively simple patterns. The sentiments are pro-America: "There riches, here poverty"; "there liberty, here slavery and bureaucracy." Or they are the reverse: "There money-grabbers and greed, here true friends"; "there a foreign country, here the fatherland"; "there dangers, here the security and warmth of family." These songs uphold stereotypes and prejudices. Clichés can be recognized in set phrases: "Lieber in der Heimat sterben als in fremdem Land verderben" ("Better die at home than perish abroad"). Or, the other side of the coin: "Better a slave in America than a citizen in Germany."

The description and the distribution of labor are also clichéd: "The sweet life is over, brothers; now we have to work." This set character appears again and again, in, for example, rhyming pairs such as *fort* and *Heimatort*, *Not* and *Brot*, and *Amerika* and *hurrah* and *Victoria*.

Our century has become sentitive to the problem of emigration and immigration. Key phrases like "imported labor" and "political refugees" have shown us just how relevant these problems are. In a society familiar with refugees and those who have lost everything, with imported labor and those seeking political asylum, we are especially able to understand people on the move, subcultures and minorities, and the desire for a new home. Unfortunately, the mass unemployment of today and the fear of a new world war cannot be solved by immigrating to a new world. On the contrary, West Germany has itself become the goal of millions of immigrants.

Research into emigrant songs belongs to those empirical and demographic methods of investigation that write history from the bottom up. Moving, precisely because they deal with the human and the everyday,

the songs make a real impact. Love and death, joy and sorrow, parents
and children, food and drink, success and failure, departure and return,
tearing up roots and resettling into new experiences, reactions to the
familiar and foreign—these are the important issues, and they find their
echoes in these songs.

GILBERT J. JORDAN

German Texana

THE German heritage in Texas falls into two broad areas. The first is
the material aspect of folk culture: the homes, furniture, fences, walls,
curbings, roads, cemeteries, and grave markers. In modern computer
language one might call these elements the "hardware" of culture.
Such areas of German heritage are the better known, and they have
been dealt with in books and studies more than have the less tangible
folkloric and nonmaterial traditions.[1] To continue with the computer
analogy, one can call the nonmaterial elements—the songs, poems, anecdotes, prayers, epitaphs, autograph-album verses, riddles, and so
on—the "software" of folk heritage. This is what one can call "German
Texana," though such cultural elements could also be referred to as
"Texas Germanica," inasmuch as they were for the most part produced
in German-speaking countries of Europe and then transplanted to
Texas by the immigrants.

Although not very much of this material was produced directly
in Texas, it did undergo alterations there. Some indigenous folklore
was also produced, for instance, the anecdotes about the Germans in
Texas and their language problems. Nevertheless, the cultural heritage
brought to Texas by the immigrants is basically European and remains
German to the present day. However, it took such deep roots in Texas
that it is in reality Texan. Therefore, it is surprising that, with the exception of historical studies,[2] this nonmaterial German Texana has
been neglected to a great extent by modern scholars and publishers.

[1]J. Roy White and Joe B. Frantz, *Limestone and Log* (Austin: Encino, 1968); Elsie
Kowert, *Old Homes and Buildings of Fredericksburg* (Fredericksburg, Tex.: Fredericks-
burg Publishing, 1977); Gilbert J. Jordan, *Yesterday in the Texas Hill Country* (College
Station: Texas A&M University Press, 1979); Lonn Taylor and David B. Warren, *Texas
Furniture: The Cabinetmakers and Their Work, 1840–1880* (Austin: University of Texas
Press, 1956); Hubert G. H. Wilhelm, "German Settlements and Folk Building Practices
in the Hill Country of Texas," *Pioneer America* 3, no. 2 (1971): 15–24.
[2]Gilbert Giddings Benjamin, *The Germans in Texas: A Study in Immigration*

Joseph Wilson, Fred Eikel, Jr., and Glen Gilbert, among others, have undertaken language studies,[3] while Terry G. Jordan has done geographical research in the material culture aspects of the German heritage in Texas.[4] In the field of folkloric, literary, and musical treasures very little was done before my two books, *Yesterday in the Texas Hill Country* (1979) and *German Texana* (1980).[5] What is presented in the following pages is based on or taken from these two books. For all the collected specimens of German Texana I have composed English translations—whenever possible in verse form and as nearly identical with the original German as possible.

Verses from Poesie-Alben (Autograph Albums)

During the nineteenth century and the early part of the twentieth German autograph albums, called *Poesie-Alben* or *Stammbücher*, were very popular among young people, especially girls. They were similar to American and English albums. The poems were invariably inscribed to the owner of the book; then followed the writer's autograph, sometimes with bold flourishes. Occasionally lacy floral emblems, called *Stammbuchblümchen* ("album flowerlets") were glued on beside the inscription. Girls sometimes fastened locks of their hair or small wreaths of braided hair on the pages. As such, these pictures represent a "multiple" sort of cultural heritage.

Of primary interest are the great number of handwritten poems in

(1909; reprint, Austin: Jenkins, 1974); Rudolph L. Biesele, *The History of the German Settlements in Texas, 1831–1861* (Austin: Von Boeckmann-Jones, 1930); Moritz Tiling, *History of the German Element in Texas from 1820–1850* (Houston: M. Tiling, 1913).

[3] Joseph Wilson, "The German Language in Central Texas Today," *Rice University Studies* 63, no. 3 (1977): 47–58; Glenn G. Gilbert, *Linguistic Atlas of Texas German* (Austin: University of Texas Press, 1972); Glenn G. Gilbert, "Origin and Present Location of German Speakers in Texas: A Statistical Interpretation," *Rice University Studies* 63, no. 3 (1977): 21–34; Fred Eikel, Jr., "New Braunfels German," *American Speech* 41 (February, 1966): 5–16; (December, 1966): 254–60; and (May, 1967): 83–104; Gilbert J. Jordan, "The Texas German Language of the Western Hill Country," *Rice University Studies* 63, no. 3 (1977): 59–71.

[4] Terry G. Jordan, *German Seed in Texas Soil* (Austin: University of Texas Press, 1966); Terry G. Jordan, *Texas Graveyards: A Cultural Legacy* (Austin: University of Texas Press, 1982), pp. 89–116; Terry G. Jordan, "German Folk Houses in the Texas Hill Country," in *German Culture in Texas*, ed. Glen E. Lich and Dona B. Reeves (Boston: Twayne, 1980), pp. 103–20.

[5] Gilbert J. Jordan, *Yesterday in the Texas Hill Country* (College Station: Texas A&M University Press, 1979); *German Texana* (Burnet, Tex.: Eakin, 1980).

these albums. Most of them were probably copied from albums brought to Texas by the immigrants or taken from written sources, but others may be imitations. Some are derived from poems transmitted by parents to children, and a few seem to be original compositions. The earlier, nineteenth-century German-Texan albums were frequently written in the decorative German script. These albums "have their own ethnic flavor, particularly the sentimental verses with recurring themes of love, friendship, nature, . . . joy, piety, . . . peace, beauty, loyalty, nostalgia, serenity, solitude, heartache, remembrance, hope, and trust" (p. 3).[6] Some of the albums have found their way into public places, like the New Braunfels Sophienburg Museum, but many are still in private hands. The small sampling of the poems shows how evident the favorite themes of the lyrics are:

> Rosen blühen weiss und roth,
> Liebe dich bis in den Todt;
> Wahre Liebe endet nicht,
> Bis der Tod das Leben bricht.

> [Roses blossom red and white;
> I love you truly with all my might.
> Love that's true will never break
> Till death at last our lives will take.] [p. 5]

> Dein Glück sei gross; / Dein Leiden klein;
> So sollen meine Wünsche sein.

> [Your happiness be great; / Your suffering be small;
> So shall my wishes e'er be all.] [p. 8]

There are also a few verses with a slight touch of humor, like this one:

> Lebe glücklich, lebe froh,
> Wie die Maus in Hafer Stroh.

> [Live happily and be gay
> Like a mouse in the oats and hay.] [p. 7]

The autograph-album poems quoted above are good examples of the more successful lyrics in the *Stammbücher*. Their poetic quality points to some sort of printed source as an inspiration.

---

[6]All quotations are reproduced from my *German Texana*. Page numbers in the text refer to pages in that book.

The Religious Heritage

Religion and the church relate strongly to much of the German cultural heritage in Texas. Of course, there was a great difference between the church-oriented groups, on the one hand, and the non-church or anticlerical people, like the freethinkers, on the other. Also, the various church groups—the Roman Catholics, the Lutherans, the Reformed Evangelicals (now the United Church of Christ), and the pietistic Methodists—had their own liturgies, songs, prayers, and catechism training, yet there is considerable similarity and overlapping. For the most part these church groups remained German well into the present century. German hymnals and other church literature were printed and distributed in America. The best-preserved and most generally accepted Texas church Germanica can be found in the hymns.

The churches in the German settlements were known for their singing, and much of this tradition, now in English, lives on. Most churches had excellent choirs, and under their leadership the congregations had good singers. This church singing was reflected in the homes, where the families often stood around pump organs and sang their hymns. Some of the men even sang while they did their work on farms and ranches and the women, while they worked in the homes and gardens. The singing also carried over into the midweek home prayer meetings.

Today some of these old customs have disappeared. It is important to note, however, that there is a renewed interest in church songs. In some rural and small-town churches German hymn festivals have been held in recent years. The following are typical German church songs, well known in Texas. The first is a familiar Catholic hymn:

> Maria zu lieben / Ist allzeit mein Sinn;
> Hab' ihr mich verschrieben, / Ihr Diener ich bin.
> Mein Herz, o Maria, / Brennt ewig zu dir,
> Vor Liebe und Freude, / O himmlische Zier.

> [Mary to love / Is always my sigh,
> I gave her my promise, / Her servant am I.
> My heart, oh Mary, / Burns ever for Thee,
> With love and with joy / Thy glory I see.] [p. 51]

Many of the German Protestant songs are unique because English versions are not known. This makes them all the more a pure aspect of

Germanica. The following songs, well known in German Protestant churches, are otherwise unknown or unfamiliar in Texas Protestant circles:

> Lasst die Herzen immer fröhlich
> Und mit Dank erfüllet sein.
> Denn der Vater in dem Himmel
> Nennt uns seine Kinderlein.
> Immer fröhlich, immer fröhlich,
> Alle Tage Sonnenschein.
> Voller Schönheit ist der Weg des Lebens,
> Fröhlich lasst uns immer sein.

> [Let our hearts be always joyful
> And be filled with thanks and cheer.
> For our Father who's in heaven
> Calls us all his children dear.
> Always joyful, always joyful,
> Sunshine every day we see.
> Full of beauty is life's pathway always,
> Joyful may we ever be.] [p. 46]

The hymn quoted below was sung to the tune of "O Worship the King," and in this respect it relates to the Anglo traditions:

> Mein Hirt ist der Herr,
> Dess bin ich so froh;
> Denn niemand, wie Er,
> Erbarmet sich so.
> Es kann ja den Seelen,
> Die Jesus regiert,
> Kein Gutes je fehlen,
> Der Herr ist mein Hirt!

> [My shepherd, the Lord,
> Of this I'm so glad;
> No one, only He,
> Has mercy on me.
> And nothing is wanting
> For souls Jesus won;
> No good ever faileth;
> The Lord is my own.] [p. 46]

Prayers were an intrinsic part of the church-oriented German-Texans, especially the evangelicals. Some church groups—for example, the pietistic Methodists—held midweek prayer meetings in the homes of the church members. Also, morning and evening devotionals consisting of Bible readings, prayers, and sometimes the singing of hymns were held regularly in many homes. For the most part the prayers were self-composed and memorized through constant repetition, and they represent a form of indigenous culture. Because it was an oral tradition, little or none of this heritage has survived. On the other hand, a number of children's prayers, usually in verse form, have come down to us and are preserved in the memories of elderly people and also in various books. In addition to the familiar prayer "Ich bin klein, / Mein Herz ist rein," there was also:

> Lieber Gott, mach' mich fromm,
> Dass ich zu Dir in'n Himmel komm'.
>
> [Dear God, let me pious be
> That I may get to heaven with Thee.] [p. 54]

Table prayers or blessings were spoken everywhere in church-oriented communities. There do not seem to have been numerous versions of these blessings. As the family members folded their hands and bowed their heads at their places around the table, blessings like the ones below were recited:

> O Herr, segne diese Gaben,
> Die wir von Dir empfangen haben.
>
> [Bless, o Lord, these gifts we see,
> That we have received from Thee.]
>
> Segne, Vater, was wir essen;
> Lass uns Deiner nicht vergessen.
>
> [Bless, our Father, what we eat,
> And let us Thee not forget.] [p. 56]

There are also a few religious poems preserved in Texas that for the most part exhort the people to give thanks to God and ask him for his guidance. The most interesting one has a refreshing, though perhaps unintentional, touch of humor:

> Wer ohne Gebet zu Tische geht,
> Wer ohne Gebet vom Tische aufsteht,
> Der ist dem Ochs und Esel gleich,
> Und kommt auch nicht ins Himmelreich.
>
> [Who without prayer at the table will sup,
> Who without prayer from the table gets up,

He's like an ox and a donkey, dumb,
And will never to the kingdom of heaven come.] [p. 57]

The above hymns, prayers, and table blessings constitute a rich aspect of the cultural heritage of the German settlements in Texas. "Although much of the material is slowly fading from the memories of the people, the influence continues even after the German language culture gradually shifts to an Anglo tradition. Outsiders coming to the Texas German Belt can still detect this religious influence to the present day in the communities with a German background" (p. 58).

Nursery Rhymes and Children's Verses

Texas-German poems and songs for juveniles show only slight deviations from the original German versions, no doubt because this heritage material was well memorized and transmitted to the children by their parents. Such poems often accompany play activities, like the English "One, two, buckle my shoe" and various German counting-out verses, for example, the following ditty:

Eins, zwei, drei, vier, fünf, sechs, sieben,
Meine Mutter kochte Rüben;
Meine Mutter kochte Speck,
Ich oder du musst weg.

[One, two, three, four, five, six, seven,
My mother cooked turnips in the oven,
My mother cooked the bacon slow,
Either I or you must go.] [p. 14]

Then there is the well-known finger-counting game and the song "Hier ist der Daumen" ("This Is the Thumb"), and the less familiar game called "Hier ist eine Maus." While the first couplet of this poem is spoken, a circle is drawn with the finger on the child's forehead. Then while the second is spoken, the bridge of his nose is touched, and for the third couplet his chin is pinched or tickled:

Hier ist eine Maus,
Die baut sich ein Haus.

Hier ist eine Mück,'
Die baut sich eine Brück.'

Hier ist ein Floh,
Der macht so.

[Here is a mouse;
She builds herself a house.

Here is a midge;
She builds herself a bridge.

Here is a flea;
He does this to me.] [p. 15]

A number of knee-bouncing songs also existed in Texas, like "Hopp, hopp, hopp, / Pferdchen lauf Galopp" ("Trot, trot, trot, / Horsie run a lot"), "Hoppe, hoppe, Reiter" ("Trotting, trotting, rider"). During these songs the child rides on the knees of the singer and is bounced up and down as if he or she were riding a trotting horse:

Wenn die Kinder kleine sein,
Reiten sie auf Stöckelein;
Wenn sie grösser werden,
Reiten sie auf Pferden.
Dann geht das Pferdchen tripp und trap,
Und schmeisst den kleinen Reiter ab;
Plumps! Da liegt er unten.

[When the kids are small and wee,
A stick horse will their horsie be;
When they're big and stronger,
They'll ride their horses longer.
Then the horse goes pit-a-pat
And throws the rider tit-for-tat;
Bump! he hits the bottom.] [p. 17]

Then there are two well-known German-Texan lullabies. The first is "Schlaf, Kindchen, schlaf" ("Sleep, Baby, Sleep"), which appears in three versions in Texas, and the song "Eia, Popeia, / Was raschelt im Stroh?" ("Eia, Popeia, / What's rustling in the straw?" p. 19).

One pain-easing child's verse, three variants of which were discovered in Texas, reads:

Heile, heile, Segen,
Drei Tage Regen,
Drei Tage Sonnenschein,
Wird alles wieder heile sein.

[Healing, healing, blessing,
Three days of rain,
Three days of sunshine,
And all is well again.] [p. 20]

Many other German-Texan "Mother Goose" poems existed, such as "Muh, muh, muh, so ruft die bunte Kuh" ("Moo, moo, moo, so calls the pretty cow," p. 21).

For children in the bilingual schools many delightful poems were printed in the old-fashioned German eclectic readers, like the books by Bacon, Fick, Grebner, and Weick.[7] The pupils read and memorized these lyrics; thus they became a part of the German-Texan tradition. Some of the elderly people in the German settlements of Texas can still quote these poems from memory. The popular children's verses "Häschen sass im grünen Gras" ("Rabbit Sat in the Green, Green Grass"), "Fuchs, du hast die Gans gestohlen" ("Foxy, You Stole Our Goose"), and "Kommt ein Vogel geflogen" ("Comes a Birdie a Flying") also appeared in Texas. There were likewise counting-out ditties similar to the nursery rhymes: "Ich und du und Müllers Kuh; Bäckers Esel, das bist du" ("I and Thou and Miller's Cow; Baker's Donkey, That Art Thou"); a few alphabet rhymes, like "A, a, a, / Der Osterhas' ist da" (A, a, a, / Easter Rabbit Comes Today"); and verses about the seasons, like "Im Winter, wenn es friert" ("In Winter, When It Freezes"); and "Der Mai ist gekommen" ("May Has Come"; pp. 24–32).

The first stanza of the following poem can be considered an ideal specimen of the verse for older children:

> Hänschen klein geht allein
> In die weite Welt hinein.
> Stock und Hut stehn ihm gut,
> Ist gar wohlgemut.
> Aber Mutter weinet sehr,
> Hat ja nun kein Hänschen mehr.
> "Wünsch ihm Glück," sagt ihr Blick,
> "Kehr' nun bald zurück!"
>
> [Hänsel, small, not too tall,
> Goes into the world alone,
> Hat and cane are his gain,
> Give him style and tone.
> Mama cries and sheds a tear,
> Now she has no Hänsel, dear.

---

[7] Paul Valentine Bacon, *Vorwärts* (Boston: Allyn and Bacon, 1915); H. H. Fick, *Hin und Her: Ein Buch für die Kinder* (New York: American Book Co., 1913); W. H. Weick and C. Grebner, *Deutsches Erstes, Zweites, Drittes Lesebuch für amerikanische Schulen*, 3 vols. (New York: American Book Co., 1886).

"Wish him luck," says her glance,
"Come back soon, my Hans."] [p. 27]

Christmas and New Year's Songs and Verse

Some of the most striking and widely accepted elements of the
cultural heritage brought to Texas from German-speaking countries
and Holland are the Christmas, New Year, and Easter customs, songs,
and poems. Examples of this transplanted culture are Santa Claus
(from Sankt Nikolaus, who comes on December 6); the Weihnachtsmann, the Christmas man who brings the Christmas presents; Kriss-
kringle (derived from Christkindlein, the Christ Child, who brings the
presents in some parts of Germany), and the decorated and lighted
Tannenbaum (fir tree, or cedar tree in Texas); the Osterhas' (Easter
rabbit) and the Easter nests made of grass and flowers in which the
rabbit deposited the Easter eggs (a custom then unknown among
Anglos).[8]

Of special concern here are the many Christmas songs and poems.
The best known song is, of course, "Stille Nacht, heilige Nacht" ("Silent
Night, Holy Night"). Three versions of this song existed in Texas. One of
the variants is perhaps a Methodist version, since it is included in the
German Methodist hymnal. This variation contains lines like these:

> Durch gebrochene Wolken von fern
> Glänzt der Heil verkündene Stern,
> Wo der Erlöser erschien.
>
> [Through broken clouds we see from afar
> The redemption proclaiming, saving star,
> Where our Redeemer was born.] [pp. 35–36]

Among the other most beloved Christmas songs are "O du selige,
o du fröhliche" ("O Thou Blessed, O Thou Joyful"), "O Tannenbaum"
("O Christmas Tree"), "Alle Jahre wieder" ("Every Year Again"), "Morgen kommt der Weihnachtsmann, kommt mit seinen Gaben" ("Tomorrow Comes Old Santa Claus, Comes with All His Presents"),
"Ihr Kinderlein, kommet ("Ye Children, O Come Ye"), and "Der Christ-

---

[8] See Francis Edward Abernethy, "Deutschtum in Texas: A Look at Texas-German
Folklore," in *German Culture in Texas*, esp. pp. 214–16.

baum ist der schönste Baum" ("The Christ Tree Is the Fairest Tree")
(pp. 37–40).

There is also this semihumorous poem:

> Der Weihnachtsmann ist ein guter Mann;
> Er bringt den Kleinen, was er kann.
> Die Grossen lässt er laufen;
> Die könn'n sich selbst was kaufen.
>
> [Santa Claus is a good old man;
> He brings the children all he can.
> The grown-ups he will leave alone;
> They buy their presents on their own.] [p. 41][9]

Other familiar holiday poems extant in Texas are "Lieber, lieber
Weihnachtsmann" ("Dearest, Dearest Santa Claus"); "Morgen, Kinder,
wird's was geben" ("Tomorrow, Children, Things Will Happen"); a New
Year's poem, "Wenn's Neujahr ist" ("When New Year Comes"); and

> Das alte Jahr ist verflossen;
> Das neue wird angeschossen.
>
> [The old year has passed away;
> We'll shoot in the new today.] [pp. 41–42]

Epitaphs in Verse Forms

Terry G. Jordan's *Texas Graveyards: A Cultural Legacy* gives a
thorough account and description of ethnic rural Texas graveyards, including those of the German areas of Texas.[10] He characterizes various
unique cultural elements in the German-Texan cemeteries, such as the
use of wooden and cast-iron grave markers in addition to the usual
tombstones; excellent carvings of various figures, folk motifs, and signs;
the characteristically German attention to order, neatness, and geo-
metric layouts; the manner of burial in a *Kirchhof* (churchyard) or in a
Friedhof or a *Gottesacker*, both euphemisms for graveyards; the location of graves and the kinds of curbings, fences, and walls used; the
grave decorations and plantings; and, what is especially important for
our discussion here, the extensive use of German verse epitaphs.

[9] See also Jordan, "German Cultural Heritage in the Hill Country of Texas," in
ibid., pp. 176–87.
[10] Jordan, *Texas Graveyards*, pp. 89–122.

These German verse inscriptions on grave markers were used extensively in the nineteenth century and well into the twentieth. The amazing thing is that the custom was so widespread and persistent. It existed through the anti-German prejudice of World War I and even through World War II. There is, for example, in Comfort a grave marker as late as 1951 with one of the familiar inscriptions.

These grave poems show both variety and a certain amount of repetition. The even quality of the lyrics and the similarity indicate common book sources and copying. There are differences between Catholic and Protestant verses and between the poems found on grave markers in church-oriented communities and those of the freethinkers.

Here are a few examples. First, a child's epitaph:

> Sein Leben war ein Augenblick,
> Ein Frühlingstraum, sein Erdenglück.
>
> [His life was but a moment's play;
> A dream in spring, his earthly stay.] [p. 63]

The themes of love, piety, and great loss are common in the epitaphs:

> Du warst so fromm, voll Liebe, treu bescheiden
> Mit dir entflohen unsere Freuden.
>
> [You were so pious, loving, modest, true;
> Our joys all went away with you.] [p. 64]

Now, finally, an epitaph from a tombstone beautifully engraved in old Gothic-German letters:

> O, lieber Freund, gedenke mein,
> In dein Gebet mich schlüsse [schliesse] ein.
> Lebe stets als frommer Christ,
> Der seine Pflichten nicht vergisst.
> Bereite dich zu jeder Zeit
> Und sorge für die Ewigkeit.
>
> [Oh, dear friend, I want to be
> Remembered in a prayer by thee.
> Live as a Christian, without fear,
> Who ne'er forgets his duty here,
> Be ready at all times and be
> Concerned about eternity.] [p. 73]

There are literally hundreds and thousands of such German poetic inscriptions in the various cemeteries. Since some of the headstones are crumbling and the words are difficult to read, special efforts should be made now to record these German poetic epitaphs while they are still legible.

Traditional Singing and Drinking Songs

The German settlers and their descendants in Texas are known for their singers' clubs and singing societies, some of which have remained active to the present day. They bear names such as the Frohsinn (Good Cheer) Club of Dallas; the Sängerbund (Choral Club) and the Damenchor (Ladies' Chorus) of Houston; the Sängerunde (Singing Circle) of Austin; the Beethoven Männerchor (Beethoven Men's Chorus), the Teutonia group, and the Mendelssohn Club of San Antonio; the Germania, the Echo, the Concordia, and the Liedertafel (Glee Club) of New Braunfels; the Salamander Club of Galveston; the Walhalla Group in Sattler; the Eintracht (Concordia) Singers of Grapetown; and the Arion Männerchor (Arion Men's Chorus) of Fredericksburg.

These singing clubs were organized into two state singers' groups: the Deutsch-Texanischer Sängerbund (German-Texan Singers' League) and the Gebirgssängerbund (Hill Country Singers' League). They have held annual festivals for many years. These singing societies have been the chief preservers of the German-Texas song tradition.[11]

There are two related groups of songs: familiar, traditional songs and drinking songs. Some of the songs are correctly called folk songs, but others were written and composed by well-known poets and composers. The nostalgic flavor of the songs and the immigrants' yearning for their fatherland caused these songs to survive in Texas, in some cases better than abroad.

Some of the songs sung in Texas are well known: "Freut euch des Lebens" ("Relish Life's Pleasures"), "Du, du liegst mir im Herzen," ("You, You Are in My Heart, Dear"), "Horch, was kommt von draussen rein" ("Hark, Who's Coming Walking By"), "Das zerbrochene Ringlein" ("The Broken Ring"), "Ach, wie ist's möglich dann" ("Oh, How Is It Possible Then?"), "Muss i denn, muss i denn" ("Must I Then, Must I Then?"), "Nach der Heimat möcht ich wieder" ("To My Homeland I

[11] Oscar Haas, *A Chronological History of the Singers of German Songs in Texas* (New Braunfels, Tex.: New Braunfels Zeitung, 1948).

Would Wander"), "Herr Schmidt, Herr Schmidt, / Wir haben eine Bitt'" ("Herr Schmidt, Herr Schmidt, / We Want to Talk a Bit"), and "Droben auf grüner Heide" ("Yonder on the Green Meadow").

The immigrants' loneliness and isolation in the New World are well expressed, for example, in the following song:

> Verlassen, verlassen,
> Verlassen bin i,
> Wie der Stein auf den Strassen
> So verlassen bin i
> Drum geh i zum Kirchlein,
> Zum Kirchlein weit draus,
> Dort knie i mi nieder
> Und wein mi halt aus.
>
> [Forsaken, forsaken,
> Forsaken am I,
> Like the stones in the pavement,
> So forsaken am I.
> For the church in the wildwood,
> For the small church I'll start,
> And I'll kneel down and weep there
> And cry out my heart.] [p. 90]

As I wrote in *German Texana*: "The custom of singing beer-hall and wine-cellar songs, as well as the songs themselves, was easily transplanted to Texas by the German colonists. . . . Then after a . . . slow-down during the prohibition years, they were revived and preserved to the present day" (p. 100). Among the better-known drinking songs are "Bier her, Bier her" ("Beer Here, Beer Here"), "Trink man noch ein Tröpfchen" ("Just Drink Another Droplet"), "Lauter schöne Leut' sind wir" ("None but Pretty Folk Are We"), and "Die Schnitzelbank" ("The Carver's Bench").

The following song, quoted in its entirety, has been especially popular in Texas:

> Im Himmel gibt's kein Bier,
> Drum trinken wir es hier.
> Und sind wir nicht mehr hier,
> Dann trinken die andern unser Bier.
>
> [In heaven there is no beer,
> That's why we drink it here.

And when we're gone from here,
The others will drink our beer.] [p. 108]

Humorous Poems, Light Verse, and Nonsensical Ditties

To quote again from *German Texana*: "Germans are not generally known for their sense of humor, partly because their serious bent of mind so often overshadows the humorous element. Nevertheless, there is a sizable body of whimsical and popular literature" (p. 109) among Germans, and some of this material may be indigenous to Texas. There are many examples of humorous poems and light verse in currency in Texas (pp. 109–23). Among these are such titles as "Wie weh tut mein Finger" ("My Finger Is Hurting"), "Regen, Regentropfen" ("Rain and Raindrops, Fleeting"), "Wenn meine Mutter wüsste" ("If My Mother Only Knew"), "Wenn der Schneider reiten will" ("When the Tailor Wants to Ride"), "Du bist wie der Schneider Puff" ("You Are Like Tailor Pooh"), "O, es sitzt 'ne Fliege an der Wand" ("Oh, There Sits a Fly on the Wall"), "Zwei Knaben gaben sich einen Kuss" ("Two Boys Gave Each Other a Kiss"), and "Jetzt geh ich nach Haus und brat' mir 'ne Maus" ("Now I Go to the House and Fry Me a Mouse").

An old quatrain that was incorporated into a musical composition offers a good illustration of this humorous verse:

> Sauerkraut und Rüben,
> Die haben mich vertrieben.
> Hätte die Mutter Fleisch gekocht,
> Dann wär' ich noch geblieben.
>
> [Sauerkraut and beets each day
> Drove me from my home away;
> If Mother had cooked me meat, somehow
> I would have stayed at home till now.] [p. 110]

The following humorous poem has a good Texas flavor, and it may be indigenous:

> Durch einen Ochsenstoss
> Flog ich in Abrahams Schoss;
> Ich ging zur ewigen Ruh
> Durch dich, du Rindvieh du.
>
> [By a wild ox I was gored,
> So to Abraham's bosom I soared;

To eternal rest I flew
Through you, dumb ox, through you.] [p. 111]

In addition to the poems above there are also some tongue twist-
ers (*Zungenbrecher*) with a humorous flavor, but their number is not
great in Texas.

Proverbs and Riddles

German-Texans, like other people almost everywhere in past centuries, were very fond of proverbs. In his book *Oma & Opa: German-
Texan Pioneers*, Curt Schmidt points out how important proverbs and
aphorisms (*Sprichwörter* and *Sprüche*) were to the German-Texans.[12]
Through constant repetition of these sayings children were indoctri-
nated by the proverbs, and thus they served an effective pedagogical
purpose. The following illustrate this genre:

Geteilter Schmerz ist halber Schmerz;
Geteilte Freude ist doppelte Freude.

[Shared pain is only half a pain;
Shared joy is double joy.]

Was du nicht willst, das man dir tu,'
Das füg' auch keinem andern zu.

[What you don't want others to do to you,
That you should never to others do.] [pp. 127, 133]

Although German proverbs were immensely popular in Texas,
riddles did not share the same degree of popular favor. Some good
riddles existed, but their number was relatively small. Children generally like riddles, but the elderly informants seem to have forgotten
most of them. Among those found in Texas are "Erst weiss wie Schnee"
("First White as Snow"), "Einer kam gegangen" ("A Fellow Came Walking Along"), and "Es sassen zehn Sperlinge auf dem Dach" ("Ten Spar-
rows Were Sitting on the Roof"; pp. 136–38).

---

[12]Curt E. Schmidt, *Oma & Opa: German-Texan Pioneers* (New Braunfels, Tex.:
Texas Folkways Publishing Co., 1975), pp. 53–57.

Anecdotes

German-Texan anecdotes are a popular form of entertainment, and they are good illustrations of indigenous Texas folklore. In a few instances the anecdotes contain names of participants and the locale—for example, "Sheriff Alfred Klaener of Fredericksburg"—but most of them have only a general reference. Often the humor results from misunderstandings, and the anecdotes are illustrations of language problems among the German ethnic groups. The following illustrates this motif:

> A German-Texas family of Fredericksburg sent their son to the University of Texas before World War I. After the boy arrived in Austin, he learned that, among other subjects, he had to study a foreign language. Because he did not know what to take, he wrote his parents at home and asked them what he should do. Papa and Mama thought things over a while and then wrote to their son: "Take Englisch, Son: de people arount hier haf schtartet schpeaking it already." [p. 142]

In conclusion, as I have written, "the German settlements of Texas have preserved to the present day a large store of heritage material that was brought to Texas by the early settlers. These treasures were kept in the minds of the people and passed on to their children" (p. 145). As time passes, however, this cultural possession of songs, poems, and stories will be forgotten. They are like endangered species in the plant and animal world, and we must make special efforts to collect and preserve this heritage. It is my hope that this chapter will help perpetuate our German Texana and encourage others to add to the collections of these treasures.

Three Literary Perspectives on the German in America: Immigrant, Homeland, and American Views

SCHOLARLY perspectives on the German in America are predominantly nonliterary. It is mainly the history of German immigrants and the contributions the immigrant has made to this country's settlement, society, culture, religion, and technology that have occupied scholarly attention.[1] There have been studies of the literary perspective, but the German in an American setting as portrayed by literary means has not been a continuous subject of interest. This is perplexing since American and German literatures abound in both empirical presentations and imaginative creations of Germans in this country.[2]

[1] Albert B. Faust, *The German Element in the United States*, 2 vols. (Boston: Houghton Mifflin, 1909; New York: Houghton, 1927, 2nd ed.); German edition: *Das Deutschtum in den Vereinigten Staaten in seiner Bedeutung für die amerikanische Kultur* (Leipzig: Teubner, 1912); Henry A. Pochmann, *German Culture in America 1600–1900* (Madison: University of Wisconsin Press, 1957); Günter Moltmann, ed., *Deutsche Amerika-Auswanderung im 19. Jahrhundert: Sozialgeschichtliche Beiträge*, Amerikastudien/American Studies 44 (Stuttgart: Metzler, 1976); Don Heinrich Tolzmann, *German-Americana* (Metuchen, N.Y.: Scarecrow Press, 1975); Don Heinrich Tolzmann, *German-American Literature* (Metuchen, N.Y.: Scarecrow Press, 1977); Willi Paul Adams, ed., *Die deutschsprachige Auswanderung in die Vereiningten Staaten: Berichte über Forschungsstand und Quellenbestände*, Materialen 14 (Berlin: John F. Kennedy Institut für Amerikastudien, Freie Universität Berlin, 1980).

[2] Preston Albert Barba, "Emigration to America Reflected in German Fiction," *German-American Annals*, n.s. 12 (1914): 193–227; F. E. Coenen, "W. Raabe's Treatment of the Emigrant," *Studies in Philology* 34 (1937): 612 ff.; Nelson Van de Luyster, "Emigration to America as Reflected in the German Novel of the Nineteenth Century, Especially in the Fiction of Bitzius, Laube, Gutzkow, Auerbach, Freytag, Storm, Keller, Spielhagen, Heyse, Raabe" (Ph.D. diss., University of North Carolina, 1943); Harold S. Jantz, "Amerika im deutschen Dichten und Denken," *Deutsche Philologie im Aufriss* (Berlin: Erich Schmidt, 1957), III, 310–71; Hans Galinsky, *Amerikanisch-deutsche Sprach- und Literaturbeziehungen: Systematische Übersicht und Forschungsbericht 1945–1970* (Frankfurt: Athenäum, 1972), pp. 40–42, 154–57; Fritz Martini, "Auswan-

One of the reasons for this relative neglect by scholars may be the bewildering variety of vantage points. Consequently, for this chapter I have selected three of them: the immigrant, the homeland, and the American perspective. I have restricted them to the German immigrant view and to the view from the homeland as expressed by two kinds of back-home writers, those who have never been to America and those who have, but merely for a short time (in the latter group the freshness of impressions was of primary interest, though I know that no duty is payable on prejudices imported and so easily found confirmed).[3] For the American perspective I confined myself to the oldest, the Anglo-American one.

Individual representatives of these three kinds of observation and vision are limited to two German immigrants, Francis Daniel Pastorius, Franconia-born father of the late seventeenth-century Germantown, Pennsylvania,[4] and Westphalia-born Mathilde Anneke, mid-

---

derer, Rückkehrer, Heimkehrer: Amerikaspiegelungen im Erzählwerk von Keller, Raabe und Fontane," in *Amerika in der deutschen Literatur: Neue Welt-Nordamerika—USA*, ed. Sigrid Bauschinger, Horst Denkler, and Wilfred Malsch (Stuttgart: Reclam, 1975), pp. 178–204. See also Denkler's essay in n. 4. For the immigrant in general literature, included in Percy Boynton, *The Rediscovery of the Frontier* (New York: Cooper Square, 1970), is a section on "The Immigrant Pioneer in Fiction." See also A. Abramson, *The Immigrant Experience in American Literature*, BAAS Pamphlets in American Studies 10 (London: British Association for American Studies, 1982). It offers a useful bibliography on pp. 37–40.

[3]Cf. Günter Kunert, *Der andere Planet: Ansichten von Amerika* (Munich: Hanser, 1975).

[4]Other pertinent material includes Augustus Gottlieb Spangenberg, *Von der Arbeit der evangelischen Brüder unter den Heiden* (Barby: Laux, 1782). For the Forty-eighters, see also Carl Schurz, *Reminiscences*, 3 vols. (New York: McClure, 1907–1908); and Carl Schurz, *Speeches, Correspondence, and Political Papers*, 6 vols. (New York: G. P. Putnam's Sons, 1913); Frederic Bancroft, ed., *Die Briefe von Carl Schurz an Gottfried Kinkel: Beihefte zum Jahrbuch für Amerikastudien* 12 (Heidelberg: Winter, 1965); Patricia Herminghouse, ed., with Carol Jean Poore, *German-American Crosscurrents: Writings of Political Emigrés in Nineteenth Century America* (New York: Kraus International Publications, 1984). Eligible novelists would have been Pomeranian Reinhold Solger, *Anton in Amerika*, serialized in the weekly *New Yorker Criminal Zeitung und Belletristishes Journal*, March 21–September 5, 1862; and Berlin-born child immigrant (1890) Ludwig Lewisohn, *The Island Within* (New York, Harper and Brothers, 1928). For Solger, see Horst Denkler, "Die Schule des Kapitalismus: Reinhold Solgers deutsch-amerikanisches 'Seitenstück' zu Gustav Freytags *Soll und Haben*," in *Amerika in der deutschen Literatur*, pp. 108–23. Concerning the immigrant view on the German in America and its lyrical expression, see Lisa Kahn, *David am Komputer und andere Gedichte* (Providence, R.I.: Trebush Press, 1982); *Utahs Geheimnisse: Gedichte* (Berlin:

nineteenth-century refugee and immigrant to Milwaukee, Wisconsin. The two kinds of homeland view are represented by Goethe, who never visited America,[5] and the contemporary poet and prose writer Günter Kunert, who visited the United States in 1972.[6] As with Pastorius and Anneke, two different periods are represented, Goethe standing for the turn of the eighteenth century and Kunert for the later twentieth century. The twentieth-century physician-writer William Carlos Williams, blessed with a German immigrant's daughter for a wife, provides the Anglo-American literary view of the German in America.[7]

Specific reasons for this contestable choice of "quintuplets" will, it is hoped, emerge in the following.

Stoedner, 1981); her contributions to *Terra Poetica: A Multilingual Magazine of Poetry* 2, nos. 1–2 (1983): 31–38; and her anthology *Reisegepäck Sprache: Deutschschreibende Schriftstellerinnen in den USA, 1938–1976* (Munich: Fink, 1979) deserve special mention.

[5] Instead of Goethe many others might have been chosen. The German as inmigrant, actual or prospective, shows up in Friedrich Maximilian Klinger's play *Sturm und Drang* (1776) and in two novels, Ernst Willkomm, *Die Europamüden* (1838; reprint, Göttingen, 1968); and Ferdinand Kürnberger, *Der Amierka-Müde* (1855; reprint, without the hyphen in the title, Weimar, 1973). For these and further earlier and later variants of the immigrant,—e.g., the German participant, voluntary or involuntary, in the American War of Independence and the subsequent settler in the United States or returnee to Germany after the end of hostilities; the political refugee; the packed-off (to avoid social stigmatization at home), and the escaped criminal—see Jantz's indispensable survey above). Franz Kafka's *Amerika* and Theodor Fontane's *Quitt* would have made excellent choices for the latter two categories. For the returnee, Thomas Mann's *Königliche Hoheit* (1909) offers two interesting comical examples.

[6] Besides Kunert and Gerhart Hauptmann in 1894 and 1932; Klaus Mann in the 1920s; and Wolfgang Koeppen, Ingeborg Bachmann, Hans-Magnus Enzensberger, Rudolf Hagelstange, Günter Grass, and Peter Handke after 1945 would have exemplified the short-term visitor. On purpose I am excluding here the "American resident alien" and "U.S. citizen" Germans, e.g., Friedrich Gerstäcker and Uwe Johnson, on the one hand, and Charles Sealsfield and Thomas Mann, on the other.

[7] By "Americans," in the framework of this chapter, any native-born person in America and their descendants are understood. They include second-generation Germans but also Americans of English or Irish descent who, like Henry James or T. S. Eliot, became British citizens. In all these respects the area of choice open to the scholar is extensive. Benjamin Franklin, Benjamin Rush, and Charles Brockden Brown represent fairly early, mainly eighteenth-century views on America's Germans. James Fenimore Cooper, Henry Wadsworth Longfellow, Herman Melville, Sidney Lanier, and Henry James make up but a sample of nineteenth-century portrayers or commentators on this subject. The twentieth century offers German-descended novelists like Theodore Dreiser, Gertrude Stein, Willa Siebert Cather, Ruth Suckow, Thomas Wolfe, John Steinbeck, and Kurt Vonnegut, Jr.; a dime-novel–style "western" writer like Zane (Zahn)

Francis Daniel Pastorius

Francis Daniel Pastorius focuses on the German in the new world of Pennsylvania—new in the geographical, socioeconomic, and linguistic but also religious sense. His well-known promotional tracts of 1684, 1692, and 1700,[8] as well as his cross-Atlantic correspondence with his parents and friends, were, of course, written in prose.[9] But these tracts have quite different, poetic neighbors in Pastorius's total repertory. Of primary interest are his epigrams, addressed to the first native born and their parents in their new interethnic situation as fellow colonists of the English. The German immigrant with his natural

---

Grey; essayists like H. L. Mencken; poets like Theodore Roethke; and dramatists like Lillian Hellman. Among non-German presenters of Germans in America, the American twentieth century has at its disposal novelists and storytellers such as Sinclair Lewis, Katherine Anne Porter, Howard Fast, Randall Jarrell, Walker Percy, and J. D. Salinger; the poet T. S. Eliot; and the dramatist Tennessee Williams. Even a best-selling writer, Hervey Allen, author of the historical romance *Anthony Adverse* (1933), belongs here. A one-time New Orleans resident, German financial genius Vincent Nolte, is among the novel's chief figures. Cf. Otis W. Coan and Richard G. Lillard, "Minority Ethnic Groups," in *America in Fiction*, 3rd ed. (Stanford, Calif.: Stanford University Press, 1949), sec. 4, pp. 172–81. For Eliot, see Hans Galinsky, *Deutschland in der Sicht von D. H. Lawrence und T. S. Eliot: Eine Studie zum anglo-amerikanischen Deutschlandbild im 20. Jahrhundert*, Akademie der Wissenschaften und der Literatur, Mainz, Abhandlungen der geistes- und sozialwissenschaftlichen Klasse, Jahrgang, 1956, no. 1 (Wiesbaden: Steiner, 1956), reprinted in Hans Galinsky, *Amerika und Europa* (Munich: Langenscheidt, 1968), pp. 199–243. With regard to Jarrell, see Galinsky, "The Give-and-Take of an American Section: Literary Interrelations between the American South and Germany in the Early Post-War Period (1945–1950)," in *Die amerikanische Literatur in der Weltliteratur: Themen und Aspekte*, ed. Claus Uhlig and Volker Bischoff (Berlin: Erich Schmidt, 1982), pp. 363–91, esp. pp. 381, 384. For Porter, see Hans-Joachim Lang, "Katherine Anne Porters Einladung auf *Das Narrenschiff*, in ibid., pp. 458–75.

   [8] Francis Daniel Pastorius, *Umständige Geographische Beschreibung/Der zu allerletzt erfundenen Provintz PENSYLVANIAE* (Frankfurt: n.p., 1700). For this edition and a shorter one printed in Nuremberg in 1692 and appended to Pastorius's father's "Description of Windsheim," see Oswald Seidensticker, *The First Century of German Printing in America 1728–1830, Preceded by a Notice of the Literary Work of F. D. Pastorius* (Philadelphia: n.p., 1893; Millwood, N.Y.: Kraus Reprints, 1980), p. 2.

   [9] *Copia, eines von einem Sohn an seine Eltern auss America, abgelassenen Brieffes*, dated Philadelphia, March 7, 1684. See letter reprinted in Marion Dexter Learned, *The Life of Francis Daniel Pastorius, the Founder of Germantown* (Philadelphia: William J. Campbell, 1908). *Sichere Nachricht auss America wegen der Landschafft Pennsylvania/ von einem dorthin gereissten Teutschen/de dato Philadelphia, den 7. Martii 1684*; with regard to reprintings in Tentzel's *Monatliche Unterredungen einiger guten Freunde von allerhand Büchern und andern annemlichen Geschichten* (1689–1706), see Learned, *Life of Pastorius*, p. 62.

wish to hand down the values inherent in his customs and manners is
behind the following pieces. One of them stresses the value of learning
through the reading of books:

> Dear Children! Come and look
> Often in your Father's book;
> Not only look, but understand,
> For Learning's more than house and land.
> A house may burn, the land be spent,
> True Learning never has an end:
> True Learning is most excellent.[10]

Another piece, also written in Pietist "plain style," teaches sexual discipline—fortunately, however, by way of a whimsical, punlike analogy:

> Cowslips never hurted none;
> But let Girls' lips alone:
> Thereby many were undone.[11]

The immigrant presenting himself as teacher is accompanied
by the immigrant as ethnic observer and comparatist. The pleasures of
the table and the limitations of national literary tastes provide an opportunity for epigrammatic wit, for chiastic patterning and punning
ingenuity:

> The English can eat flesh both without herbs and bread,
> Flesh without herbs and bread to Germans is black Lead.[12]

> *Hans Sachs* and *David Lindsay* write,
> And all is Verse what they indite,
> But Verse per verse, which Modern's [sic] loath.
> Pray! tell me WHO is best of both?
> The German doubtless will say Sachs,
> The English of his Lindsay cracks.[13]

These three features upon which the immigrant perspective of Pastorius fixes, the handing down of national values, the good-humored
statements of ethnically different eating habits and literary tastes, will
persist over the centuries.

So will the verse expression of the immigrant's mind and his place

[10] In Harrison T. Meserole, ed., *Seventeenth-Century American Poetry* (New York:
Norton, 1972), p. 301.
[11] Ibid.
[12] Ibid., p. 302.
[13] Ibid., p. 303.

of refuge, the private garden. The view of the German colonist that emerges from these poems is a strikingly European one, that of the happy house owner and cultivator of his garden:

> Let Kings and Princes keep the wide Earth-Ball,
> I would not change my Garden with them all.[14]

This kind of immigrant does not consider himself a bearer of an imperial mission; rather, his attitude is significantly quietist. The possible establishment of "ein Klein Teutschland" ("a little Germany") that Pastorius speaks of in a letter to his parents in 1684 is tied to a political existence: ". . . unter unserem Recht and Gerechtigkeit liebenden Gouverneur Können wir ein Friedsames und stilles Leben in aller gottseligen Dankbarkeit Führen. Amen!" (". . . under a law- and justice-loving [English] governor, we can lead a peaceful and quiet life, in godly gratitude. Amen!").[15] These quietist prose and verse examples are in keeping with what Pastorius calls "Rare Garden Meditations."[16] They follow the customary ascent of the religious spirit from the "Creatures" to the "Creator."[17]

But the poetic mind of Pastorius does not stay within the confines of house and garden.[18] It also operates as an imaginary traveler. Partly it is stimulated by the experience of the Atlantic voyage, partly it feeds on memories of Pastorius's grand tour of Europe as travel companion and tutor of a German nobleman's son, partly it falls back on pure imagination, delighting in near-puns and internal rhymes:

> When I solidly do ponder,
> How thoughts wander; I must wonder
>   And for Shame exclaim, and own,
>   Mine are ranging up and down. . . .
> Thro' Great Britain, France and Holland,
> Denmark, Moskovy, Spain, Polland [sic],
>   Portugal and Italy,
>   Oft'ner yet thro' Germany

[14] Ibid., p. 302.

[15] Pastorius, *Copia, eines . . . Brieffes*, reprinted in Armin B. Brandt, *Bau deinen Altar auf fremder Erde. Die Deutschen in Amerika—300 Jahre Germantown* (Stuttgart: Seewald, 1983), p. 95. This and subsequent translations by the author.

[16] "On His Garden Book," in Meserole, *Seventeenth-Century American Poetry*, p. 296.

[17] "As often as some where before my Feet," ibid., p. 298.

[18] Ibid., p. 301.

Hence returning to Braganza;
To the Cape of Bon Speranza;
So, by way of Africa,
Home to Penn Silvania.[19]

Pennsylvania has become home.

The German fellow immigrant is occasionally mentioned in Pastorius's poetry. With a fine sense of adequacy, that is, with full awareness of the bilingualism of colonial Pennsylvania, Pastorius composes the following poem on the unreliability of a German craftsman or merchant in English and German, a German with a Main Valley Franconian touch and a bilingual pun (*Hanns:hands*):

Hanns has his hands and tongue at his command,
He keeps most fast, what he did promise, and
Verspricht,
und lieferts nicht,
Das ist ein Schand.

[Promises,
and doesn't deliver;
that is a disgrace.][20]

The German in colonial America is also referred to in the prose of Pastorius in his role as lawyer, promoter, and administrator. The humor permeating many of the previous poems is occasionally replaced in the prose by a slightly angered tone of Germantown's first mayor. With varying success he tries to persuade his countrymen to share the burden of public service for the sake of the immigrant community.[21] Total seriousness prevails in America's first Germantown-made declaration against slavery, probably penned, and definitely signed, by Pastorius.[22] His linguistic environment shows particularly clearly: it is multilingual and multidialectal. The example quoted reveals his grasp of English and his love of dialectical Franconian German. Other examples could

---

[19] Ibid., p. 294.

[20] "Francis Daniel Pastorius, his Life, . . . Begun Anno Domini . . . 1696," photostat of manuscript in the Harris Collection, Brown University, Providence, R.I., [no.] 69.

[21] Learned, *Life of Pastorius*; Faust, *The German Element*, passim.

[22] Reprinted in Learned, *Life of Pastorius*, p. 262; German translation in Oswald Seidensticker, *Die Erste Deutsche Einwanderung in Amerika und die Gründing von Germantown im Jahre 1683: Festschrift zum deutsch-amerikanischen Pioneer-Jubiläum am 6. Oktober 1883* (Philadelphia, 1883), pp. 81–82.

be cited to prove his knowledge of Hebrew, Greek, Latin, Dutch, and French, as well as the Lower Rhine German dialect of his Krefeld fellow settlers. The partial adoption of English from the very first helps explain why so many German-American contributions to American literature have gone unheeded as *German*-American literary achievements.

Mathilde Anneke

Pastorius provides the best illustration of the colonial immigrant's literary perspective of the German immigrant in America at that time. An answer to the question how this literary perspective subsequently changed can be found in another vantage point of German-American history: the 1848–49 period and its political refugees and, specifically, in the point of view of a woman, Mathilde Anneke. Anneke was born into an upper-class family in Münster, Westphalia's leading Roman Catholic city. She was well acquainted with aristocratic circles and married a French emigré aristocrat whom she, however, subsequently divorced. Cut off by her own acquaintances, she was received into the fringe group of religious and political freethinkers. Her second husband, a former Prussian officer, was dismissed for similar views, and Mathilde herself became acquainted with German pre–March, 1848, revolutionary theory. Revolutionary practice followed in the armed uprisings of the German southwest. The revolt failed, and the Annekes escaped to the United States.[23] The fight for their middle-class survival began. Although this fight was never won by the husband, a journalist and colonel in the American Civil War, it was fought successfully, though late in life, by Mathilde herself. Two years in Milwaukee; six years in Newark, New Jersey; two more in Milwaukee; five in Switzerland; and another nineteen in Milwaukee mark the main stations of her life struggle.

Anneke's literary perspective on the German in America is recorded primarily in journalistic prose, sometimes objectively descriptive, often propagandistic. As a self-trained journalist, Anneke also wrote private, epistolary prose, lucid and vivid, at times colored by her

---

[23] Maria Wagner, *Mathilde Franziska Anneke in Selbstzeugnissen und Dokumenten* (Frankfurt: Fischer Taschenbuch Verlag, 1980).

journalism. A third area of her literary activity includes imaginative prose and poetry.

It was characteristic of Anneke, formerly a German revolutionary and later a member of American abolitionist circles, that not the German but the black slave first appealed to her imagination. She experimented with the German immigrant as a literary figure in an unpublished three-volume novel, *Der Sturmgeiger* (*Fiddler in the Storm*), a piece of wildly political romanticism.[24] The figure of the immigrant also appears in her short novel *Uhland in Texas* as well as in her poetry. *Uhland in Texas* was serialized in the *Illinois Staatszeitung* in April, 1866.[25] Its subtitle promised "Ein deutsch-amerikanisches Lebensbild aus Texas" ("A German-American Portrait from Texas"). This "portrait" was painted by an author, as it were, twice removed from Texas. During her first eleven years in the United States she had never been to Texas, let alone to Uhland, a small village in east-central Texas, and when she was writing the novel, she was staying in Switzerland. In this "portrait" the Texas-German functions as helper and fellow sufferer of the black. "Dutchman und Nigger, alles ein Teufel" ("Dutchman and Nigger, both one devil") is used or self-coined as a slogan by the author and put into the mouths of Anglo slaveholders. This spectacular phrase is paralleled by a spectacular scene. A German and a black are roped to the hooves of a wild horse and chased into the plains. They are stopped by a band of Texas Indians. "Seht, wir Wilden sind doch bess're Menschen" ("Look, we savages are the nobler men, aren't we?").[26] That proverbial lesson first expressed by Johann Seume's Huron in his well-known German poem on the North American Indian "Der Wilde" ["The Savage"] underlines this symbolic episode in Anneke's Texas novel.

In the poetry of Pastorius discussed earlier, the interethnic theme included only white immigrants. In Anneke's prose tale it expands into an interracial one (as it does indeed in Pastorius's epistolary prose).[27]

[24] Ibid., pp. 152, 159, 161.
[25] Ibid., p. 434.
[26] Ibid., p. 386.
[27] For Pastorius's view of the Indian, see *Sichere Nachricht auss America* (1684), p. 4, as reprinted in Learned, *Life of Pastorius*, and inserted between pp. 128 and 129. See also letter to his father, dated June 1, 1693, available in English translation in Albert Cook Myers, ed., *Narratives of Early Pennsylvania, West New Jersey, and Delaware, 1640–1707*; Albert Cook Myers, ed., *Original Narratives of Early American History*

The Texas-German pioneer's attitude toward slavery as depicted by Anneke is largely in keeping with Texas history.[28] Though embellished slightly, her presentation of Indian-German relations is equally correct.[29] The setting, the region north of Indianola, had been well known to German-American and back-home readers as the Carlshafen area, the debarkation site for the settlers attracted by the Society for the Protection of German Immigrants in Texas.[30] The fourfold constellation comprising Anglos, Germans, blacks, and Indians in which the German immigrant finds himself in Anneke's *Uhland in Texas* is rather rare, however, in literary renderings of Germans in nineteenth-century America by German immigrants themselves.

In Anneke's poetry the Germans appear as an ethnic group but not as individuals. In a poem occasioned by the opening of the Milwaukee Civic Theater, the German community is addressed as a collective, and Milwaukee, predominantly German at the time, is praised in a characteristic style. The poem fuses themes from German pre-1848 freedom poetry with the equally persistent classicist revival of antique values:

Wie ihr die Freiheit führt' auf der Standarte,
So hebet unter eurer Freiheit Schutz
Empor, der alten Tyranney zum Trutz
Das Schöne, Ewige auf Eure Warte.

[As you carry freedom on your standard,
Under the protection of your freedom,
In defiance of the old tyranny,
Also raise up on your watchtower, beauty and that which is everlasting.][31]

This oratorical flourish carried over into Anneke's political speechifying. The subject of this oratorical prose, however, is woman in general and American woman in particular. In her fight for the rights of women, especially voting rights, the political role of the German

(New York: Charles Scribner's Sons, 1912), p. 419; letter to high-school principal Model (1697), in ibid., p. 435.

[28] Rudolph Leopold Biesele, *The History of the German Settlements in Texas* (Austin: Von Boeckmann-Jones, 1930), p. 196; T. R. Fehrenbach, *Lone Star: A History of Texas and the Texans*, 2nd ed. (New York: American Legacy Press, 1983), pp. 294–95.

[29] Ibid., p. 190.

[30] Ibid., pp. 108, 110, 128–29.

[31] Wagner, *Mathilde Franziska Anneke*, p. 376; Frank Trommler, "Vom Vormärz zum Bürgerkrieg: Die Achtundvierziger und ihre Lyrik," in *Amerika in der deutschen Literatur*, ed. Bauschinger et al., pp. 93–107.

woman in America may have been more significant than the Anneke material as yet published actually reveals.[32]

Anneke's epistolary prose rounds off impressions gathered from her imaginative and nonimaginative public prose. In this very personal mode of expression judgments on German-Americans either withheld or formulated more cautiously in public are not suppressed. The reader quickly learns that the unconscious self-presentation of this fascinating immigrant woman is often more enlightening than what she has to say about the other Germans in America.

Immigrant to America, American resident in Europe, returnee to America mark three changing perspectives on these "others" and herself from the time Anneke, aged thirty-two, first set foot on American soil. Such changing vantage points, so different from Pastorius's fixed points of Germantown and nearby Philadelphia, as well as differences of historical time and American region, concepts of religion, and woman's place in society, do not seem to make for a meaningful comparison of our two selected immigrant views on the German in America. Nevertheless, there are similarities. Both Pastorius and Anneke were articulate and produced literature as immigrants because they were not pioneer farmers or craftsmen but urban intellectuals, founders of German schools, and community leaders. In the writings of both, objective description focuses on the needs of education and on living with other ethnic groups while each of these groups adheres to its transplanted preferences. The common focus is also on squabbles within the German element and its antipathies toward shouldering public responsibilities. Agreement also prevails on the rejection of slavery. Self-presentation in both writers fixes on the love of nature, home, children, and books, and also on a wanderlust, a love of travel, remembered or merely imagined. Pastorius's "Home to Penn Silvania" has its parallel in Anneke's "Heimat, die in unserem Gemüte stets am Michigan See festgehalten wurde" ("home which in our minds was always fixed at Lake Michigan").[33]

Naturally there are also differences between these two immigrant writers. These differences are less pronounced in their imaginative

[32] Some of it has been reprinted in Wagner, *Mathilde Franziska Anneke*, pp. 331–32, 338–39, 345–46. Repository of pertinent material: State Historical Society of Wisconsin, Madison, Wisconsin.

[33] Wagner, *Mathilde Franziska Anneke*, p. 217.

than in their nonimaginative presentation of the Germans in America (including themselves). What is most strikingly different from Pastorius's view is Anneke's multifaceted picture of German women in America. The recently immigrated German household help; the *Hausfrau*, that is, Anneke herself; her immigrant mother and daughter; her children of the first native-born generation; the freshly imported German private-school teacher; the German woman as importer of Friedrich Froebel's *Kindergarten* ideas, as member of the Vassar College faculty, as actress, poet, and translator—what a portrait gallery opens in Mrs. Anneke's correspondence![34] It also comprises group portraits like "German women of the Union" as hoped-for readers of her *Deutsche Frauenzeitung (German Women's Paper)*, founded by her in 1852 and the first publication of its kind in the United States.[35] The nightmare of prospective women voters casting their vote for Prohibition apparently rose in her pragmatic—and prophetic—mind as early as 1869. We also owe to this newspaper the following defensive characterization of Wisconsin Germans loving their beer:

> Die meisten von ihnen sind intelligente, ehrliche, schaffende Bürger der besten Art, die es lieben, die Natur und ihre Gaben zu geniessen, ohne dass sie es Circe gestatten, Tiere aus ihnen zu machen.

> [Most of them are intelligent, honest, hardworking citizens of the best kind, who love enjoying nature and her gifts, without permitting Circe to turn them into animals.][36]

Decorum, no doubt, prevented Anneke from staying closer to Homer and writing "swine."

In one final respect Anneke remained more German than did Pastorius: she nearly always felt the need to express herself in German. The literary work of Germantown's founder, as has been pointed out, was bilingual, even at times multilingual. Although Anneke had translated an English-language novel in the 1840s, and English outlines of some of her speeches are extant, her writing was monolingual practically throughout. Naturally, lexical and, more rarely, syntactic Americanisms crept into her German.[37]

[34] Ibid., pp. 288, 108, 111, 245–46, 288, 265, 293.
[35] Ibid., pp. 316–17.
[36] Ibid., pp. 339.
[37] Ibid., p. 411: "Ich gewinne täglich" (cf. "I am gaining [weight]"). See also p. 349: "Ich sprach nach Noten" (cf. "notes" meaning "Notizen").

Goethe

Goethe is the first and the most illustrious example of the home-based observer, the one who relies on the imagination supported by written or oral information, furnished by books about America, by American visitors to Germany, or by returnees to Europe and especially Germany. It is fascinating to watch the slow emergence in Goethe's works of the figure of the immigrant, both the prospective and the actual one, through its antecedents and their transmutations.[38] From Lili Schönemann's readiness to immigrate to America with young Goethe, her fiancé, the motif of the voyage to America and subsequent settlement there could be pursued through such plays as *Stella* and *Der Gross-Cophta*.[39] For reasons of space, however, only the novel *Wilhelm Meisters Lehrjahre* (*Wilhelm Meister's Apprenticeship*, 1796) and its sequel, *Wanderjahre* (*Wilhelm Meister's Travels*, second version, 1829), are discussed here.

In the *Lehrjahre*, Lothario is a German participant in the American War of Independence. He is a German officer, just returned from the New World, where in company with some Frenchmen he had served with distinction under the flag of the United States. Fundamentally a German intellectual, Lothario had gone overseas for the sake of an idea: ". . . war eine Handlung nicht mit tausend Gefahren umgeben, so schien sie mir nicht bedeutend, nicht würdig" (". . . action, if not surrounded by a thousand dangers, is not important, is not worthy"); and he had thought that only by going overseas could he be "nützlich und notwendig" ("useful and necessary").[40] In America, however, he learned a lesson: not what is exotic but what is nearest can provide a setting for being "useful and necessary." ". . . hier, oder

---

[38] Walter Wadepuhl, *Goethe's Interest in the New World* (Jena: Frommann, 1934); Ernst Beutler, "Von der Ilm zum Susquehanna: Goethe und Amerika in Ihren Wechselbeziehungen," in his *Essays um Goethe* (Bremen: C. Schünemann, 1957), pp. 580–629; Johannes Urzidil, "Goethes Amerika und Amerikas Goethe," *Amerikanische Rundschau*, no. 20 (1948), pp. 69–81; Victor Lange, "Goethes Amerikabild: Wirklichkeit und Vision," in *Amerika in der deutschen Literatur*, pp. 63–74; Karl E. Wipf, *Elpuis: Betrachtungen zum Begriff der Hoffnung in Goethes Spätwerk* (Berne: Francke, 1974).

[39] *Dichtung und Wahrheit*, in *Sämtliche Werke* (Zurich and Munich: Artemis and DTV [Deutscher Taschenbuch Verlag], 1977), X, 829–30; *Stella*, in ibid., IV, 886; 890; *Der Gross-Cophta*, in ibid., VI, 609, hereafter cited as *SW*.

[40] Ibid., VII, 282.

nirgend ist Amerika!" (". . . here or nowhere is America!"), with "here" meaning Germany, encapsulates the lesson.[41] The young returnee and landowner, though still in debt, entertains plans of profit sharing with his farm laborers. This is Goethe's new and mildly ironic perspective of the returned fighter for freedom.

Lothario is flanked by two figures who are also interested in going to the United States. One of them is a variation of Lothario the "idealist," and once again the frame of reference is historical. This time it reaches beyond revolutionary to colonial, post-Pastorius America. Lothario's brother-in-law, the "Count," is a supporter of the Moravian, or "Herrnhuter," Brethren. For their benefit the Count intends to sell his estate and go on a trip to America. Modeled on Count Nikolaus Zinzendorf, the founder of the Brethren's settlement at Bethlehem, Pennsylvania, this saintly man is mockingly supposed to yearn secretly for a glamorous martyrdom as an Indian missionary.[42]

Fortunately, a down-to-earth materialist is not lacking in this company. During the critical years between the War of Independence and the impending French Revolution, Major Jarno, grown worldly-wise in his former days as a courtier, is considering a reinvestment of his financial interests. Jarno has established a mutual insurance company and, like a secularized Pastorius, is about to go to the United States to look around for suitable investments. He invites Wilhelm Meister to accompany him. While Jarno will be touring America, his friend the "Abbé" will visit Russia.[43] What a glorious anticipation of economic and political modernity! The proverbial "Go west, my boy!" is counterbalanced by a less proverbial "Go east, my boy!" However, neither emigration nor immigration is presented as an accomplished fact in the *Lehrjahre* (completed in 1796). In this volume of *Wilhelm Meister*, Lothario is the only person who has been across the ocean and returned.

In the following thirty-three years Goethe composed the first version of the *Wanderjahre* and recast it (especially during the period

[41] Ibid., p. 464; cf. Johann Gottfried Herder, *Briefe zur Beförderung der Humanität, Sämtliche Werke*, ed. Bernhard Suphan (Berlin, 1877–1913), XVII, 10: ". . . das Philadelphia, für welches diese Gesellschaft gestiftet ist, kann überall liegen" (. . . the Philadelphia for which this society was created can be anywhere.")
[42] SW, VII, 567–68.
[43] Ibid., pp. 604–605.

from 1825 to 1829). New sociopolitical ideas in both Goethe's times and Goethe's imagination, came to the fore.[44] Emigration, merely a concomitant motif in the earlier novel, shifted toward its sequel's center. The cultural-historical aspect of such a comprehensive theme as "Europe and America" and the philosophical, anthropological aspect of "Man, a migratory being by his very nature," entered the second novel.

Curiously enough, Lothario's role in the *Lehrjahre* of the returnee from America reappears with an interesting variation. Once again the role is rooted in the authentic history of German-American relations. The landowner who entertains Wilhelm Meister as a guest and newcomer to the "Pedagogical Province" is fittingly called "der Oheim" ("the Uncle"). This "Oheim" is the proverbial "uncle from America," and rich he is indeed. He is the returned grandson of a German diplomat who in the late seventeenth century gave up his London post under the influence of William Penn. Like Pastorius the diplomat immigrated to Pennsylvania. His Philadelphia-born son expanded his father's estate to near the Ohio frontier. The grandson, heir to these family lands, paid a visit to the Old World, and its cultural life recaptured this third-generation German-American. But, like Lothario, this returnee transplants to Old World Germany enlightened American farming concepts and agrarian political notions. He becomes the philanthropic "steward" of his German estate, which he runs "freisinnig," that is, in the spirit of a liberal, and with great efficiency.[45]

In the framework of this German-American family history, told in a flashback, the authorial narrator of the *Wanderjahre* for the first time comes to reflect on immigration and the problems of immigrants. To him they are problems of European, not merely German, scale. It is this American-European aspect that leads to a comparison of the two continents. In Europe a homogeneous nation had come to be seen as depending on conformity of manners and religion, whereas in America toleration of the pluralism of moral and religious concepts was felt to be necessary for the settlement of a continent.[46]

Goethe's third-generation German-American grows aware of an

[44] Ibid., VIII, 888–92 ("Einführung").

[45] Ibid., p. 92. For the term "Pedagogical Province" see p. 265. Concerning the "returnee," see Alfred Vagts, *Deutsch-Amerikanische Rückwanderung*, Beihefte zum *Jahrbuch für Amerikastudien* 6 (Heidelberg, Winter, 1960).

[46] SW, VIII, 91.

option. On the one hand, he may participate in a continuously living and reborn culture of "mehreren tausend Jahren" ("several thousand years"), "in der grossen, geregelt tätigen Masse mitwirkend sich zu verlieren" ("losing himself in large multitudes of regulated activity"). On the other hand, he may, in America, "um Jahrhunderte verspätet den Orpheus und Lykurg . . . spielen" ("play the roles of Orpheus and Lycurgus centuries late")—in other words, lay the foundations of poetry and law long after the mythical stage of European history.[47] This option is less the idea of the "cultural lag," embedded in an overall theory of progress, than it is the cyclically repetitive theory of cultural history formulated here. Such a choice is also meant to underpin the choice that confronts the German-American returnee to Europe. Aside from the terminology borrowed from Greek mythology, the returnee's impression of life in America is conveyed to the reader in the returnee's own words: "dass ich mich mit den Irokesen herumschlage . . . oder sie durch Kontrakte betrüge, um sie zu verdrängen, aus ihren Sümpfen, wo man von Moskitos zu Tode gepeinigt wird" ("having skirmishes with the Iroquois or cheating them by treaties in order to drive them out of their swamps, in which mosquitoes make you suffer until you die"). [48]

The authorial narrator reconciles this image, which runs counter to that of an Arcadian frontier America, with the concept of a near-American Europe. The agricultural activities of the "Uncle" are described as follows:

> . . . innerhalb der kultivierten Welt, die in einem gewissen Sinne auch gar oft eine Wildnis genannt werden kann, ein mässiges Gebiet zu erwerben . . . , das für die beschränkten Zustände immer noch utopisch genug ist.
>
> [. . . within the cultivated world, which likewise, in some sense, may very often be called a wilderness, to acquire a modest area . . . , which, in view of restricted conditions, is surely utopian enough.] [49]

Orpheus and Lycurgus, exemplary figures from Greek mythology, are beautifully counterbalanced by wilderness and utopia, concepts closely connected with early American history and myth and recurrent in the

---

[47] Ibid., p. 91–92.
[48] Ibid., p. 92.
[49] Ibid.

poetry of such an early German-American as Pastorius. In this way Goethe's German-Pennsylvanian returnee is a more sophisticated variation of the soldier Lothario's personification of the German returnee from the United States.

In the reverse direction Jarno, the immigration planner of the *Lehrjahre*, resumes his function in the *Wanderjahre*. In the second volume Jarno has become an experienced mineralogist and has assumed the fitting name "Montanus"—no bad preparation for pioneer mining and prospecting in the New World. Emigration, formerly thought of by Jarno as a safety device for the wealthy few, now changes into a large-group movement. It is conceived of as a settlement association of needy farmers and craftsmen directed by aristocrats and by the Abbé, the clergyman. It is not the returned grandson of the old Pennsylvania immigrant but the fourth generation, the returnee's nephew, Leonardo,[50] who is supervising the group-emigration scheme jointly with Lothario, now going to America for a second time, presumably for good.

Goethe's imaginative change from emigration as a small "Band" ("group") undertaking[51] of the 1780s to a large-group enterprise of the 1820s is in exact keeping with the actual increase of German emigra-

[50] For Jarno's name change, see ibid., p. 282; for his intended activities in the uninvestigated areas, see ibid., p. 476. In Gerhard Küntzel's interpretation ("Einleitung," ibid., p. 943): "Zusammen mit Lydie und Philine bildet Montan eine ironisch betrachtete Gruppe der Auswanderer und Amerika-Fahrer inmitten der europäischen Gesellschaft um Makarie" ("Along with Lydie and Philine, Montan forms an ironically regarded group of emigrants and travelers to America in the midst of the European society around Makarie"), the interpreter comments on an antiemigration complex which he follows up in interpreting Lenardo on pp. 950–952: "Bei Lenardo hängt sie [eine unechte Entsagungs- und Tat-Maxime] zusammen mit dem Auswanderer-Gedanken, den Goethe im Zusammenhang mit utopischem Ferndrang als einen Flucht-Gedanken verstanden wissen will" ("In the case of Lenardo, it [a false maxim of renunciation and activity] is associated with the idea of emigration which Goethe could understand, together with the utopian desire for distant lands, as an idea of flight") (p. 950). See p. 952: "Das Operose war als die bedenkliche Kehrseite des Auswanderer-Unternehmens gemeint." ("The operation was intended as the questionable opposite side of the emigration undertaking.") This interpretation would seem to be debatable. For Montanus, see also Goethe, "Tag-und Jahreshefte 1818," ibid., XI, 900: "Durch besondere Gelegenheit kommt die Geognosie der Vereinigten Staaten uns näher: Was für Vorteil daher entspringt, wird auf freundliche und solide Weise erwidert" ("Because of a special opportunity, the knowledge of the geology of the United States is made more accessible to us: what ensues from this advantageously is mentioned in a friendly and substantial fashion"), and II, 405: "Den Vereinigten Staaten."
[51] Ibid., VIII, 334–43.

tion statistics at that time.[52] So does the projected settlement near the Ohio frontier correspond to one of the preferred areas of actual German settlement. Similarly, the imagined aristocratic management accords with one actual administrative type of German emigration, the Mainzer Adelsverein, the Society for the Protection of German Immigrants in Texas.[53]

The elderly Goethe's search for some, if not total, historical objectivity in the presentation of his prospective immigrants to the United States shows most convincingly in the way he sets against America two other options. The first recalls the Abbé's reconnaissance trip to Russia. The emissary of an unnamed state at the fringe of Europe is given a chance to address the prospective immigrants to the United States. Colonization in the European east is offered as a contrastive attraction.[54] The second option is homemade. A clever administrator of a large agricultural domain is willing to hire craftsmen for a new plant intended to produce machine-made furniture.[55] Only one small group is deviated by each of these two rival options. Most of the prospects stay fixed on the notion of immigrating to America. In the *Wanderjahre*, therefore, America as the overseas option is suspended in a kind of classical balance. In the one scale is the projected immigration to the United States; in the other are what amount to three individual counterweights: (1) staying in an old world of culture governed by an aristocracy gradually liberalizing under the influence of America-enlightened German returnees, (2) colonizing less-developed areas within Europe, and (3) entering the industrial age in Germany.

One must keep in mind, however, that Goethe's vision of the German in America is a homeland author's perspective. Typically it concen-

[52] U.S. Bureau of the Census, *Historical Statistics of the United States, Colonial Times to 1957* (Washington, D.C.: U.S. Government Printing Office; 1960), pp. 56–57. Cf. (years) 1827: 432; 1828: 1,851; 1829: 597; 1830: 1,976; 1831: 2,413; 1832: 10,194.

[53] See Biesele, *The History of the German Settlements in Texas*, pp. 66–110; Fehrenbach, *Lone Star*, pp. 291–95.

[54] *SW*, VIII, 412, 421–22, 425, 433, 438–43, 486; cf. Dietrich Gerhard, "The Frontier in Comparative View," in *Proceedings of the Second Conference of the European Association for American Studies, Held at the Fondation des Etats-Unis, Paris, September 3–6, 1957*, ed. Dietrich Gerhard, pp. 74–82, esp. pp. 80–82.

[55] For the "Möbelfabrik" ("furniture factory") see *SW*, VIII, 486–87; cf. pp. 343, 412.

trates on emigration, and this much more in the planning stage than in that of actual performance. In the next-to-last chapter of the *Wanderjahre*, Goethe is quite explicit about this crucial point. Facets of life in America are not presented but reported or conjectured.[56] On the whole Goethe omits what he has not observed at first hand, though secondhand information was available to him in a very large measure.[57]

Examining Goethe's activities not only as a novelist but also as a book critic and the explicator of his own poetry likewise yields insight into the writer's thoughts on German ethnicity and interethnicity in American history. His review of the report of 1822 on German emigration by Ludwig Gall, the "commissar" of a German emigration society who had been in America in 1819–20, illustrates this point.[58] So does a much more surprising passage, Goethe's comments on "Tύχη, The Accidental," one of the poems constituting the cycle "Urworte: Orphisch."[59]

Seen as a whole, Geothe's is the most comprehensive late eighteenth- and early nineteenth-century literary attempt to combine under a homeland perspective three facets of the German in America: the military volunteer, the emigrant (much more prospective than actual), and the returnee. All three are subordinated to a perspective that goes beyond the theme itself. The German in or to or back from America serves as a symbol of Man, that migratory being, that *homo viator* of medieval thought. It is into this dimension that the contemporary

[56] Ibid., pp. 262–63, and, with an undertone of mild mockery, pp. 473–74 ("ein ganzes Volk von Hausfrauen" ["a whole nation of housewives"]). See also pp. 412–20, 433–37.

[57] Cf. n. 38 and Harold S. Jantz, "The View from Chesapeake Bay: An Experiment on the Image of America," *Proceedings of the American Antiquarian Society for April 1969* (Worcester, Mass., 1969), pp. 155–56.

[58] "Ludwig Galls Auswanderung nach den Vereinigten Staaten Trier 1822," in "Stoff und Gehalt zur Bearbeitung vorgeschlagen," SW XIV, 380–81; see also p. 1071.

[59] "Tύχη, das Zufällige," SW II, 618: ". . . europäische Nationen, in andere Weltteile versetzt, legen ihren Charakter nicht ab, und nach mehreren hundert Jahren wird in Nordamerika der Engländer, der Franzose, der Deutsche gar wohl zu erkennen sein; zugleich aber auch werden sich bei Durchkreuzungen die Wirkungen der Tunche bemerklich machen, wie der Mestize an einer klärern Hautfarbe zu erkennen ist." (". . . when European nations are removed to other parts of the globe, they do not lose their character, and after several hundred years in North America the Englishman, the Frenchman, and the German will certainly be recognizable; at the same time, however, because of crossbreeding, the effects of whitewashing will be noticeable in the way that a mestizo is recognizable because of a clearer skin color.")

tradition of the "emigration song" has also been raised in *Wilhelm Meister*:

> Bleibe nicht am Boden heften,
> Frisch gewagt und frisch hinaus,
> Kopf und Arm mit heitern Kräften
> Überall sind sie zu Haus:
> Wo wir uns der Sonne freuen,
> Sind wir jede Sorge los:
> Dass wir uns in ihr zerstreuen,
> Darum ist die Welt so gross.

> [Don't be sedentary,
> Dare to take a fresh start,
> Head and arms happily vigorous,
> We are at home everywhere:
> Where we enjoy the sun,
> We are rid of every care:
> So that we can scatter ourselves in it,
> That's why the world is so large.][60]

Günter Kunert

In what respect does the homeland view of the German in America change or continue if the back-home author has enjoyed a brief stay in that country? *Der andere Planet: Ansichten von Amerika*, a travel book of 1975, by the then East German poet Günter Kunert, provides a preliminary answer.[61] In 1972, Kunert traveled fairly extensively in the United States. For part of that time his base was the Department of

[60] Ibid., VIII, 342.

[61] See n. 3. For the title of Kunert's travel book, see the same metaphorical expression in a different context in Brecht's *Arbeitsjournal*, vol. 2, 1942–55, ed. Werner Hecht (Frankfurt: Suhrkamp, 1973), p. 721: "20.1.45 mitunter ruft Dessau an und spielt mir übers telefon einen neuen vierzeiler vor, da kommt er wie von einem andern Planeten." ("20.1.45. once in a while, Dessau calls up and plays a new quatrain over the telephone for me, like he's from another planet.") For Kunert, his relationship to American literature, and his image of America, see Jack Zipes, "Die Freiheit trägt Handschellen im Land der Freiheit: Das Bild der Vereinigten Staaten in der Literatur der DDR," in *Amerika in der deutschen Literatur*, pp. 344–46, 349, 351; in the same volume, Sigrid Bauschinger, "Mythos Manhattan: Die Faszination einer Stadt," pp. 384, 396; Wilfried Malsch, "Vom Vorbild zum Schreckbild" in *Die USA und Deutschland*, ed. Wolfgang Paulsen (Berne: Francke, 1976), pp. 34–35; Manfred Durzak, *Das Amerika-Bild in der deutschen Gegenwartsliteratur: Historische Voraussetzungen und aktuelle Beispiele*, Sprache und Literatur 105 (Stuttgart: Kohlhammer, 1979), pp. 59, 62, 70–72, 76–77, 82, 112–28, 147, 214, 218–19.

122   HANS GALINSKY

Germanic Languages of the University of Texas at Austin. Thus, contrary to Goethe, his chief medium of expression in this experience is not the novel but the travel sketch.

Kunert's picture of the German in America unfolds along regional lines. The Southwest and the South come first, with Austin for a base and excursions to, for example, San Antonio and New Orleans. An invitation takes Kunert to Iowa, where he visits the Amana group of German settlers. Trips to Washington, D.C., and New York make for further contacts with Germans and their descendants in the New World.

This picture also unfolds in time. Nineteenth- and twentieth-century Texas-Germans and eighteenth-century Louisiana-Germans are followed by mid-nineteenth-century members of the Amana Society and their present-day progeny.[62] A contemporary Austrian resident, a schoolteacher in Washington, D.C., precedes New York Germans or German-Americans. A local seventeenth-century flashback resurrects the German colonist Peter Minuit (or Minnewit) who purchased Manhattan in the service of the Dutch.[63] Kunert's great-grandfather and his large family, short-term immigrants to postbellum Tennessee and returnees to Germany,[64] are at the end of this long row of individual or group pictures.

Kunert's awareness, however momentary, of America's seventeenth- and eighteenth-century German immigration history is similar to Goethe's. Like Goethe's "German-American uncle" figure, Kunert is interested in the financial dealings with American Indians.[65] Contempt for cheating is the characteristic mood of both. Kunert bypasses the religious, missionary issue in German immigration but takes up a psychological one. Fittingly, a countryman of Freud's, the aforementioned Austrian schoolteacher, introduces the so-called guilt aspect of immigration into America and its appearance in his dreams about American Indians.[66]

Both Goethe and Kunert exhibit a number of similarities on the

[62] Kunert, *Der andere Planet*, pp. 31, 66, 76, 86, 132–34.
[63] Ibid., p. 153: "diese den Indianern für ein paar Dollar abgekaufte Halbinnsel" ("this peninsula bought from the Indians for a few dollars"). There is no explicit reference to a German as purchaser (in Dutch guilders, not, of course, in dollars).
[64] Ibid., pp. 204–208.
[65] See n. 63.
[66] Kunert, *Der andere Planet*, pp. 148–49.

topic of the German in America. To both authors the effect of the German Pietists on America is a fact, and both evaluate it ambivalently. For Kunert in particular admiration for Amana craftsmanship in the manual production of old-style furniture is tinged with mild mockery at "gemütliche Gestrigkeit," the mood of "those heart-warming yesterdays."[67] Kunert also presents the German-American as a returnee. He discusses two implicit literary returnees, Brecht, the political refugee, and Uwe Johnson, the New York publisher's temporary assistant.[68] They are matched by two explicit returnees. One is Kunert himself; the other is his great-grandfather. Even the stock figure of "the uncle from America," one of Goethe's two returnees, with Kunert undergoes a brutal but unforgettably moving transmutation.[69] Finally, the views of both writers on the German in America are wide enough to see him in the company of other immigrant groups. In Kunert's impressions of the United States National Museum of History and Technology he extends Goethe's French and English company of German immigrants to include the Dutch, Spanish, Indian, black, Japanese, and Chinese contributions to American culture.[70]

Disagreement arises when Goethe and Kunert view German ethnic stability in the United States. Goethe conceived of a continuing distinction of the European nations colonizing America, though he anticipated instances of ethnic mixture.[71] Kunert focuses on self-destructive forces within the German immigrant element. He singles out, for example, the disillusionment of the Forty-eighters when the dream of

[67] Ibid., p. 134.

[68] Ibid., pp. 173, 175.

[69] "Ein Enkel des Dokumentierten, mein Onkel also, vornamens Kurt, nahm das Original (des grossväterlichen amerikanischen Passes) ebenfalls auf eine Reise mit—nur führte die nach Auschwitz (war aber als Ziel nicht angegeben)—um notfalls das Papier vorzuzeigen, sich als potentieller Ausländer nachzuweisen—in der unsinnigen Hoffnung, Hitlers Helfer, Komplikationen mit einer Weltmacht befürchtend, würden akzeptieren, in case of need to give him lawful Aid and Protection, anstatt ihn auszulöschen." ("A grandson of the one who was documented, that is to say, my uncle, with a first name of Kurt, likewise took along the original [the grandfather's American passport] on a journey, which however, was to Auschwitz [even though it wasn't indicated as a destination]. He did this, to be able to present these papers, if necessary, in identifying himself as a potential foreigner, in the insane hope that Hitler's helpers, fearing complications with a major world power would accept 'in case of need to give him lawful Aid and Protection,' instead of liquidating him.")

[70] Kunert, Der andere Planet, p. 139.

[71] See n. 59.

the establishment of a German democratic state in America failed.[72] He also observed a German self-hate among the immigrants which impeded concentration and growth of the German element in one or two states of the Union: "Sie lebten über den ganzen Kontinent verstreut, zum grössten Teil auf dem Lande" ("They lived in continent-wide dispersion, mostly in the rural areas").[73] Something like post-1945 resentment may be responsible for this bitter diagnosis.

Kunert, however, fills two gaps in Goethe's view of the German in America: the German living in America as a political refugee[74] and as speaker of his native language.[75] Kunert's sensitivity to American-English interference with the German that is spoken and written in America today seems to have been sharpened by his limited familiarity, in the East Berlin of the early 1970s, with the many similar interference items in West German parlance. He has a fine feel for the Amana German dialect and its regional and local back-home components.[76]

Kunert's visit to the United States a century and a half after the writing of *Wilhelm Meister* is, of course, a major reason for the differences between the two writers' perceptions. It is the more surprising, then, that a few remarkable continuities have persisted over the years. Thus the homeland view of the German in America has persevered. But there are also certain links of Kunert's with the immigrant perspective on the German in America, especially regarding Kunert's attitude toward the German language and the political refugee, when one remembers those of Pastorius and Anneke.

William Carlos Williams

The American view completes the triad of perspectives. Compared with the previous observers from Pastorius through Kunert, the

[72] Kunert, "der nationale Selbsthass," p. 66.

[73] Ibid.; but cf. Kathleen Neils Conzen, "Die Assimilierung der Deutschen in Amerika: Zum Stand der Forschung in den Vereinigten Staaten," in Adams, ed., *Die deutschsprachige Auswanderung in die Vereinigten Staaten*, pp. 33–64, the comment on it by Reinhard R. Doerries, ibid., pp. 65–72, and the "summary of discussion," ibid., pp. 73–80; Hartmut Keil and John Jentz, "The Chicago Project: A Study in German Ethnicity," *American Studies International* 20, no. 4 (1982): 22–30, esp. p. 23.

[74] Kunert, *Der andere Planet*, pp. 53–55, 155, 173.

[75] Ibid., pp. 66, 159.

[76] Ibid., pp. 53–54, 133.

physician and writer William Carlos Williams yields not only entirely
new insights but also old ones, though sometimes with a new intensity.
The German immigrant in America, working as physician or scientist,
is a phenomenon of which Williams had become aware in the course of
his medical and scientific training. In his *Autobiography* and *Selected
Letters* the reader meets Dean Christian Gauss, of Princeton,[77] and the
brilliant young New York pathologist Charles Krumwiede. For Williams
the latter embodied that "German devotion to detail, that thorough-
ness, that relentless determination to come at the evasive core of a
problem until it has been laid bare."[78] But in the short stories of
Williams there is also room for such a "poor brat" and "living skeleton"
as Jean Beicke, an eleven-month-old baby girl of German immigrants,
a baby doomed to die in a Paterson or Passaic, New Jersey, children's
hospital.[79]

Albert Einstein's first visit to America is, furthermore, the subject
of a poem whose tone differs strikingly from the melancholy mood of
the Beicke story. "St. Francis Einstein of the Daffodils" provides for
bizarre comedy. The poem subtly juxtaposes and fuses Einstein the
physicist's attitude toward nature, and that of Saint Francis, lover of
God, mankind, and animals. Thus Einstein is presented as "tall as a
blossoming peartree."[80]

Also of thematic newness is the description of the German immigrant as skilled industrial worker and his relations with his American
employer and with labor unions. Against this socioeconomic background Williams narrates the family saga of Joe Stecher, immigrant
printer from Silesia in the days of pre-1914 imperial Germany. It is not
a typical rags-to-riches story that Williams tells but the sober and humorous tale of moderate success with failure admixed. By way of a tril-

[77] William Carlos Williams, *The Selected Letters of William Carlos Williams* (New
York: McDowell, Obolensky, 1957), p. 176.
    [78] William Carlos Williams, *The Autobiography of William Carlos Williams* (New
York: New Directions, 1951), p. 86.
    [79] William Carlos Williams, *Life along the Passaic River* (Norfolk, Conn.: New Di-
rections, 1938), reprinted in William Carlos Williams, *The Farmers' Daughters: The Col-
lected Stories of William Carlos Williams* (New York: New Directions, 1961), p. 159.
    [80] William Carlos Williams, *The Collected Earlier Poems of William Carlos Williams*
(New York: New Directions, 1951), pp. 379–80. See also ". . . Aigeltinger/Mathematical
Genius," in William Carlos Williams, *The Collected Later Poems*, rev. ed. (New York:
New Directions, 1963), pp. 65–66.

ogy it transmutes into art the life of Williams's immigrant father-in-law, son of a forester near Breslau, and the lives of the immigrant wife and their three children.[81] In the novels composing the trilogy—*White Mule* (1937), *In the Money* (1942), and *The Build-Up* (1950)—the most successful treatment of the immigrant theme is in *White Mule*. Nowhere else has a German-Norwegian baby girl of the first native-born generation been portrayed so intimately and comically, and nowhere else have the descriptions of immigrant family life and of immigrant working conditions, dramatically culminating in a New York printers' strike, been balanced so well.

Unparalleled too is Williams's perceptivity of what World War I meant to America's immigrant Germans.[82] Also of striking newness is the encounter of a post-1945 German in America. Williams tells of it in a short poem whose syntactically broken lines render the speaking voice:

> The young German poked his head
> in at the door, handed me
> an advertising leaflet for some
> drug manufacturer and left,
> coloring furiously after a few
> thinly spoken words. My
> attention was sharply roused.
> It seemed a mind well worth
> looking into. And beneath that
> another layer, Phoenix-
> like. It was almost, I confess,
> as though I envied him.[83]

I do not know of any briefer and more hopeful image of young Germany in America in recent Anglo-American literature.

New, but only in the intensity of perception, not because of its subject, are Williams's views on the language of America's Germans, their place in an interethnic society, and their contribution to the arts in the United States. Pastorius and Anneke, mostly by self-representation, and Goethe and Kunert, by authorial comment or

---

[81] Williams, *Autobiography*, p. 154: "Pa Herman, by birth an East Prussian [*sic*] from near Breslau." But see also William Carlos Williams *The Build-Up* (New York: Random House, 1952), p. 22: "His father had been a forester near Breslau."

[82] Williams, *The Build-Up*, pp. 324–25, 329–33.

[83] Williams, "The Rare Gist," in *The Collected Later Poems*, p. 253.

quotation, had afforded insight into the language of America's Germans. Williams was the son of an English father who had immigrated to the Virgin Islands (at that time still Danish), and of a Spanish- and French-speaking mother from Puerto Rico. As a literary artist Williams, consequently, was unusually sensitive to the phenomenon of linguistic interference and the way it signaled stages in the process of acculturation and assimilation.[84]

The interethnic environment of America's immigrant Germans is represented by Williams with special care. Joe Stecher's Norwegian wife, her relatives, and her black help in the Stecher home are more than matched by the multiethnic work force in the printshop.[85] Occasional frictions and, in the Stecher family as seen from the younger daughter's viewpoint, a persistent feeling of "foreignness," are not glossed over:

> That was a strange feeling that ran through the whole family and its relationships in the town where they had come to live or any town where they might live. It made for internal solidarity, but it was, for a child at least, something to live down. And they knew it. They all knew it.[86]

Heightened to the point of the stereotypical is Williams's emphasis on the efficiency, punctuality, and honesty, the "work for the work's sake" ethic of the German-immigrant skilled worker. For Anneke it was a German characteristic imported into the United States; for Kunert it was a relic to be admired in the Amana furniture makers. Likewise, the role of the German immigrants and of their descendants in the American life of the arts is by no means overlooked by Anneke and Kunert. But it is illustrated in richer detail in Williams's autobiog-

---

[84] See, e.g., William Carlos Williams, *The White Mule* (Norfolk, Conn.: New Directions, 1937, 1967), pp. 20 ("Nun ja"), 22 ("Ja"), 23 ("Hausfrau"), 25 ("Ein Blitzmädel"), 35 ("Ach"), 37 ("'Ya,' said Joe"), 55 ("Gott in himmel"), 45 ("Gott sei dank"), 53 ("Götterdämmerung"), 53 ("'Yah,' said Joe"), 55 ("Yah"), 60 ("Yah"), 73 ("Gott"), 74 ("Gott in himmel"), 75 ("*Ein, Zwei . . . Ein, Zwei . . . at Drei*"), 76 ("Auf Wiedersehen!"), 80 ("Wunderschön!"), 84 ("Was der Bauer nicht kennt, das frisst er nicht"), 85 ("Gedul' bring' Rosen!"), and many other examples. See also Williams, *The Build-Up*, pp. 6 ("Es stinkt!"), 28 ("Echt deutsch"), 36 ("Ya, Donnerwetter"), ("Ya"), 40 ("Um Gotteswillen," "Du bist verrückt"), 46 ("Na, na"), 66 ("Mein Gott in Himmel!" "Turnverein"), 67 ("Obstgarten"), 67 ("Hausfrau . . . sauerbraten"), and other items of linguistic interference.
[85] William Carlos Williams, *In the Money* (New York: MacGibbon & Kee, 1966), pp. 152–53.
[86] Williams, *The Build-Up*, p. 22.

raphy, letters, and essays. There one finds the German element in the changing avant-garde of "modern" American literature, from Gertrude Stein, Maxwell Bodenheim, and Ben Hecht to Theodore Roethke, Peter Viereck, and Allen Ginsberg. Nor does Williams forget the organizers of progressive literary "little magazines" and their contributors, people like Walter Arensberg, cofounder of *Others*; Lincoln Kirstein, cofounder of *Hound and Horn*; and George Oppen, cofounder of the Objectivist Press. Beyond literary people like these one encounters painters, musicians, art dealers, and photographers of German descent, a long line from Charles Demuth through Alfred Stieglitz.[87]

The mildly bizarre touches that Kunert added to the German group portrait and the equally mild mockery with which the picture of Goethe's would-be Moravian missionary was tinged recur with Williams in a broader and more intense variation. In Klaus Ehrens, the evangelist shouting in the Paterson park, he achieves a partly narrative, partly scenic presentation of a German religious immigrant. The figure of Ehrens dominates a whole section of Williams's long poem *Paterson*. The first part of the evangelist's story is one of material success. He rose from poverty to modest wealth in the Old World to more considerable wealth in the New. The second part tells the climactic event: Ehrens's conversion by God's personal call and the Almighty's advice to give away all of one's earthly riches.

Why make a German immigrant such as Ehrens the hero of this didactic confessional? An answer might be found in the interethnic aspect of this German-American episode. A Polish-American among the Paterson Sunday-afternoon crowd comments on this open-air preacher in a significant way:

> What kind of priest
> is this? Alarmed, goes off scowling,
> looking back.
> This is a Protestant! protesting—as
> though the world were his own.[88]

Protestantism, the name and the concept, brings back sixteenth-century Germany, the cradle of the Reformation. One of its overseas

---

[87] Hans Galinsky, "An American Doctor-Poet's Image of Germany: An Approach to the Work of William Carlos Williams," *Studium Generale* 21 (1968): 80.

[88] William Carlos Williams, *Paterson* (Norfolk, Conn.: New Directions, 1963), bk. 2 (1948), sec. 2, pp. 81–82.

offshoots was Pastorius's Germantown. We are back full circle to the immigrant German's view of the late seventeenth century and to Goethe's
German disciple of William Penn in *Wilhelm Meister's Travels*.

From this vantage point of an American's view on the German in
America one can finally realize not only what is new by theme or by
intensity of treatment but also what is traditional. Traditional, and in
this respect linking Williams with Goethe, Anneke, and Kunert, is
Williams's emphasis on the role of the German in the War of Independence. With Goethe and Anneke it is the pre-Revolutionary role; with
Kunert and Williams, the enforced, mercenary, and anti-Revolutionary
role, the role of the Hessians. The *Paterson* poem has a niche for "Hes-
sian deserters" who escaped to the mountains and mixed with the Indian, black, and white population of New Jersey.[89] Traditional too is
Williams's awareness of the German part in the western and southwestern settlement. Williams once again shares this awareness with Goethe,
Anneke, and Kunert. In the Stecher trilogy Joe's brother, an immigrant
to the West, adds this touch.

Persistent as well is an old reason for emigration: the desire to "escape" military service at home. Young Joe Stecher has it in common
with what probably was the intention of Kunert's great-grandfather.[90]
Williams, however, ascribes to Joe's emigration yet another motive, a
political one: ". . . he had renounced [his fatherland] willingly, to take
his place beside the rest of those who had come here across the seas to
dedicate themselves to a better, a more democratic country."[91] But this
in itself is in line implicitly with both Pastorius and Anneke. Equally
persistent is the much more romantic reason for emigration. For
Goethe, America beckoned as a land of escape for lovers in social di-
lemmas and a place of new economic beginnings. Williams also sees
this sentimental but useful function of the New World. He makes Joe's
dashing brother Oswald elope with the wife of his captain "in the Kaiser's Dragoon Guards."[92]

Not quite so melodramatically comical is a final traditional element
in Williams's perspective on America's Germans. What to Pastorius was
"little Germany" to be established under Penn's benevolent govern-

[89] Ibid., bk. 1, sec. 1, pp. 21–22.
[90] Kunert, *Der andere Planet*, p. 206.
[91] Williams, *The Build-Up*, p. 324.
[92] Williams, *The White Mule*, p. 80.

ment, what to Anneke was the German coloring of Milwaukee, and what to Kunert was New York's "Sauerkraut Boulevard"—East Eighty-sixth Street—turns up again with Williams. Aging Joe Stecher encounters "Kronstadt," half-pseudonym for Carlstadt, New Jersey:

> Kronstadt was an old German-speaking community, a freethinking town founded by a Carl Weiss, in the middle of the last century. It was independent, believed in small enterprises and stayed conservative, with no church allowed in its precincts—but for the past fifty years good beer to be had on nearly every corner. . . . It . . . fascinated [Joe]. Here, if his eyes did not deceive him, was a part of old Germany.[93]

Once again we are back to a founder like Pastorius, but unlike him in the matter of religion. Here Carl Weiss resembles Anneke, his contemporary.

Thanks to Williams, a keenly observant physician-writer and a second-generation American, the fullest view on the German in America has emerged from an Anglo-American. His Stecher trilogy has come closest in its way to the ideal Euro-American emigration and immigration prose epic envisioned by Goethe in his review of Ludwig Gall's report on emigration.

In summary, in the limited material presented on the German immigrant's perspective, the Protestant lawyer Pastorius and freethinker-journalist Anneke fixed respectively on the German as founder of Pennsylvania's first German agricultural community of the late seventeenth century and on the German immigrant in an agricultural and gradually industrializing Midwest of the middle and later nineteenth century. The German homeland author Goethe provided a bridge between the two periods and regions. Goethe focused on emigrants, prospective rather than actual, military volunteers, and returnees from late seventeenth-century Pennsylvania through the early nineteenth-century western-frontier period. He offered alternatives to Atlantic migration and made the migrant a symbol of mankind.

---

[93] Williams, *The Build-Up*, pp. 66–67. For Joe's "fortress" Spandau, see ibid., p. 314. Cf. the Stecher girls, who "could go to the Turnverein," ibid., p. 66; and Dr. Williams joining it, ibid., p. 321; and Williams, *Autobiography*, p. 155. Additional information on Williams as seen from the angle of American-German literary interrelations is supplied by Hans Galinsky, *Wegbereiter moderner amerikanischer Lyrik: Interpretations- und Rezeptionsstudien zu Emily Dickinson und William Carlos Williams* (Heidelberg: Winter, 1968); Galinsky, *Amerikanisch-deutsche Sprach- und Literaturbeziehungen*, p. 253, index, sub "Williams, William Carlos."

The short-term visitor Kunert—guest lecturer, tourist, and writer—emphasized the twentieth-century, predominantly post-1933 immigrant, refugee, resident, and returnee. He had some memory of early seventeenth-century colonial history and an eye for what he considered to be "survivors" or relics of nineteenth-century Southwest and upper Midwest immigration. The Anglo-American physician-writer Williams combined many of these historical facets with his view as an ethnic outsider, non-German but close to German ethnic and interethnic immigrant life. He did not describe German immigration in the seventeenth century, but he did describe details of regional New Jersey in the eighteenth and nineteenth centuries. The German immigrant as skilled industrial worker and his rise to the position of manager and owner were emphasized with World War I overshadowing German-America and its interethnic context. German-American contributions to the nation's sciences, arts, and religious thought were also traced by Williams from the period of World War I to the present time.

Thus our threefold perspective on the German in America, an immigrant, homeland, and American perspective, has spanned three centuries. It will surely go on stimulating—and taxing—the imagination of authors both in German lands and in America.

HUBERT P. HEINEN

The Consciousness of Being German: Regional Literature in German Texas

IF we take some liberties with our definition of German Texas, we can date the beginning of regional literature in German Texas to a song by Prince Carl von Solms-Braunfels from 1845.[1] In some ways we could extend the beginning over a dozen years back and call Friedrich Ernst's letter detailing the delights of life in Texas the first published German-Texan fiction.[2] Charles Sealsfield's *Das Kajütenbuch* (*The Cabin Book*, 1841) certainly qualifies as regional literature, but it was written *about* rather than *in* Texas.[3] Of course, considering the love of song and literature exhibited by many of the pioneer settlers, and in view of the popularity of occasional verse to mark special festivities, it is quite likely that the earlier settlers had been writing such verse throughout the 1830s.[4] At any rate, by the mid-1840s at the latest we find German settlers in Texas writing creatively.

Let me begin with a discussion of the prince's song, even though I would not normally consider the literary efforts of a visitor to Texas ap-

---

[1]As does Selma Metzenthin-Raunick, *Deutsche Schriften in Texas*, 2 vols. (San Antonio: Freie Presse für Texas, 1935–36), I, 6; see also Hermann Seele, *Die Cypresse und Gesammelte Schriften* (New Braunfels, Tex.: Neu-Braunfelser Zeitung, 1936), p. 176, trans. Edward C. Breitenkamp as *The Cypress and Other Writings of a German Pioneer in Texas* (Austin: University of Texas Press, 1979).

[2]See G. G. Benjamin, *The Germans in Texas: A Study in Immigration* (1910; reprint, Austin: Jenkins, 1974), pp. 17–19.

[3]Charles Sealsfield, *Das Kajütenbuch*, ed. Alexander Ritter (Stuttgart: Reclam, 1982); see review by Glen E. Lich, *German-Texan Heritage Society Newsletter* 5 (1983): 92–93.

[4]See, for example, Dorothy E. Justman, *German Colonists and Their Descendants in Houston* (Wichita Falls, Tex.: Nortex, 1974), pp. 35–36; Ottilie Fuchs Goeth, *Memoirs of a Texas Pioneer Grandmother*, ed. and trans. Irma Goeth Guenther (Burnet, Tex.: Eakin, 1982), pp. 99, 105–109, 112–13, 154–61, 195–97, 206–207, 212–21, 238–

propriate to my topic—and even though he may not have even written it: Theodore Gish has suggested that this authorship of the song is simply one of the legends that have sprung up around him.[5] Still, he is associated with the song, and as the official of the Adelsverein, the Society for the Protection of German Immigrants, which was responsible for the founding of New Braunfels, he must be considered more than just a simple tourist:

> Durch des Weltmeers Wogen,
> Getrennt vom Vaterland,
> Sind wir hergezogen,
> Von manchem Liebesband.
> Auf muthigen Rossen durchzieh'n
> Wir Texas['] heisse Prairien,
> Und kürzen den Weg mit Gesang,
> Der schallet in diesem Klang:
> Hoch Deutschland, Deutschland hoch!

> Lagern wir im Kreise
> Ums helle Feuer hier,
> Gedenken in der Ferne
> Der trauten Lieben wir,
> Und spiegelt den seltnen Wein [der seltene?]
> Des Feuers Widerschein;
> Wir würzen den Trunk mit Gesang,
> Der schallet in diesem Klang:
> Hoch Deutschland, Deutschland hoch!

> Geht es nun zum Kampfe,
> Mit Indiern wild und graus,
> Zum blutigen Schlachtentanze
> Dann Du deutsches Schwert heraus!
> Und wer den Tod hier fand
> Starb auch für's Vaterland.
> Er kämpfte und starb mit Gesang,
> Der schallet in diesem Klang:
> Hoch Deutschland, Deutschland hoch!

---

48. To be sure, Flora L. von Roeder has called into question the authenticity of the letter cited in Justman and elsewhere, with good arguments; see her *These Are the Generations* (Houston: author, 1978), pp. xi, 279–81. Still, the love of many early German settlers for literature is unquestionable.

⁵Theodore Gish, "Carl, Prince of Solms-Braunfels, First Commissioner-General of the Adelsverein in Texas: Myth, History and Fiction," *Yearbook of German-American Studies* 16 (1981): 70–87.

[Separated by the waves of the ocean from our Fatherland, we've come here, (drawn) by many a bond of love. We cross Texas' prairies on spirited steeds and shorten our way with song that resounds with a toast to Germany!

When we're drawn around bright campfires, we remember my dear one(s), and the choice wine reflects the fire. We spice our drink with song that resounds with a toast to Germany.

If it now comes to a fight with wild and terrible Indians, then you'll be drawn, O German sword! And whoever found death here died for the Fatherland as well; he fought and died with song that resounds with a toast to Germany.]

Neither this text, reported by Hermann Seele at the conclusion of a humorous sketch, nor the even less satisfactory one presented by Selma Metzenthin-Raunick makes complete sense—both seem to show signs of corruption through oral transmission—but this very fact suggests that the song, with all its blemishes, may indeed have been written by the prince and set to music by Alexis Baur, as Seele claims. For it seems likely that the two texts represent separate, and corroborating, traditions. The variants could well represent independent, and unsuccessful, efforts to "repair" flaws in the prince's song. Be that as it may, the song is a clear example of its author's consciousness of being German on Texas soil—the clichés that are also realities of German song, German loved ones left behind, the convivial enjoyment of wine (albeit not necessarily German wine: the choice or rare wine of this version corresponds to strange wine, "der seltsame Wein," in the version that Metzenthin-Raunick prints), and the scarcely less common toast to Germany are commonplaces of German drinking songs easily and often transplanted to foreign soil. But the exhortation to defeat the Indians in bloody combat by sword, a German sword, to the glory of the fatherland reflects a German consciousness rather atypical of most of the German settlers, especially those of a slightly later period, following John Meusebach's relatively successful treaty with the Indians, but one perfectly consistent with contemporary reports of the attitude of Prince Solms.[6] Surely the notion of fighting Indians with a

[6] Irene Marschall King, *John O. Meusebach: German Colonizer in Texas* (Austin: University of Texas Press, 1967), pp. 105, 110–23, 155–56, 175–76. Gish's skepticism about the authenticity of individual anecdotes regarding Prince Solms is justified, but

sword reflects an aristocratic disdain for practicality; the text given by Metzenthin-Raunick is closer to the reality of later encounters with the Indians:

> Geht es dann zum Kampfe
> Mit Indianern wild und graus
> In dichtem Pulverdampfe
> Dann deutsches Lied heraus!

[If it then comes to a fight with wild and terrible Indians in the midst of puffs of gunsmoke, then join the fray, O German song!]

If Indians are to be fought, they will be fought with firearms, not with swords. The improbable employment of German song to conquer the savages is almost certainly not authentic; it is hard to believe that even the worst efforts of the *Gesangvereine* could be used as lethal weapons. Seele recounts how he himself broke into song one evening upon approaching a human habitation, only to find it deserted. Later he learns that its owners had thought that he was a marauding Indian.[7] So even the song of one of the founders of the New Braunfels singing society could terrorize those who did not expect it. Some such anecdote as this might lie behind the exchange of a song for a sword; Prince Solms would have scarcely been so clever.

Johannes Romberg, perhaps the most gifted pioneer poet in German Texas, rarely praised Germany and things German, but the Franco-Prussian War inspired a flurry of jingoistic German patriotism; witness, for example, poems entitled "1870–71" and "Nach dem Friedensschluss zwischen Deutschland und Frankreich," as well as a response to a subsequent flare-up of hostility between Bismarckian Germany and France, "An Deutschland," the tone of which can be characterized by a typical strophe:

> Doch du brauchest nicht zu zittern
> Vor des Franken droh'nder Hand,
> Auch in Kampfes-Ungewittern
> Hält die deutsche Eiche Stand.

[But you need not tremble at
the Frenchman's threat;

---

there can be little doubt that Solms was very conscious of his aristocratic status and favored subduing the Indians with force.

[7] Seele, *Die Cypresse*, pp. 148–49.

> even in the storms of battle
> the German oak stands fast.]

He has a poem commemorating the death of Kaiser Wilhelm; "Am 9. März 1888." In "Ein Traum" ("A Dream"), one of his late poems from around 1890, he praises Germany for concentrating on consolidation rather than colonies. The closest he comes to commenting on American politics or political figures (in the published collection of his poems, from which such topics may have been excised) is in his "Bacchus und die Prohibition." However, at the time he wrote his long, humorous rejection of those who would forbid the consumption of wine, his opponents would have been religious rather than political leaders, and his poems are full of good-natured attacks on organized religion.[8]

Romberg's strongest consciousness of his German heritage is evident in "Die Deutschen":

> Das Herz Europas sendet aus
> Sein Blut in alle Zonen,
> Die Welt, die ist des Deutschen Haus,
> Er will es auch bewohnen.
>
> Der eis'ge Nord, der Wüste Sand,
> Die können ihn nicht schrecken,
> Er pilgert fort im Sonnenbrand
> Mit seinem Wanderstecken.
>
> Bald merkt er sich ein Plätzchen an,
> Sagt, dass er bleiben wolle,
> Nimmt einen Pflug und wendet dann
> In sich vergnügt die Scholle.
>
> Geduldig ist der Deutsche sehr,
> Lässt viel mit sich geschehen,
> Doch setzt er endlich sich zur Wehr,
> Wird man ihn mutig sehen.
>
> Ja, tapfer ist der deutsche Mann,
> Wie and're Nationen,
> Der Franke das bezeugen kann
> Und Varus['] Legionen.
>
> Die deutsche Treue ist ein Wort,
> Das nie vergessen werde,

[8]Johannes Romberg, *Gedichte*, ed. Alfred Wagner (Dresden: Pierson, 1900).

Wohin ihr wandert, pflanzt es fort,
Es wächst in jeder Erde.

[The heart of Europe sends
its blood out to all regions,
the world is the German's house,
and he wants to move in.

The icy north wind, the
desert's sand, cannot
make him afraid; he goes
out in the blazing sun
with his pilgrim's staff.

Soon he finds a little
spot, says he wants to
stay, takes a plow, and
turns, full of content-
ment, the furrow.

The German is very patient;
he lets himself be pushed
around, but when he finally
defends himself, you'll
see his courage.

Yes, the German is brave,
like other nations. The
Frenchman can witness to
that, and Varus's legions.

German loyalty is a word
that should never be for-
gotten. Wherever you
roam, spread it. It
grows in every soil.]

German wanderlust and industry combine to help the immigrant establish his new home—an echo of Romberg's experience. But still more
of his experience can be heard in the mention of German patience in
response to aggravation: when pushed hard enough, the German will
fight back. The Germans were not welcomed with open arms, especially not by the bottomland slaveholders whom Romberg encountered. Finally, German loyalty is recommended to Romberg's readers
as their foremost contribution to their new land. The poet's choice of

ideals says something about his perception of the Anglo-American attitudes that were dominant in Texas when the settlers arrived. Industry
and loyalty seemed to be missing; hostility was obvious.

Unlike Romberg, Fritz Goldbeck came to Texas while he was
young.[9] Although his collection *Seit fünfzig Jahren* (*For Fifty Years*) is
similar in form and style to the samples quoted, it shows less range and
sophistication than Romberg's work as a whole. Nevertheless, Goldbeck's narratives and vignettes show a remarkable sharpness of vision,
and he does not hesitate to criticize as well as praise his new homeland.
And though the forms and language of his poetry are cruder than Romberg's, his range of topics is broader. He waited out the Civil War in
Mexico and traveled through the American desert to California; his observations on his experiences are anecdotal. He does not refer to specific historical events except in a few commemorative poems. Even in
these his personal involvement is mentioned only in connection with
the history of the settlement of New Braunfels and Comfort. Nowhere
does he comment on developments in Europe after his departure, and
his mention of things German is generally restricted to German industry, German song, and German conviviality; even these are rather
sparingly mentioned. Still he does on one occasion stress his consciousness of being German, with his poem "Ein Germane bin ich":

> Fort mit dem trügerischen Schein,
> Ein Deutscher bin ich, will es sein!
> Ob ich auch englisch reden kann,
> Bin ich darum kein and'rer Mann.
>
> O Muttersprache, süsser Laut,
> Wie klingst du mir doch so vertraut!—
> Wo ich im Leben immer bin,
> Mein Denken ist ein deutscher Sinn!
>
> Was in der Kindheit ich geseh'n
> Bleibt treu und fest im Herzen steh'n
> Solange, bis mein Auge bricht,
> Bleib ich ein Deutscher, läug'n [*sic*]
>   es nicht!

[9] A discussion (in English) of Goldbeck's life and works is given in Robert Robinson-
Zwahr, *Die Bremerverwandtschaft in Deutschland und in Texas* (Wichita Falls, Tex.:
Nortex, 1977), I, 76, 166–69; see also Robert A. Govier, "German Verse Written in New
Braunfels, Texas" (Master's thesis, University of Texas, 1962).

Das Land, wo an der Mutter Brust
Ich einst geruht, noch unbewusst,
Es ist und bleibt mein Vaterland.
Ob ich ein neues Heim auch fand.

Die Zeit hat längst gebleicht mein Haar,
Soll ich vielleicht mich schämen gar?
Das müss ich doch, wollt ich zum Schein
Ein Andrer, als ein Deutscher sein!

Ein Bürger, wie es Pflicht und Recht—
Nicht jener Überhebung Knecht—
Der bin ich, und der bleib ich auch!—
Es ist so ein Germanen Brauch.

Wer sieht es gern, wenn dummer Stolz
Ihn formen möcht, wie ein Stück Holz?
Wer dienet gern als Hampelmann,
Mit dem die Einfalt spielen kann?

[Away with deceiving appearances:
I am and want to be a German. Even though
I can speak English, I'm not
someone else because of that.

O mother tongue, sweet
sound, how familiar you
sound! Wherever I am in
life, my thought is
German!

What I saw as a child
remains in my heart, as
long as I live—I'll
stay German,
I don't deny it!

The country where I once
rested on my mother's
breast is and will be my
Fatherland, even though I
found a new home.

Time has long since
bleached my hair; should
I then be ashamed? I'd
have to be if I wanted to
pass for anyone but a
German!

> A citizen, as is one's
> duty and one's right, not
> the servant of that effrontery,
> that's what I am and mean to stay!
> That's the Teuton custom.
>
> Who likes to see stupid
> arrogance try to shape
> him like a piece of wood?
> Who wants to serve as the
> puppet of simpletons?][10]

The apologetic tone is striking; clearly Goldbeck felt constrained to defend himself for his Germanness, perhaps because he had been a public official, the appointed mayor of New Braunfels from 1867 to 1872 during Reconstruction. Perhaps too his outspoken opposition to slavery, though not uncommon among the German-Texans, caused him some problems in New Braunfels, where most of the German-Texans had sided with the Confederacy.[11] Only a few of his poems touch on these questions, and then in retrospect; in all likelihood they were written after the Civil War. At any rate, in stressing his German heritage, he does not dwell on the purity of his ideals, as one might expect.

. August Siemering was an even more outspoken abolitionist. When he depicts the Civil War period in his novella *Ein verfehltes Leben* (*A Failed Life*, 1876),[12] he makes no secret of where his sympathies lie; the only Southern partisans portrayed are strongly negative figures. Still, he is restrained in his overt praise of German abolitionist virtue; one of the strongest figures is an American slaveholder and planter who supports the Union he served and serves in the Union army.[13] Although most of the positive figures are German immigrants, largely intellectuals or at least well-educated men who settle in Sisterdale, and al-

[10] Fritz Goldbeck, *Seit fünfzig Jahren* (San Antonio: author, 1895–96), I, 49–50. Both volumes are reproduced in Robinson-Zwahr, *Die Bremerverwandtschaft* I, 528–630.

[11] For a remarkable insight into "Confederate" New Braunfels, see Minetta Altgelt Goyne, *Lone Star and Double Eagle* (Fort Worth: Texas Christian University Press, 1982), esp. pp. 177–99.

[12] San Antonio: Freie Presse für Texas, 1876.

[13] In her strange translation-adaptation, May E. Francis (who allowed the title of the book she translated to be transcribed as *Ein verstehltes Leben*) changes this American into an enthusiastic supporter of the Confederacy; see August Stemering, *The Hermit of the Cavern*, trans. May E. Francis (San Antonio: Naylor, 1932).

though the fact is glossed over that at least one of the Germans was a paid spy for the Confederates, the thrust of Siemering's melodramatic tale is not the glorification of his German heritage. Indeed, it is a skillful example of the genre of the emotionally charged novella suitable for the lending library or newspaper serialization. Siemering was the editor of the *Freie Presse für Texas* (*Texas Free Press*) at the time his story was published, though he wrote it for a contest sponsored by the *Cincinnati Volksblatt* (*Cincinnati People's Voice*), which he won. As such its political message is used as atmospheric background, much in the way that E. Marlitt, the extremely popular German exemplar of such writings, allowed her feminism and freethinker philosophy, though they were important to her, to be overwhelmed by rather silly, sentimental plots.[14]

Hermann Seele, in his "Die Cypresse," follows much the same generic constraints with less success. His short, fantastic tale utilizes the same sort of exotic notions about hidden Indian civilizations that Friedrich Armand Strubberg had already used for his wild account of life in Fredericksburg.[15] Such stories were popular in both Germany and America. Seele's literary talents were much more effectively employed in a series of autobiographical and historical sketches; his collected poems have not been published. As one would expect, his praise of his German heritage is strongest when he is treating the history of the German settlers, as when he suggests that the purpose of such a history is to prove

> wie deutscher Männer Muth, Fleiss und Ausdauer selbst diesen weniger von der Natur begünstigten Landstrich in so ausgedehnten [*sic*] Masse der Cultur gewonnen haben, dass durch sie schon jetzt hunderte von Familien Heimstätten und Wohlhabenheit erworben haben, auf deren Grundlage deutsche Sitte und freier, froher Sinn sich aufgebaut haben und sich noch lange erhalten mögen!

[14] See Bertha Potthast, *Eugenie Marlitt: Ein Beitrag zur Geschichte des deutschen Frauenromans* (Bielefeld: Rennebohn; & Hausknecht, 1926).

[15] Friedrich Armand Strubberg, *Friedrichsburg: Die Colonie des deutschen Fürsten-Vereins in Texas* (Leipzig: Fleischer, 1867); see also Preston Albert Barba, *The Life and Works of Friedrich Armand Strubberg*, Americana Germanica 16 (New York: Appleton, 1913). Only slightly less fantastic is the novel by Pater Alto Hörmann, *Die Tochter Tehuan's oder Texas im vorigen Jahrhundert* (Cincinnati: Benziger, 1866), characterized briefly by Winfred Lehmann, "One Star German," *Rice University Studies* 63, no. 3 (1977): 76–79.

[how the courage, industry, and tenacity of German men has cultivated even this clime, little graced by Nature, to such an extent that because of these hundreds of families have gained homesteads and prosperity, on the basis of which German customs and free, joyful thought have been established and may, one hopes, long remain!][16]

Industry, the establishment of homesteads, and the perpetuation of German customs and morality are traits mentioned by previous authors and echoed by subsequent ones. Another such commonplace is slightly less apparent. The "free, joyful thought" that Seele praises is specifically the delight in beer, wine, dances, and singing-society concerts (*Frohsinn* occurs, for example, as the name of a *Gesangverein*) on Sundays that so frequently incurred the enmity of the Germans' Anglo-American, Calvinist neighbors. Thus even an apparently innocuous praise of positive traits can have an apologetic purpose.

Two of the numerous German-Texan newspaper editors who were also active as creative writers were William Andreas Trenckmann and Hugo Moeller. The former, in his play *Die Schulmeister von Neu-Rostock*, which he published in the Christmas, 1903, issue of his *Bellville Wochenblatt*, does not portray just "good" Germans and dubious Americans (actually, the only non-German figures who appear are a drunken Irishman and a black boy who speaks Low German) but rather has villainous Germans confronting farcically upright and virtuous protagonists. It is significant, perhaps, that one of the villains speaks a hair-raising mixture of bad English and abysmally corrupted German, as do his two insufferable children; however, his wife and the other villain speak as correctly as the other characters. All the minor characters speak dialect, with virtually every linguistic area represented—a great deal of the humor of the play derives from the use of language, as is appropriate to a *Volksstück* ("folk play").

Without putting too much weight on what is intended as a slight, humorous piece, one can still remark Trenckmann's pride in German traditions and virtues. His serialized novel *Die Lateiner am Possum Creek* deals with the problems of the Austin County Germans during and immediately after the Civil War.[17] In this somewhat later work

[16] Seele, *Die Cypresse*, pp. 164–65.
[17] Charles Trenckmann, a grandson of William Andreas Trenckmann, has made available to me copies of the play and the novel. The novel was serialized in the weekly issues of *Das Bellville Wochenblatt*, December 25, 1907, to November 19, 1908. Trenck-

Trenckmann has his main character, Kuno Sartorius, fall out with his former teacher for several reasons. In the first place he breaks an oath he had made to his teacher to escape into the bushes rather than allow himself to be conscripted into the Confederate army; in the second he becomes "Americanized." When Kuno asks for the hand of his former teacher's daughter, the upright old man forbids the marriage, relenting only when Kuno gives an eloquent oration at a festival celebrating the German victory in the Franco-Prussian War and warmly advocates the maintenance of Germanness combined with American patriotism. Although Kuno's experiences have led him to interact with Americans, he has also learned that a German-Texan is most at home among other German-Texans.

Hugo Moeller, longtime editor of the *Freie Presse für Texas*, is the most skillful short-story writer among the German-Texans. His *Aus Deutsch-Amerika* (1894) and *Grand Prairie* (1909) are collections in the spirit of Gottfried Keller's *Leute von Seldwyla*, though his stories and sketches tend to be slighter than Keller's novellas.[18] Moeller's work is well worth a more extended examination than would be appropriate here. He came to Texas in the 1880s, later than the other German-born authors discussed up to this point, and first settled in Austin County, whose earlier German settlers, especially those around Cat Spring and Millheim, provide an inspiration for his tales and subjects for his character sketches. There are virtually no general or theoretical statements about national characteristics, though Moeller does not hesitate, for example, in "Der grosse Prozess von Grand-Prairie," his longest story or novella, to characterize groups of settlers—in this instance the three groups that came to the locality at different times and only gradually intermingled: the freethinkers, the Roman Catholics, and the Lutherans.

The action of the story begins as Bremer, the Lutheran pastor, is forced, contrary to his convictions, to pray for rain to break a drought.

---

mann had already written and published a history of Austin County as a supplement to *Das Bellville Wochenblatt* for 1899. For another, nonfictional picture of the same locale and period, see Charles Nagel, *A Boy's Civil War Story* (Saint Louis: author, 1935), pp. 39–56, 71–263.

[18] Fredericksburg: Penniger, 1894, 1909. Moeller printed another edition of *Aus Deutsch-Amerika* (San Antonio: Freie Presse für Texas, 1895); all the works cited are from *Grand Prairie*.

His doing so is mocked by the most outspoken freethinker, whose opposition to religion is heightened by his son's interest in a Lutheran girl, and Bremer actually agrees with his adversary. When it does indeed start to rain, the pastor asks God for forgiveness for being reluctant, the freethinker curses, and the Catholics wish that they had held a procession so that they could share the credit for the miracle. When it continues to rain for months, despite repeated prayers for the rain to cease, the joy sours, and the anger turns to bitterness. The freethinker brings suit against the Lutherans for ruining his wool (which gives Moeller a chance to describe the machinations of the Anglo-American shysters—typically the lawyers and judge are the only important figures who are not German-Texan), and the suit polarizes the town. Against all expectations the freethinker seems on the verge of winning his suit when a character witness, a worthy successor to Frau Marthe in Heinrich von Kleist's *Der zerbrochene Krug* (*The Broken Pitcher*), makes it obvious that he is acting from antireligious fanaticism rather than from a sense of injury, and the jury decides against him. When he appeals the decision, his son leaves him to marry the daughter of the most prominent Lutheran layman. Pastor Bremer arranges a reconciliation, though not a conversion, and the story ends with the marriage. None of the groups depicted are idealized, though Bremer and Father Rottenbühl are portrayed sympathetically. The Anglo-Americans are caricatured, to be sure, but no more so than are most of the Germans, and less so than are several of the main figures.

Moeller does treat the problems of adjustment from the Old World to the New in several of his pieces, for example, in "Drei Frauen-Portraits" ("Three Women-Portraits") and in "Weihnachten in der Fremde" ("Christmas Abroad"). In general he suggests that the less one remains bound to the fatherland the better; his comments on the hardships the women suffered as pioneers are especially interesting.

One story, "John Reinhardt's erste Liebe," has at its center a conflict between an Anglo-American planter and a poor German-Texan farm boy who woos and wins the heart of the planter's daughter but is chased off the plantation. The boy leaves the state, fights for the Union in the Civil War, is nursed to health by a Confederate farm girl after being wounded in battle, marries her, and makes his fortune, only to have his children and then his wife die. He returns to Texas, finds his first love barely surviving as a seamstress, her father a ruined man. Despite the continuing animosity of the father, he and the girl agree to marry, and they look forward to an autumn and winter bathed in sunlight. As summarized, the story is frightfully sentimental, and the summary does it justice—the satirical wit that lends most of Moeller's stories distance and counteracts the ever-present sentimentality is largely lacking in this one. Be that as it may, the narrator of this well-told story does not dwell on the central conflict in such a way that the fact of the hero's being German is emphasized. To be sure, his Germanness is never completely forgotten; the girl learned to speak German when they were childhood sweethearts, he naturally joins the Union army because he is German, and the old planter's continuing animosity is largely due to his being a "damned Dutchman." Nevertheless, the action is presented as the fates of individuals rather than as a generalization of national characteristics. Moeller is concerned with German-Texans because he is one and is writing for others, not because he sees in them something extraordinary.

The mood is quite different in the works of several roughly contemporary poets. Ferdinand H. Lohmann wrote an impassioned plea for a revitalization of the use of German in America (1904), a sketch of Comfort in commemoration of the fiftieth anniversary of its founding (1904), a volume of poems in German (1906), and one in English (1910), two-thirds of which are translations from German.[19] As a peripatetic schoolteacher he was active in teaching German and praising the glories of all things German. A characteristic poem, one not in his collection, was composed as a prologue to a festivity commemorating the sixteenth anniversary of Magnolia Lodge No. 7 of the Sons of Hermann in Houston in 1906:

Die Sendung der Deutschen

Ein Engel einst zur Erde niederstieg
Gesandt vom Schöpfer alles Schönen.
"Geh," sprach der Herr, "und führe ewig Krieg
Mit allen, die des Lichtes höhnen."

[19] Ferdinand H. Lohmann, *Die deutsche Sprache* (Chicago: Koelling & Klappenbach, 1904); *Comfort* (Comfort, Tex.: Fellbaum, 1904); *Texas-Blüten: Gedichte* (Utica, N.Y.: American Author's Agency, [1906]); also published in German (Leipzig: H. G. Wallmann); *To My Darling and Other Poems* (New York: Broadway Publishing, 1910). For a brief biographical sketch of Lohmann, see Selma Marie Metzenthin-Raunick, "Was haben die deutschen Einwanderer und deren Nachkommen in Texas auf dem Gebiet der Dichtkunst geleistet?" (Master's thesis, University of Texas, 1922), pp. 224–25.

Gehorsam dem Gebot der Engel flog
Hinab zur nachtbedeckten Erde,
In raschem Fluge er das Land durchzog,
Dass Licht der blinden Menge werde.

Wohin er kam, ward ihm nur Spott zu Teil,
Er wandte zürnend sich mit Grausen:
"Nicht spriesst den kommenden Geschlechtern Heil
Vom Ort, wo wilde Rotten hausen."

Schon sinken wollte ihm sein hoher Mut,
Als er von fern ein Volk erspähte,
Aus blauen Augen sprühte Himmelsglut,
Die Häupter goldig Haar umwehte.

Den Gottesboten haben sie erkannt,
Empfingen ihn mit frommem Danken;
Fürs göttlich Schöne war ihr Sinn entbrannt,
Ins Herz des Engels Worte sanken.

Der Engel sprach: "Ihr hegt so hohen Sinn,
Als Lohn dafür will ich [euch] lehren,
Den andern Erdbewohnern zum Gewinn
Mit hehren Geistern zu verkehren."

"Dann teilt den fremden Völkern mit vom Licht,
Dass sie von euch d i e Sprache lernen,
Durch die der Mensch mit reinen Geistern spricht,
Dem Himmel und den lichten Sternen."—

So ward berufen zu dem lichten Sein
Das Denkervolk im deutschen Lande;
Und rein bewahrt es hat der Wahrheit Schrein,
Gelöst des Aberglaubens Bande.

Und wir, die alle deutschem Blut entstammt,
Wir folgen treu der Väter Spuren;
In unsern Händen licht die Fackel flammt,
Zu hellen hier die dunklen Fluren.

Treu pflegen [wollen (handschriftlicher
Zusatz des Dichters)] wir des Lichtes Saat,
Zum Himmel lenken die Gedanken;
Von unserm Tun soll zeugen deutsche Tat,
Bis sinken alle Geistesschranken.[20]

[20] Clipping from the *Texas Deutsche Zeitung* (Houston), March, 1906, with a handwritten correction by the author, found with a number of letters and other unpublished
(uncollected) poems by Lohmann in the papers of my grandfather, Hubert Heinen, now
in my files under Lohmann; also in Metzenthin-Raunick, "Einwanderer," pp. 73–74, as

[*The Mission of the Germans*

An angel once descended to Earth, sent by the creator of all that is beautiful. "Go," the Lord said, "and wage eternal war against all that scorn the light."

Obedient to the command, the angel flew down to the benighted Earth; rapidly he flew across the land to bring light to the blind masses.

Wherever he arrived he was greeted scornfully, whereupon he angrily turned away, shuddering [and said], "No good will accrue to the coming generations where these savage hordes reside."

His high spirits were flagging when he espied in the distance a people from whose heads golden hair was streaming.

They recognized the angel of God and received him with pious thanks; their senses were receptive to divine beauty, and the angel's words entered their hearts.

The angel spoke: "You are so high-minded that I will teach [you] the art of communing with exalted spirits, to the profit of the other denizens of Earth.

"Then you should share the light with the other nations, so that they learn from you that language with which mankind speaks with pure spirits, heaven, and the bright stars."—

Thus the nation of thinkers in Germany received its vocation. It has preserved the shrine of truth and dissolved the bonds of superstition.

And we, who are all descended from German blood, follow our forefathers' footsteps faithfully. In our hands the torch burns brightly to shed light amidst the somber regions here.

We want to tend this light's seedlings and direct men's thoughts toward heaven. German deeds shall bear witness of our actions until all intellectual barriers are lowered.]

This poem, which transfers Friedrich von Schiller's notion of God's special grace for poets in his "Teilung der Erde" to an assertion of a similar special grace for Germans as the freethinking emancipators of humanity from the bonds of superstition and, Lohmann probably intended to be understood, the tyranny of religiously inspired prohibition, also considers it the mission of German emigrants to spread the glories of

---

are a number of other otherwise unpublished poems by Lohmann. I am preparing a study of the Gesangverein in Texas in the first seventeen years of the twentieth century in which I discuss this poem briefly in a different context.

the German language to all ends of the earth. It is a remarkable concession to the reality of his position in an English-speaking Texas, albeit for the most part in German-speaking enclaves, that Lohmann also wrote poetry in English. Many of his poems reflect his bitterness that reality failed to live up to his ideal.

A generation later John Ulrich commented with a sigh wrapped in a smile on the loss of German:

Die Kinder

Gottfried Trautmann war gestorben,
Ein alter deutscher Pionier.
Kam mit seinen Eltern 'rüber
In achtzehnhundertvierzig vier.

Er war vom Scheitel bis zur Sohle
Ein Ehrenmann, ein deutscher Mann.
Und er hielt auch seine Kinder
Zum Reden dieser Sprache an.

Ob er auch Englisch gut beherrschte
Hielt er doch ein deutsches Blatt.
Wofür er den Abonnementspreis
Immer prompt entrichtet hat.

Als ihm nun der grosse Schnitter
Das Aug' für immer zugedrückt,
Hat der Zeitungsmann ihm einen
Ehrenruf noch nachgeschickt.

Die Kinder kamen um zu danken,
Als der Vater lag im Grab.
Und mit verweinten, nassen Augen
Bestellten sie—die Zeitung ab!

[The Children

Gottfried Trautmann, an old
German pioneer, died. He'd
come over with his parents
in 1844.

He was a solid citizen, a
good German, from head to
toe, and he made sure his
children spoke German.

Although he knew English
well, he subscribed to a Ger-

man paper and always paid for
his subscription promptly.

When the grim reaper closed
his eyes forever, the editor
wrote an obituary full of
praise in his honor.

The children came to thank
him as their father lay in
the grave, and with tears in
their eyes they—canceled
the subscription!][21]

In Lohmann's eyes such a lighthearted treatment of the topic would
have been tantamount to treason, and he was by no means alone in this
attitude. Karl Emil Max Nürnberg, of Westhoff, De Witt County, for
example, dedicates his collection of war poems and songs celebrating
the flurry of German success on the western front in the early stages of
World War I to the German-American youth: "Möge es die deutsch-
amerikanische Jugend begeistern und sie im Geiste hinführen nach
dem Wunderland am Rhein"[22] ("May it inspire German-American
youth and lead them in spirit to the wonderland on the Rhine"). The
slender volume, *Es schlug Deutschlands grosse Stunde* (*Germany's
Great Moment Arrived*), appeared late in the year in 1915 in San Antonio, almost a year after the beginning of hostilities. Two of its thirty-
two poems give a sense of Nürnberg's consciousness of being German.
Since quantity is more characteristic of Nürnberg's verse than quality,
I have relegated the poems themselves to an appendix to this chapter (choosing to present two here, nonetheless, since the author has
been neglected by subsequent scholars), and I restrict myself to a
few remarks.

"Das Land, wo meine Wiege stand" ("The Land Where My Cradle
Stood") asserts the total innocence of the fatherland of all warlike traits
and intentions. Nürnberg blames the other nations of shameless slander
and hypocrisy in their attacks on Germany and proclaims the certainty
of a just German victory. Although when viewed by itself the poem

[21] Metzenthin-Raunick, *Schriften* I, 74.
[22] Karl Emil Max Nürnberg, *Es schlug Deutschlands grosse Stunde: Kriegsgedichte
und Lieder* (San Antonio; Lone Star, 1915); Nürnberg is the only older poet not mentioned in Metzenthin-Raunick, *Schriften*.

seems unbearably jingoistic, when compared with the hyperbole of hate and the excesses of chauvinism characteristic of most poetry from all camps of the period, it is almost remarkable for the restraint of its protestations of German innocence of any war guilt and for the absence of slurs against France, England, and Russia, some of which can be found in other of Nürnberg's poems. The stress the author places on Germany's isolation may well reflect his own sense of isolation in Columbia, as the United States was commonly called at the time. Another of his poems expresses such a sense of isolation more directly. In "Der Heimatlose" ("The Homeless Man") he chooses to have a water sprite, a sort of allegorical figure of Germania, address him and ask him why he has not joined in his fatherland's glorious battle. As the last poem in the collection this lament does not provide very effective propaganda for German-Texan youth. There is no clear call to action and no consistent characterization of the relationship between the fatherland and the foreign land in which the author now finds himself. His failure to return (if we can equate him with the persona of the poem) is not explained or justified but simply lamented. The predominant emotion is, however, less sorrow than guilt. The obtrusive and apparently fortuitous mixture of past and present tenses the poem exhibits does lend a greater immediacy to the dream vision, but the victory hymn of the heroes has been transformed into a reproach. The poet's consciousnes of being German can be equated with a guilty conscience—not, however, because he is German but because he is not in Germany in its time of need.

The events of World War I evoked a number of poems, though not, to my knowledge, any stories—I have found little postwar prose in any event.[23] Metzenthin-Raunick includes a considerable number of poetic reactions to the war in the first volume of her *Deutsche Schriften in Texas* (1935), not the least accomplished of which are several of her own poems. Although she wrote both English and German poetry, as did Clara Rummel[24] and, of course, Ferdinand Lohmann, her English poetry (and the two German poems) in her *Verses from an Invalid's Pen*, which she privately published in 1923 with her name lightly veiled by

---

[23] All the prose writings cited up to this point and a good number more are listed and briefly characterized in Metzenthin-Raunick, *Schriften*, vol. 2. I am preparing a study of some German Texan reactions to World War I.

[24] See Metzenthin-Raunick, *Schriften*, pp. 45–47.

the use of initials (Selma M. R.), shows no obvious consciousness of her German heritage. She is all the more outspoken in the poems that she includes in her subsequent anthology; her brother, a professor of German at the University of Texas and an indifferent poet in his own right, was active between the two wars in promoting the teaching of German in the schools. An example of her German patriotism is her role poem "Die deutsche Grossmutter":

Die deutsche Grossmutter

Rah, rah—bum, bum—tei, tei!
Amerikas Jugend marschiert vorbei,
Darunter viel tausend Deutsche,
Darunter auch du, mein Enkelsohn,—
Ach Gott, ach Gott, welch' Spott und Hohn—
Zu Schlagen die "deutschen Barbaren,"
Mit den englisch-französischen Scharen.

Halt ein, halt ein, du töricht Volk,
Du verblendete Jugend!—Um Geld geht's, um Geld.
Um die Kästen der Reichen zu füllen
Sie schlau euch die Wahrheit verhüllen,
Halt ein, halt ein, mein Enkelsohn!
—Ach, er ist weit von dannen schon.
Vorbei mit all den Scharen
Die der Teufel hält zu Narren.

Rah, rah—bum, bum—tei, tei!
Amerikas Jugend marschiert vorbei,
Darunter viel tausend Deutsche,
So stolz und so sicher und eben
Als gält es nicht Leben um Leben,
Als gält es nicht Schwester und Bruder Tod.
Dies Blut—ihr Blut—es färbt alles rot—.
Ein Schrei entringt sich der Alten—
Es siegen die schwarzen Gewalten.

[*The German Grandmother*

Ta-ra-ra boom! America's youth is filing in parade, among them thousands of Germans, among them you, too, my grandson. Oh God, what mockery and scorn to beat the "German barbarians" along with the English and French throngs.

Desist, you stupid people, you blinded youth! It's all a matter of money. To fill their coffers the rich conceal the truth from you. Desist, my grandson! Alas, he's already gone away, gone by with all the throngs the devil deceives.

Ta-ra-ra boom! America's youth is filing in parade, among them thousands of Germans, as proud and sure and straight as if it weren't life against life, as if it didn't mean death to their brother and sister. This blood, their blood, dyes everything red. The old woman gives out a cry; the dark powers have won.]

Only the next-to-last line, in which the grandmother is described from outside, reveals that the entire poem has a mixture of perspectives: the grandmother's immediate reaction to the parade is mingled with the narrator's observations on the stupidity of Germans lining up to fight Germans. The "enemy" is not, explicitly at least, the Anglo-Americans but rather the plutocrats, the American war profiteers. German-Americans typically saw America's entry into the war as an ally of England and France as having been dictated by business interests. But the hate directed toward the opponents of the Germans is quite virulent, nonetheless. It is no wonder that Metzenthin-Raunick had such a high opinion of Lohmann's poetry.

After the highly personal poetry of Clara Matthaei Palacios Reyes (who wrote under the pen names Gertrud Hoff and Walter Gray), poetry whose creator never displays an overt consciousness of being a descendant of Germans and rarely reflects the German poetic traditions of the nineteenth century to which most German-Texan poets were indebted, after the often tendentious poetry of Lohmann and Nürnberg, the affirmation of German middle-class values typical of the verse of Hulda Saenger Walter, and after the fervently Germanophile poetry of Pedro Ilgen, G. F. Neuhäuser, and, of course, Metzenthin-Raunick, reading the novella *Else: Ein Lebensbild aus Texas*, by Hedwig Klappenbach Schroeter[25] is almost like being transported into another world. This charming, well-told work reads astonishingly like a novella by Adalbert Stifter rather than like a story appearing in 1926. It is as though one had stepped outside the twentieth century into another age. Only with the concluding paragraphs does it become clear that this lack of contemporaneity is part of the conscious message of the au-

---

[25](San Antonio: Texas Free Press, 1926). See Gertrud Hoff, *Vineta-Lieder* (Leipzig: Volger, n.d.; also Dresden-Leipzig: Pierson, 1911); and the later poems in Metzenthin-Raunick, *Schriften*; there too and in her "Einwanderer" are poems by and information about Walter, Ilgen, Neuhäuser, and herself. See also Bob Brady, "The Discovery of Pedro Ilgen," *German-Texan Heritage Society Newsletter* 1, no. 2 (1979): 34–41.

thor. An innocent young country girl living on an out-of-the-way farm in the hills west of New Braunfels loses her heart and nearly her virtue to a trifling, self-centered German dandy but is rescued by a stalwart German-Texan farmer, himself an intellectual German immigrant who is devoting his life to agriculture according to the most scientific methods. Soon afterward her father, realizing that he was not cut out to be a farmer, moves with his family to Austin to be a teacher. About nine years later the girl, who is helping her father make ends meet by taking in sewing (her father's pay as a teacher is not enough to support a family—some things never change), meets the farmer again at a picnic in the hills west of Austin. They realize that they love each other, they get married, and in the final paragraphs husband and wife hope and trust as they gaze on their grandchildren that these grandchildren and their children will find their way back to natural simplicity in the hectic and luxurious modern world. Although the decisive actions take place in the 1860s, no mention is made of the Civil War; interactions are completely personal, not political. Social interaction, on the other hand, is prominently depicted, and it is presented as self-evident that all the important associations of the characters are with Germans, both in the country and in Austin. The conflict in the novella is not between German-Texans and Anglo-Americans but between the questionable morals of the city and the positive values of the country. Although the plot is trite and the decisive events are strongly sentimental, the skillful depiction of nature and people rescues the novella from the trivial superficiality common to most such works. The author's consciousness of her German heritage is never stated overtly, but it clearly pervades the presuppositions on which the novella is founded and the narrative conventions employed.

H. K. Houston [Heinrich] Meyer's novel *Konrad Bäumlers weiter Weg: Ein Texas-Deutscher Roman (Konrad Bäumler's Distant Journey: A Texas-German Novel)* has some affinities with the works of Hans Grimm and Josef Ponten that celebrate the German colonists, and it enjoyed some initial popularity in Nazi circles, though Meyer later asserted, doubtless correctly, that he wrote it to counter the racial assertions of Nazi ethnographers; its appearance in 1938, shortly before the outbreak of hostilities in Europe, may well have contributed to the conflicts with the administration that led to Meyer's leaving Rice Institute, in Houston, where he had been a professor of German.[26] Meyer, who received his doctorate in German studies before immigrating to the United States in 1930, obviously researched his novel carefully, though a few minor errors of detail occur.

The basic plot is quickly told. Konrad, yearning to escape the petty officialdom for which his university training has fitted him, leaves his fiancée in Nürnberg, sets sail from Bremerhaven for New York, and meets a vital north German peasant girl on board whom he marries in New York, where he also meets the plutocrats who really control American life and restrains a young Georgia planter, Roger, from committing suicide. He and his new wife visit Roger in Georgia, where Konrad meets Roger's sister, Angelina, toward whom he feels a powerful attraction. The Bäumlers, Roger, and Angelina move to Texas in 1844, together with a number of slaves, and establish plantations along the Brazos, not far from Cat Spring. Konrad soon emancipates his slaves and discovers that the former slaves make far better hired hands, since anyone who refuses to work can be fired. His marriage is a living hell from which he escapes by means of a largely platonic dalliance with Angelina, and he is relieved when his wife dies many years later, leaving him with a teenage son whom he and his second wife, Angelina, rear as a wild and free but well-educated young man. The son decides to study law, but he leaves Judge Pease in Austin after a quarrel about the constitutionality of secessionism and arrives home just in time to make his way north, where he joins the Union army and is subsequently killed in battle during the Civil War. Konrad and Angelina, however, survive the war and are able to help Roger and his wife avoid the worst excesses of the Reconstruction.

The last two-thirds of the novel, some four hundred pages, are filled with comments about German-Texans and their relationship to Americans, and although many of these are historical reflections on the attitudes and actions of the pioneer settlers, a number of the authorial asides probably reflect Meyer's own feelings about his status in his chosen country. Anyone who knew Meyer or knows his other works could predict that many of the comments are designed to refute con-

---

[26] Stuttgart: Deutsche Verlags-Anstalt, 1938; see also Heinrich Meyer, *Was bleibt: Bemerkungen über Literatur und Leben, Schein und Wirklichkeit* (Stuttgart: Hans E. Günther, 1966), pp. 11, 118–22, 131–32, 165.

ventional wisdom. The very fact that his hero starts out, at least, as a slaveholder reflects Meyer's delight in opposing commonly held views. Konrad has a beautiful singing voice, but he uses it to join with Angelina in a spiritual union, not to participate in a singing society. According to Meyer, the industry and love of the land that characterized the German immigrants also accounts for the fact that they never amounted to much; if they had been lazy and had spent their time on the porch chatting with their neighbors, they would have been able to participate in American political life, which is governed by uninformed opinion and idle rumor rather than ideals or ideologies, and would have speculated in land and profited from graft. In short, they would have become rich and influential rather than comfortable and provincial. When they did waste time, they did so feeling homesick in the company of their countrymen, singing and drinking beer and spinning fantastic cloud castles about their superior intellectual status.

Meyer has a delightful scene in which he explains the notion of Latin farmers as a hoax through which crude former aristocrats enhanced their feeling of superiority by flummoxing their less educated countrymen into thinking that they still remembered the Latin they had been exposed to in their youth. Meyer's hero succeeds, to the extent that he does succeed, by not conforming to the usual pattern; he uses slaves and hired hands, he stays fairly aloof from his fellow Germans, his marrige to an American succeeds, and so on. Still, despite his joy in playing the devil's advocate and his impatience with the image German-Texans of the 1930s had of themselves and their ancestors, Meyer exhibits a nostalgic, sentimental attachment to these pioneer settlers. What at times seems like an attack on the German-Texans develops into something more like an affectionate apology for their failings. The recurrent theme of the ambivalent status of the immigrant, neither German nor American, acts as both a commentary on history and a reflection on the author's own position. The novel is different from the other works discussed up to this point in that it clearly is written for a German audience rather than a German-Texan one. Nevertheless, there were many German-Texans in the 1930s and 1940s who could have and might have read it.

Herman Toepperwein, a younger relative of Ferdinand Lohmann, has continued the family tradition of creative writing, but he and the other members of his family of his generation write in English. Nevertheless, since his novel *Rebel in Blue* (1963) deals with the German-Texans during the Civil War, it deserves at least a brief mention in this context.[27] The hero is an American, but he falls in love with a German-Texan girl from San Antonio and helps her father in an elaborate plot to spy for the Union and debase the Confederate currency while pretending to serve the Confederacy, circumventing the Northern blockade with trade through Mexico. The positive figures are American, Mexican-American, and German; the scoundrels, American, German, and English. Captain Nimitz, an ancestor of the author, is an admirable German-Texan supporter of the Confederacy; the German-Texan Unionists killed in the Nueces Massacre are portrayed as foolish, stubbornly idealistic, and in part cowardly. In short, although the author is keenly aware of his German heritage, he has no desire to glorify inherited German virtues. The only apologetic tone one perceives reflects an apparent uneasiness about the role of Captain Nimitz.

Some few German-Texans still read and write German; more have learned German as a foreign language. Still, to the extent that speaking of German-Texan literature implies not only an author but also an audience, German-Texan literature in the last decades has been and will have to be written in English. Having made that statement, I want to qualify it with an apparent counterexample. Lisa Kahn is a distinguished German writer with a home in and close ties to Texas. Her poem "Mitgift" can serve as an example of her intense involvement with the implications of the German-Texan heritage:

Mitgift

Eicherne Truhe handschmiedeeisern beschlagen
aus unbekanntem Dorf in Westfalen
nach Texas verschifft—wann?—
einst selbstgesponnenes Linen bergend
grossmüttervererbt
auch Schmuck in einem schmalen Seitenfach
jetzt voller veralteter Sammlungen
Briefmarken
Ansichtskarten
Münzen
Kinderfotos herzzugeklappt

---

[27] New York: Morrow, 1963; see also, for example, Fritz A. Toepperwein and Emilie Toepperwein, *Donkey Day* (Boerne, Tex.: Highland, 1950); and their *José and the Mexican Jumping Bean* (Boerne, Tex.: Highland, 1965).

hat ein faustgrosses Schloss
das schaut aus
wie ein Frauengesicht:
alt
abgenutzt
zugeschlossen
Der Schlüssel
ging schon lange verloren.[28]

Trousseau

Oaken chest fitted with hand-wrought iron from an unknown village
in Westphalia shipped to Texas—when?—at one time holding hand-
spun linen from one's grandmothers and jewelry in a narrow com-
partment at the side, now full of dated collections: stamps, picture
postcards, coins, photos of children in closed, heart-shaped albums.

Has a fist-sized lock that looks like a woman's face: old, worn-out,
closed up tight.

The key was lost long ago.

This poem shares with her others Kahn's awareness of her ambivalent
position between cultures (American and German here, old and new,
but also Jewish and Christian in many of her poems). With all her em-
pathy for the joys and especially sorrows evoked by the trunk, her recognition of how it reflects the fate of the women who worked to fill it
and used it, her utilization of its lock to mirror the aging and closing up
of these women, she also perceives that it has lost its vital relationship
to the culture that needed it: "The key was lost long ago."

The consciousness of being German is certainly not lost among
those native Germans now living in Texas, but it is lost as a theme of
regional literature in German. Lisa Kahn's works serve as an example
that there can be contemporary literature in German with a strong
sense of the traditions of German Texas, and to the extent that the
poems treat Round Top, Texas, as a special place, for example, they appear to qualify as regional. Since such writers as Fritz Goldbeck and
Clara Rummel do not restrict themselves to Texas but also write of
other regions, one cannot claim that Kahn's writing about a wide range
of regions and topics disqualifies her as a German-Texan poet. What

[28] *Feuersteine: Gedichte* (Zürich: Storm, 1978), p. 20; other works by Lisa Kahn
listed on the inside back cover of *David am Komputer und andere Gedichte* (Providence,
R.I.: Trebush Press, 1982).

does do so, I would maintain, is that her audience, to the extent that it is not a general German one, is not an ethnic but rather an intellectual community. I would be glad to be wrong, to be able to speak of a century and a half of German-Texan literature.

In a few instances—Romberg, Moeller, Meyer, and Kahn—the authors bring their skills with them to America; for the most part they develop them here. Nevertheless, the dominant national characteristics most German-Texan authors evoke who display their consciousness of being German are much the same ones that Germans themselves perceive: idealism to a fault, a certain willingness to accept authority blindly, a blend of inwardness and conviviality, and industry. In many instances being German means transplanting both the good and the bad from the Old Country, though in the very act of transplanting both are transformed. Many of these writers are sustained by their awareness of their German heritage and by their devotion to their region. Their strength, however, is generally also a weakness; their dual devotion often protects them from a provincialism of spirit, but it dooms them to a provincialism of impact. The good they have to say is not heard very far; the strangeness of their traditions develops quaintness rather than hybrid vigor. Exceptionally, however, talent, topic, and tradition coalesce to create a noteworthy work of literature that is also a witness of their heritage.

Poems by Karl Emil Max Nürnberg

Das Land, wo meine Wiege stand

Ach, wie bist du so verlassen,
O mein teures Vaterland!
Sag', warum sie
Dich so hassen,
Das Land, wo meine
Wiege stand.
Das nur gewollt der
Völker Frieden,
Nie hat gehemmt der
Länder Werdelauf;
Doch ist es dir
Nicht beschieden—
Zum tödlichen Schlag
Hebt man die Hand nun auf.
Schon höret man die
Meute kläffen
Über deutsche Barbarei;
Und man möcht' ins
Herz dich treffen
Durch Lug und Trug
Und Heuchelei.

Voll Wanderlust und frohen
Tatendrang
Zog ich hinaus
Ins fremde Land.
Ach, wie schlägt mein
Herz so bange
Um dich, geliebtes
Heimatland!
Columbia, du Land
Der Freiheit,
Enthüllst den Schleier
Von dem Angesicht;

Du hältst es
Mit andern Freieren [*sic*],
Auch [Ach?] du liebst uns
Deutsche nicht!

Gott ist gerecht!
Und du wirst siegen,
Du, mein teures Vaterland.
Die Prüfungszeit
Wird auch verfliegen,
Die Sonne bricht
Durch düst're Wolkenwand.
Die Tränen der Witwen
Und der Waisen
Werden kühlen
Den blutroten Feuerbrand.
Mit Blut und Eisen
Wird man
Neu wieder schmieden
Das Land, wo meine
Wiege stand.

[*The Land Where My Cradle Stood*

Alas, how deserted you are
O my dear Fatherland!
Tell me why they
Hate you so,
The land where my
Cradle stood.
Which only wanted
Peace of the nations,
Never checked the
Development of countries;
But it was not
Granted to you—
For a deadly blow now
They are raising their hand.
One can already hear the
Pack of dogs baying
About German barbarism;
And one would like to
Wound you to the heart
With lies and betrayal
And hypocrisy.

Full of wanderlust and happy
Desire for action
I left
For the foreign land.
Alas, how my heart beats
So full of anxiety
For you, beloved
Homeland!
Columbia, you land
of freedom,
Are taking the veil
From your face;
You are having an affair
With other suitors;
Alas, you do not love
Us Germans!

God is just!
And you will win,
You, my dear Fatherland.
The time of trial
Will pass;
The sun will break through
The dismal wall of clouds.
The tears of widows
And orphans
Will cool
The blood-red blaze of fire.
With blood and iron
One will forge anew
Once more
The land where my
Cradle stood.]

Der Heimatlose

Von allen verlassen
Im fremden Land
Wandelte ich Heimatloser
Zum Meeresstrand.
Ich schaute hinein
In die schäumende See.
Da teilt sich die Flut,
Es erschien eine Fee.
Bestrahlt vom goldnen

Sonnenlicht,
Sie zu mir
Diese Worte spricht:
"Was tust du hier,
Du feiger Gesell'?"
Es erklang ihre Stimme
So scharf und hell.

"Du suchst in der Fremde
Nach Ruhm und Glück,"
Und schaute mich an
Mit strafendem Blick;
"Was irrest du hier,
Wo die Deutschen nichts gelten?
Nur in der Heimat
Gibt's wahre Helden."

"Sie kämpfen und sterben
Für heiliges Gut;
Sie lieben die Heimat
Mit inniger Glut.
Warum willst du in
Der Fremde verderben,
Wo deine Brüder
Fürs Vaterland sterben?"

Und plötzlich ertönte
Mit mächtigem Klang
Aus weiter Ferne
Der Helden Gesang.
Mit leuchtenden Augen
Blickt über die See
Zurück zur Heimat
Die Meeres-Fee.

"Vernimm nun des Liedes
Brausenden Schall
Zur Feier des Sieges
Dort in Walhall'
Wo jauchzend vor Freude
Und Siegeslust
Die Jungfrau sich schmiegt
An des Helden Brust.

Wo in den Augen erstrahlet
überirdischer Glanz,
Wenn man in glühender
Liebe sich drehet beim Tanz;

Wo man perlenden Wein
Im goldnen Pokal
Kredenzt den Helden
Beim festlichen Mahl;

Wo man dem Freunde
Entbietet treu-deutschen Gruss
Und abscheuend verachtet
Den Heuchler und treulosen Kuss.
Sag', weshalb kehrest du nicht
Zur Heimat zurück
Und suchest zu finden
In der Heimat dein Glück?

Es glühen und blühen
Noch duftende Rosen
Für euch alle,
Ihr Heimatlosen.
Weshalb soll verbluten
Vor Sehnen dein Herz?
Nur in der Heimat,
In der Heimat versteht man
     dein'n Schmerz.

Kehre zurück
Zu deiner Eltern Haus;
Raste und ruhe
Vom Wandern aus."
Und freundlich noch grüßend
Winkt mir die Hand,
Die leise rauschend
Im Meere verschwand.

Ich aber wandle
Am Strande alleine
Und schluchze
Und weine.
Da kam es mir
So recht erst in Sinn,
Wie verlassen, verlassen
In der Fremde ich bin.

[*The Homeless Man*

Abandoned by everyone
In a foreign land
I wandered, a homeless man,
Onto a beach by the sea.

I was gazing out into
The foamy waves
When the waters part
And a sprite appeared.
Bathed in the rays
Of the golden sun
She speaks
These words to me:
"What are you doing here,
You cowardly fellow?"
Her voice rang out
So sharply and brightly.
"You're searching abroad
For fame and fortune,"
And she gazed at me
Reproachfully.
"Why are you wandering about
Here where Germans are dirt?
Only in the homeland
Can true heroes be found.

"They fight and die
For a holy prize;
They love the homeland
With heartfelt ardor.
Why do you want to
Perish in a foreign land
When your brothers are
Dying for the Fatherland?"

And suddenly there rang out
With a fierce clamor
From a far distance
The song of the heroes.
With glistening eyes
She gazes back across the sea
Toward the homeland,
The ocean sprite.
"Listen now to the roaring
Sound of the song
In celebration of victory
There in Valhalla
Where, loudly jubilant and
Flushed with victory's joy,
The maiden presses up against
The hero's breast.

Where ethereal splendor
Gleams in one's eyes
When one twirls full
Burning love at the dance;
Where one toasts the heroes
With bubbling wine
In a golden cup
At the festive meal;

Where one proffers a loyal,
German greeting to a friend
And with abhorrence scorns
The flatterer and his
Faithless kiss. Tell me, why
Don't you return home
And try to find
Your fortune there?
Sweet-scented roses are still
Glowing and blooming
For all of you,
You homeless men.
Why should your heart bleed
Dry with longing?
In the homeland alone,
In the homeland your pain is
    understood.

Return to the
House of your parents,
Rest and recover
From your travels."
And with a friendly greeting
The hand waves to me
That with a quiet rushing
Disappeared in the ocean.

But I am left wandering
alone on the beach
and sobbing
and crying.
At that point I really
Became fully aware
How abandoned, abandoned
I am in a foreign land.]

German-American Contributions to Eighteenth- and Nineteenth-Century Art

WHAT is often considered typical American art is actually the work of a German immigrant. This can be shown be reviewing some of the most familiar nineteenth-century images. The heroic *Washington Crossing the Delaware*, a major icon of American patriotism, was painted by German-born Emanuel Leutze; *The Rocky Mountains* is but one of the many grandiose western panoramas painted by Albert Bierstadt, born in Solingen. Many of the lithographs by Currier and Ives, possibly the most popular Americana, were produced by German draftsmen,[1] among them Louis Maurer and the little-known Otto Knirsch. Thomas Nast, whose political cartoons exposed the corrupt bosses of New York City's Tammany Hall, came from the Rhenish Palatinate.

No doubt the very best American painters of the eighteenth and nineteenth centuries were native-born Americans of the Anglo-American schools, but, commensurate with the large German immigration, artists from the German-speaking region of central Europe made significant contributions to the development of American art. Among the seven million German immigrants about four hundred registered professions related to the arts.[2] Some of these later abandoned art to turn to more profitable occupations. It also happened that after years of working in a certain trade, a German immigrant would choose to become an artist. Many of them were well trained in their professions; some of them displayed superior talent. In the New World even

[1] Currier & Ives, established in New York in 1834, was the most renowned American firm of lithographers. It employed a number of recent German immigrants as draftsmen, lithographers, and lettering artists. The stones used in the process were imported from Bavaria.

[2] U.S. Bureau of the Census, *Historical Statistics of the United States* (Washington, D.C.: U.S. Government Printing Office, 1971), pp. 56–57.

artists of lesser skills were able to produce important pictures. At times they had the opportunity to make unique pictorial records which today are of great value to the study of cultural history. In America most immigrant artists felt less inhibited, for no glorious artworks of the past overshadowed their own achievements. The enormous dissimilarities in background and training in art and most of all in talent account for the varying quality in the work of German-immigrant artists. Their output ranged from the crudest to the most accomplished, clearly demonstrating that some were little more than skilled craftsmen while others belonged among the top painters of their day.

Bierstadt and Nast, for example, possibly the two most successful German-immigrant artists, were brought to the United States at a very early age. Thanks to their artistic accomplishments both rose from poverty to great prominence and fortune. Nast achieved great power by influencing public opinion through his drawings for *Harper's Weekly* and actually helped determine the outcome of presidential elections. Lincoln called Nast his best recruiting sergeant.[3]

The first of the professionally trained painters from the German-speaking territories of Europe came at the very beginning of the eighteenth century and worked in the royalist colonies of Maryland and the Carolinas, where rich landowners tried to imitate European aristocratic life-style. Justus Engelhardt Kühn settled in Annapolis, Maryland, sometime before 1708 and was active there until 1717. Although Kühn was only moderately talented, his work suggests that before he left Germany he was well trained in the old Baroque portrait style. His major legacy is some charming portraits of children, the daughters and sons of wealthy Maryland landowners. His pictures were probably the most elaborate portraits produced in the colonies. The extraordinary surroundings of the portrayed figures, the spatial conception, and the use of light and shade surpass anything done in New England, Philadelphia, or New York at that time. Kühn can be credited with having been one of the very first to bring the craft of professional painting to America.[4]

Another artist trained in the German Baroque portrait style was

[3] Albert Bigelow Paine, *Thomas Nast: His Period and His Pictures* (New York: Macmillan, 1904), p. 69.

[4] John Wilmerding, *The Genius of American Painting* (New York: William Morrow, 1973), p. 38.

Jeremiah Theus (ca. 1719–74), who came from Switzerland when he was about nineteen years old. Theus was well acquainted with the Baroque formula of showing the sitter in a representational, upright pose, clearly aware of the beholder. In Charleston, South Carolina, Theus played a role similar to the one John Copley was to play twenty years later in Boston. He produced a large number of portraits; in composition they are much alike, but his faces have individuality and lively expression.[5]

Of much different background was John Valentine Haidt (1700–80), a contemporary of Theus who worked in the Moravian communities of Pennsylvania. Haidt was born in Danzig, the son of a goldsmith, and learned not only his father's profession but also attended the Royal Academy in Berlin and later traveled widely. In London he joined the Moravian church when he was about forty years old. His ministry took him to Pennsylvania in 1750. There he devoted the last twenty years of his life to serving his church and producing paintings for the Moravian community. Depicting religious subject matter in the style of northern Baroque painters, his paintings are strongly derivative but nevertheless convey his sincere religiosity. (Haidt is considered to have been the first painter in America who represented religious subject matter.) More interesting, though, are his portraits of members of the Bethlehem Moravian community. His female sitters are stiffly posed, wearing the typical caps of the Moravian sisters; however, their faces are remarkably explicit likenesses, charming reflections of the active spiritual life of their community.[6]

In about 1795, John Eckstein (1736–1817) painted a group portrait of a Philadelphia family which indicates the hand of an artist of professional experience. Eckstein, who also was a modeler in wax, had worked at the Berlin court of Frederick the Great. In 1794 he came to Philadelphia, where he cofounded the Pennsylvania Academy of the

[5] Margaret Simons Middleton, *Jeremiah Theus: Colonial Artist of Charlestown* (Columbia: University of South Carolina Press, 1953).

[6] Portrait painting dominated American art even beyond the colonial period into the first decades of the new republic. Pragmatic Americans commissioned portraits less for artistic reasons than for the preservation of the likeness of a beloved or highly esteemed person. But artists with greater talents and ambitions soon sought to break away from the provincial confinement of their role, and they no longer painted only when they were commissioned to do so.

Fine Arts and taught Hiram Power, the premier American sculptor of the nineteenth century.

Influenced by the ideas of the French Revolution and in turn by the Romantic movement, which conceived art as the unfettered expression of genius, a German, Johann Ludwig Krimmel (later John Lewis Krimmel, 1786–1821), introduced genre painting into American art. Krimmel became the first painter whose pictures consistently focused on American daily life. Krimmel came to America late in 1809. Born in Württemberg, the young German merchant apprentice had come to Philadelphia to join his brother's business but changed his mind after having been in America for about six months. Like so many other people of his time Krimmel had practiced drawing and watercolor as an amateur. In his new environment he became fascinated by the looks and behavior of the American population and felt such a strong urge to depict them that he left the mercantile trade to become a professional painter. Soon his pictures were seen in the annual exhibitions held at the Pennsylvania Academy, where they aroused admiration, particularly among fellow artists. In May, 1812, Krimmel exhibited *View of Centre Square on the Fourth of July*, showing Philadelphians of all classes enjoying the national holiday in a spirit of contentment.

Subsequently Krimmel painted several other scenes showing contemporary American life. *Election Day 1815* depicts a large crowd of Philadelphians gathered before the statehouse. *Dance in an American Tavern* portrays a spirited moment of merrymaking. All of Krimmel's paintings appear at first glance to be observed events, but actually they are sophisticatedly composed with a decorative realism that took into account the current vogue of Neoclassicism.

Family problems obliged the painter to return to his Württemberg hometown, and he spent almost two years in Germany (1817–18) at the height of the Romantic movement. The impressions he gained gave new directions to his art. When he was back in Philadelphia, he resumed his work as a more mature artist but continued to paint genre scenes of American life. His finest work, a group portrait of his brother's family and himself, is actually a memorial painting depicting the living and dead members of the Krimmel family reunited by family love. It strongly shows the influence of German Romantic painting,

John Lewis Krimmel, *Procession of Victuallers*, 1821. Aquatint based
on his watercolor. This event, organized by the butchers and cattle
raisers of Philadelphia, took place on March 21, 1821. Krimmel depicted the procession in a watercolor, which was engraved by J. Yeager,
also a German immigrant. The work is an early example of American
advertising.

particularly of the portrait style of the "Nazarenes," a group of southern German Romantic painters. Early in 1821, Krimmel was elected
president of the Association of American Artists. In the summer of the
same year his very promising career came abruptly to an end; only
thirty-six years old, he drowned in a millpond near Germantown.
Krimmel had painted for only eleven years, yet the rapid development
of his talent had enabled him to leave behind a body of work that not
only pointedly illustrates American life of this period but itself became
a lasting fiber in the fabric of American art. His paintings, and the engravings made of several of his pictures, exerted a direct influence on
America's most important genre painters of the next generation, particularly on William Sidney Mount and George Caleb Bingham.[7]

Aside from the mainstream of American art and the true folk art of

[7] Anneliese Harding, *John Lewis Krimmel: Genre Painter of the Early Republic*, to
be published in 1985 by the Henry Francis du Pont Winterthur Museum, Delaware.

the Pennsylvania Dutch, there developed mostly in the thinly populated areas of the United States a rich volume of pictures that today are
classified as primitive paintings. Some of them are the work of craftsmen; most of them are done by untutored yet gifted individuals. They
are usually executed in a naive but fastidiously exact manner. This kind
of art flourished particularly during the second and third quarters of
the nineteenth century. Most of the American amateur artists remain
anonymous. Of the small number by name several were identified as
German immigrants.

One of the earliest was Frederick Kemmelmeyer, who depicted
Washington reviewing his troops on October 18, 1794. The design of his
painting was based on an engraving by Daniel Chodowiecki representing Frederick the Great reviewing his troops. Kemmelmeyer simply
adapted the same design to the American motif. He executed his painting in the hard drawing style and pure colors typical of ornament and
sign painters. Another amateur artist, Jacob Maentel (1763–1863), became known for his meticulously painted portraits of his neighbors.
Possibly educated as a medical doctor and rumored to have been a secretary of Napoleon, Maentel settled first in Pennsylvania and later in
Indiana. Heading for Texas, he stopped at the utopian colony of New
Harmony and remained there for the rest of his life. While he was in
Pennsylvania, he had portrayed people in strict profile; in Indiana he
changed his style and depicted his neighbors in direct frontal view.[8]

Jürgen Frederick Huge (1809–78), my third example, was born in
Hamburg and became best known for his pictures of ships. He is
thought to have been a ship's captain before he married a wealthy girl
from Bridgeport, Connecticut, settled down, and became a grocer. In
his spare time he painted charming pictures in a miniaturist style, at-
tending to every detail of the particular ship or Bridgeport building.[9]
Finally, the Wisconsin farm scenes of Paul Seifert (1840–1921) count
among the masterpieces of American primitive painting. Seifert, a
vegetable farmer, demonstrated a particularly fine sense for rhythmical
patterns and color.[10]

[8] Jean Lipman, ed. *American Folk Painters of Three Centuries* (New York: Hudson
Hills Press, 1980), p. 117.
[9] Jean Lipman and Alice Winchester, *The Flowering of American Folk Art, 1776–
1876* (New York: Viking Press, 1974), p. 61.
[10] Ibid., p. 160.

The opening of the western frontier aroused widespread interest in Europe. Early reports about the uncharted territories of the United States piqued the curiosity of Europeans for various reasons: artists were interested in North America as a continent of exhilarating beauty, full of unfamiliar animals and plants. The natives were handsome, fascinating people with strange customs. German immigration to America resumed strongly after the end of the Napoleonic Wars and two years of famine. In the summer of 1821 a group of German Swiss from the area of Bern embarked on a sailing vessel to settle in the area of the present site of Winnipeg. Among the colonists was a fifteen-year-old boy, Peter Rindisbacher, with a remarkable talent for drawing. He recorded the most memorable events of their long and hazardous voyage. When the travelers finally reached the Red River Colony, they were surrounded by Indian tribes. Young Peter began to draw and watercolor industriously, soon compiling a series of sketches that today are seen as the first comprehensive, highly authentic pictorial record of Plains Indians and northern frontier life. The young artist's pictures derive their impact from their uninhibited immediacy and convincing authenticity. They show that remarkable power of observation peculiar to young people. Later Rindisbacher and his family moved to the United States territories. They first tried to settle in Wisconsin but moved on to Saint Louis, where Peter established himself as a portrait painter. He died suddenly in 1834 at the early age of twenty-eight.[11]

While Rindisbacher's Indian and frontier sketches are invaluable for their early date and richly descriptive information, they undeniably show a stiffness in design. Far superior in artistic quality and of finer naturalistic definition are the sketches and watercolors of Karl Bodmer, another German-Swiss, who worked with similar subject matter about a decade later. In 1832, Bodmer was hired as an artist recorder by the German naturalist Prince Maximilian von Wied to accompany him on his expedition into the interior of the United States. Maximilian's earlier ventures had won him a reputation as an ethnologist and taught him the importance of retaining an artist. He selected Bodmer with good reason. Bodmer, who had studied in Paris, was already an established painter. At twenty-three he was still young enough for adven-

[11] Alvin M. Josephy, Jr., *The Artist Was a Young Man* (Fort Worth: Amon Carter Museum of Western Art, 1970), pp. 15–16.

ture and ready to endure the hardships of such an expedition. In April, 1833, the prince, Bodmer, and the prince's servant embarked on a steam vessel of the American Fur Company and traveled up the Missouri River. Whenever they stopped at the various forts and trading posts, Bodmer found opportunity to sketch the landscape as well as the Indians in their colorful attire. Because Bodmer's sketches were to serve as illustrations for Maximilian's book, the naturalist must have insisted on the pictures' authenticity and exactness. In fact, to please his patron, Bodmer seems often to have placed more importance on the paraphernalia and costumes of the Indians than on the rendering of an individual portrait. The prince's party returned to Saint Louis at the end of May, 1834, and soon after took a ship back to Europe. Maximilian's book appeared in 1839 in his hometown, Koblenz, under the title *Travels through the Interior of North America in the Years 1832–1834*. It contained eighty-one engravings based on Bodmer's drawings.[12]

About the middle of the nineteenth century Heinrich Balduin Möllhausen, an adventurer, artist, and writer with a proclivity for both science and fiction, joined two U.S. government expeditions as official draftsman. Möllhausen (born near Bonn in 1825) made three trips from Germany to America between 1848 and 1858. Some of his drawings were later lithographed for the official reports of expeditions. Möllhausen returned to Europe and recorded his experiences in America. He wrote novels, including *Das Mormonenmädchen*, about American pioneer life and Indians, and he died in 1905.

The most accomplished painter of Indians, superior even to the more famous and more prolific George Catlin, was Karl (later Charles) Wimar (1828–62), who came to the United States at the impressionable age of fifteen. His family settled on the outskirts of Saint Louis, where he befriended Indians who were camped in the area. Wimar's interest in and affection for the Indians never waned. Even when the young painter, then in his twenties, went to study at the art academy in Düsseldorf, he continued to depict scenes of Indian life. He painted his best pictures after his return to America in 1856. By then his style had taken on a Romantic fervor, delineated with an exact draftsman-

[12] Robert Taft, *Artists and Illustrators of the Old West* (New York: Charles Scribner's Sons, 1953), pp. 78–85. See also Maximilian, Prince of Wied, *Travels in the Interior of North America*, trans. H. Evans Lloyd (London: Ackermann & Co., 1843).

Charles F. Wimar, *Attack on the Emigrant Train*, 1860. Courtesy Joslyn Art Museum, Omaha, Nebr.

ship and a scientifically precise definition that he had learned in Düsseldorf.[13] Wimar and his fellow painters left invaluable descriptions of the newly opened western territories in their virgin state and a vivid depiction of the Indian before the white man's impact drastically diminished their numbers and destroyed their way of life.

Among the many young German intellectuals who sought safety in America after the unsuccessful Revolution of 1848 were two young painters, Richard Petri (1829–57) and Hermann Lungkwitz (1824–91).[14] Both had studied at the Dresden Academy, where they became involved in the political activities which preceded the revolution. They emigrated with their families to America and settled on a farm in Texas in 1851. City bred and accustomed to a bourgeois standard of living, they were ill prepared for the hardships and physically demanding life on the western frontier. Petri spent most of his seven years in Texas ill and bedridden but nevertheless produced some fine and unique im-

[13] Perry T. Rathbone, *Charles Wimar: Painter of the Indian* (Saint Louis: City Art Museum, 1946).

[14] See Chapter 8, by James Patrick McGuire.

ages of the settlers and of the Indians. *The Pioneer Cowpen* shows a female member of the Petri family wearing a fashionable dress brought from Dresden while she is milking the cows. A watercolor of an Indian woman holding her little child and riding a mule beautifully depicts the mother's protective movement.[15]

During the middle of the nineteenth century, German immigration to the United States grew extraordinarily, and the German influence on American artistic development increased accordingly. Between 1840 and 1865 many American painters, including those of non-German descent, went to Düsseldorf to pursue their art studies. For twenty-five years this small city in the German Rhineland, famous for its art academy, became a vital center for the development of American painting. American artists needed the professional training Düsseldorf had to offer; there they learned the basic skills of draftsmanship and anatomy, the effects of light and shade—all prerequisites for competing in the now more sophisticated art market at home. Düsseldorf art training, either at the academy or in the studio of one of the many famous painters who resided there, greatly expanded American artists' subject matter; it also taught them how to compose a landscape painting from precise preparatory sketches and how to group figures more naturally with a greater sense of motion.

The central figure of the American artists' community in Düsseldorf was Emanuel Gottlieb Leutze (1816–68), an artist admired for his drawing talent, his portraits, and his historical compositions. Born in the southern German region of Württemberg, he came with his family to Philadelphia at the age of nine. As a teenager he helped support his family by drawing pencil portraits for a small fee. In 1840, at the age of twenty-four and with seven years' experience as a painter, he returned to Germany to study in Düsseldorf. After a year at the academy he withdrew to work in the studio of Carl Friedrich Lessing, a painter renowned for his rhetorical history paintings with broad political implications. These types of paintings steered Leutze toward his own compositions, such as his large (149-by-255-inch) canvas *Washington Crossing the Delaware*.

With this painting Leutze paid tribute to a heroic event of the

[15] William W. Newcomb, Jr., *German Artist on the Texas Frontier: Friedrich Richard Petri* (Austin: University of Texas Press, 1978).

Revolutionary War that took place on Christmas Night, 1776. He began this painting in 1849, the year following the abortive German revolution, with an eye on the contemporary German political scene, intending it to be a model and inspiration to the discouraged German liberal-thinking patriot, as well as a glorification of the American spirit.

When the original painting was almost finished, it was damaged by a studio fire. Leutze painted a second picture, which was shipped to America. When it toured American cities in the early 1850s, it was enthusiastically viewed by more than twenty thousand people. Now part of the collections of the New York Metropolitan Museum, it remains a major attraction. His artist friends correctly recognized Leutze as a prophetic, rather than a retrospective, genius. His historical compositions should not be seen as a reconstruction of past events but as a symbolic projection of an heroic spirit.[16]

Düsseldorf's training prepared the American painters to interpret the American landscape with a dramatic flair. Now they were able to express in their paintings the spirit of the time, the era of rapid expansion and great national pride. Painters like Albert Bierstadt (1830–1902) first opened the eyes of the American public to the magnificence of the western panorama.

Bierstadt, who was brought to America as a two-year-old, grew up in New Bedford, Massachusetts. After working as a painter with little success, he left for Europe in 1853 to study at the Düsseldorf Academy, where his uncle was a professor of genre painting. During his four years in Europe, Bierstadt worked extremely hard, spending many weeks hiking through and sketching the German countryside. He returned to America in 1857 and in the following year joined the western surveying expedition of Col. Frederick Lander. When their party reached Wyoming, Bierstadt was so overcome by the beauty of the natural sites that he left the expedition to sketch the Wind River and Shoshone country. In 1859, after months of constant sketching, he returned east to set up his studio in New York. By working his western sketches into large, impressive paintings, he soon built a national reputation as one of America's premier landscape painters. Bierstadt's small

---

[16] Barbara S. Groseclose, *Emanuel Leutze: Freedom Is the Only King* (Washington, D.C.: National Collection of Fine Arts, 1975).

Albert Bierstadt, *The Oregon Trail*, 1869. Courtesy The Butler Institute of American Art, Youngstown, Ohio.

oil sketches as well as his large paintings have lately earned appreciation once again. His best canvases captured the poetry of the wilderness and brought American landscape painting to a grand climax.[17]

Many other German immigrant artists, before and at the same time as Bierstadt, celebrated the beauty of America's natural splendor. Some chose the picturesque vistas of intimate spots and others, the sweeping panoramas of rolling hills. Landscape painters like brothers John and Godfrey Frankenstein in Ohio, Paul Weber in Pennsylvania, Paul Roetter in Wisconsin, Hermann Lungkwitz in Texas, and Heinrich Vianden in the midwestern states painted and drew the American sites with the vision of German Romanticism.

Charles Christian Nahl (1818–78) made a major contribution to American art as a painter and illustrator. His work shows a strong influence of the Düsseldorf style, though he actually studied at the Academy of Kassel, his hometown. Financial difficulties caused his family to

[17] Gordon Hendricks, *Albert Bierstadt, 1830–1902: Catalogue for Retrospective Exhibition* (Fort Worth: Amon Carter Museum, 1972). See also Gordon Hendricks, *Albert Bierstadt: Painter of the American West* (New York: Abrams, 1974).

Charles Christian Nahl, *Sunday Morning in the Mines*, 1870. Oil on canvas. Courtesy E. B. Crocker Art Gallery, Sacramento, Calif.

move to the United States in 1849. After a short stint in New York the Nahls headed for California, arriving in San Francisco in May, 1851. Hoping to make their fortune in the gold mines, Nahl and his brother joined one of the camps, but Charles soon abandoned pick and shovel for the drawing pencil. Sketching the miners and Indians, as well as the enchanting natural environment, Nahl realized that his true chance for success and fortune lay in making a chronicle of what he saw and that no artist of skill equal to his was there to compete. In the winter of the same year he and his friend Wenderoth, also a German immigrant, established a studio in Sacramento. Nahl received commissions for paintings but reached first true recognition with his drawings for woodcuts, depicting contemporary California life and particularly focusing on life in the mines. These illustrations, appearing in newspapers and magazines, were seen with great interest not only all over the United States but also in Europe. In the 1860s and 1870s, Nahl was commissioned by the California judge Charles Crocker to produce large canvases based on his earlier sketches. He then painted one of his best-known works, *Saturday Night at the Mines*. Nahl has to be seen as the major artist of the unique historical phenomenon called the California gold rush.[18]

Another German painter who worked in the 1870s in San Francisco and produced important paintings that documented contemporary life in California was William Hahn (1827–87). Born in Dresden, Hahn studied art in Düsseldorf and Paris before coming to America. After first working in New York, where he exhibited at the National Academy of Design, he opened a studio in San Francisco. Fascinated by the life-style of the explosively growing American cities with their potpourri populations and well-designed buildings, he produced *Market Scene in San Francisco in 1872*. Three years later he painted *Harvest Time*, showing the threshing of a California grain field.

In the 1880s, American painters began to flock to Munich, which by then had become the major German art center. Painters like Frank Duveneck, Charles Friedrich Ulrich, and Charles Merit Chase carried the fluently brushed Munich style to America, while William M. Harnet perfected in Munich his Old Master–style techniques and trompe l'oeil paintings.[19] Each of these important American artists extracted from the Munich experience different elements and combined them with other European influences to develop a more personal style after their return to America. Munich-trained Joseph Decker and Ignatz Gaugengigl, after immigrating to America, practiced a personal realism that at times presaged movie stills. Decker (1853–1924), born in Württemberg, immigrated in 1867 and lived most of his life in Brooklyn, New York, where he produced some highly original pictures. William Wehner, a Munich painter and entrepreneur, established a studio in Milwaukee and with a team of ten German painters carried out commissions of huge, realistically painted cycloramas depicting historic battle scenes of the Civil War. His most famous, *The Battle of Atlanta*, served Hollywood as direct inspiration for the film epic *Gone with the Wind*.[20]

Although our contemporary taste is at times hard-pressed to appreciate fully the art these immigrant artists have produced, the ro-

---

[18]Charles Moreland L. Stevens, *Christian Nahl: Artist of the Gold Rush 1818–1878* (Sacramento, Calif.: E. B. Crocker Art Gallery, 1976).

[19]Richard V. West, *Munich and American Realism in the Nineteenth Century: Exhibition Catalogue* (Sacramento, Calif.: E. B. Crocker Art Gallery, 1978), pp. 44, 62, 38.

[20]Wilbur G. Kurz, *The Atlanta Cyclorama* (Atlanta, Ga.: City of Atlanta, 1954).

mantic realism that they brought from Germany to America was precisely right for the United States in the nineteenth century. It was a type of art accessible to anyone and thus ideally suited to satisfy the growing hunger for painting in America. In a country where large portions of the population could not or could only insufficiently speak and read the official language, the visual medium, universally understandable, played a particularly important role.

I have discussed only a small portion of the large visual treasure Germans created in America. Having experienced in their splintered German homeland the damaging and retarding effects of disunity and fragmentation, German immigrant artists instinctively supported the sweeping cultural unification that began to develop in the United States. To the best of their abilities they joined the intensive artistic productivity in which America was soon to excel.

JAMES PATRICK MCGUIRE

Observations on German Artists in Nineteenth-Century Texas

GERMAN immigrant artists who chose Texas during the nineteenth century are more limited in number and in the variety of subjects than are those who settled elsewhere in the United States. As Anneliese Harding has indicated, the late 1600s witnessed the arrival of German artists and artisans from the Rhineland regions in the English colonies.[1] It was another century and a half before Texas witnessed the presence of such artists. Most stayed a short time, finding economic conditions adverse. A few, however, including Carl G. von Iwonski, Richard Petri, and Hermann Lungkwitz, by the end of the nineteenth century had laid the foundation for the development of the fine arts in Texas.

The story of these artists in Texas begins with the period of mass immigration after the 1820s, the result of liberalized colonization laws under the Mexican Constitution of 1824. Texas was a part of that nation until 1836. Thereafter the fledgling Republic of Texas sought people to develop the virgin land of its huge territory. In 1845, Texas was annexed to the United States. Of its population of 212,592 in 1850, thousands were Germans who had immigrated under the leadership of the Adelsverein (Society for the Protection of German Immigrants in Texas) and settled along the western frontier of central Texas during and after the mid-1840s. By 1860 there were more than 20,500 native-born Germans in Texas (of a total population of 604,215, including 182,566 slaves), the largest foreign-born element in pre–Civil War Texas.

With this tide of immigrants came a score or more of German-speaking artists to the German colonies and to the new Texas ports and

---

[1]Anneliese Harding, *America through the Eyes of German Immigrant Painters* (Boston: Goethe Institute, 1976).

towns. Most stayed a while and then left, seeking better markets for their art. Among those appearing were Carl Rohrdorf (d. 1847 at Nassau Plantation, in Fayette County), a Swiss-born landscapist who completed a large panorama of New Braunfels for the Adelsverein's advertisements in Germany. Carl Nebel prepared sketches for lithographs of the Mexican War during the late 1840s, and Carl Schuchard (1827–83), a mining engineer, was a topographer with the Gray Survey of 1854. Schuchard later settled in San Antonio.[2]

Other German artists who went to San Antonio were Erhard Pentenrieder (1830–75), a Bavarian, who prepared two lithographed letterheads of San Antonio's Main Plaza. One showed camels in the plaza, marking the U.S. Army's experiment with transcontinental transportation before the Civil War. Wilhelm C. A. Thielepape (1814–1904), of Wabern, moved to Texas in the 1840s and served as a surveyor, architect, musician, politician, and artist. He operated Texas' first lithographic press in San Antonio in 1855 and is best remembered as Reconstruction mayor from 1867 to 1872.[3]

Just after the war Augustus Koch and Hermann Brossius prepared panoramas of several Texas towns, including New Braunfels, Waco, Jefferson, and Victoria. Along the Texas coast in Galveston, Matagorda, and Indianola, German artists periodically advertised their studios and services. C. O. Bahr (active ca. 1856), William Neuser (1837–1902), Augustus Behne (1828–95), the Reverend Peter A. Moelling (active ca. 1860s), Helmut Holtz (active ca. 1860), and Theodore Lehmann (active in Houston, 1839) were among those limners and painters who appeared briefly and then moved elsewhere.[4]

Among the masses of German settlers there were also a few folk artists who interpreted Texas and European subjects through their naive renderings. Louis Hoppe (active 1860s), a farm worker in Fayette and Colorado counties, left two floral watercolors and two farmhouse scenes of pioneer life. Julius Ploetz, an amateur who advertised himself as a "Painter, taught by experience," was active in New Braunfels

[2] Pauline A. Pinckney, *Painting in Texas: The Nineteenth Century* (Austin: University of Texas Press, 1967), p. 167; Carl Rohrdorf File, University of Texas, Institute of Texan Cultures, San Antonio.

[3] Erhard Pentenrieder File, Institute of Texan Cultures; Pinckney, *Painting in Texas*, pp. 151, 153, 177; Wilhelm C. A. Thielepape File, Institute of Texan Cultures.

[4] Pinckney, *Painting in Texas*, pp. 68, 73, 141–45, 152–55, 212.

as early as 1859. Two of his landscapes, including a naive view of Hermann Seele's Saengerhalle, have survived. Rudolph Mueller (1859–1929), of Saxony, settled at Castroville, where he produced a small number of landscapes of that Alsatian-immigrant village as well as of German castles remembered. These men's work, though primitive, provides a charming view of rural life in Texas a century ago.[5]

German-born or Texas-German women artists should also be mentioned. Both Ida Weisselberg Hadra (1861–85) and Lina von Rosenberg Bissel (1864–1959) were Texas-born of German-immigrant parents, and both studied in Austin under the landscape master Hermann Lungkwitz, who will be discussed later. Hadra, a landscapist and portraitist, was born in Castroville and moved to Austin in 1872. There she studied drawing and painting under Lungkwitz at the Austin Collegiate Female Institute from 1879 to 1880, producing a number of competent copies of his landscapes of the Texas capital city. After her marriage to Dr. Berthold Hadra in 1882 and their move to San Antonio, Hadra painted scenes of the San Antonio River. She died in childbirth at the age of twenty-four.[6]

A contemporary, unidentified Austin newspaper mention of Hadra's work said:

> Miss Weisselberg, a pupil of Mr. Lungkwitz, is the earnest, patient, toiling art student. It is no mere accomplishment that she seeks, but finished, profitable excellence, such as the world of art will recognize. Miss W. is said to be as patient, painstaking and faithful to truth and nature as her famous preceptor. She has devoted four or five years to the study and practice of the rules and philosophy of painting and will yet reflect credit upon the people she represents.[7]

Lina von Rosenberg, likewise a child of German immigrants, was a lifelong resident of Austin. She studied drawing and painting under Lungkwitz at the Alta Vista Institute and later took private lessons from him. She often chose to copy his scenes and worked along Shoal Creek and at Texas Military Institute. Following her marriage in 1890 to

[5] Cecilia Steinfeldt, *Texas Folk Art: One Hundred Fifty Years of the Southwest Tradition* (Austin: Texas Monthly Press, 1981), pp. 34–37, 44, 46–49.
[6] Pinckney, *Painting in Texas*, pp. 174, 177–80; Sheree Scarborough, "Women Painters in Austin (1870–1890)" (MS, University of Texas at Austin, 1982; copy, Institute of Texan Cultures), pp. 6–8.
[7] Scarborough, "Women Painters in Austin," fig. 11.

George Bissell, however, she gave up painting to rear a family. Like Hadra and Bissell, other dilettantes studied drawing and painting in Texas' German and English academies that sprang up in large German colonies in such cities as Austin and San Antonio during the mid- and late nineteenth century.[8]

Only one woman, Louise Heuser Wueste (1805–74), from Gummersbach, in Westphalia, pursued an active professional art career in Texas. Widowed young and with three small children, Wueste operated a boardinghouse before turning to art. She studied at the Düsseldorf Academy under Boser and received able assistance from two brothers-in-law, artists Karl Friedrich Lessing (1808–80) and H. L. Adolf Schroedter (1805–75), both of whom were well known in Düsseldorf and Karlsruhe. She was also influenced by August Wilhelm Sohn (1829–99).[9]

Wueste followed her three grown children to Texas, arriving in 1859 at the age of fifty-four. Residing mainly in San Antonio, she periodically visited her children and grandchildren in Pleasanton and Eagle Pass. Best known in Texas for her sensitive portraits of children, Wueste opened a studio in San Antonio in 1860, taught in the local German-English school, and gave private lessons. She died in Eagle Pass in 1874.[10]

Wueste's observation of the arts in Texas at the time of the Civil War was probably accurate for all artists seeking to make a living there. She wrote that "painting is a queer art here in America where only commerce is recognized" and that "poetry and art are of little importance here." And in a letter to relatives in 1869 she lamented: "You lucky ones who live in our German Fatherland surrounded by art treasures. . . . Life here in America is very difficult, so harassed with everyone thinking of means to earn money for a return trip to Germany."[11]

Toward the end of the century two German marine painters ap-

[8] Ibid., pp. 7–8.

[9] Pinckney, *Painting in Texas*, pp. 118–21; Ingeborg Wittichen, *Oberbergische Malerinnen des 19. Jahrunderts aus der Familie Jügel/Heuser* (Celle: Schweiger & Pick, 1980), pp. 10–13.

[10] Wittichen, *Oberbergische Malerinnen des 19. Jahrunderts aus der Familie Jügel/Heuser*, pp. 10–13.

[11] James Patrick McGuire, "Views of Texas: German Artists on the Frontier," in *German Culture in Texas: A Free Earth: Essays from the 1978 Southwest Symposium*, ed. Glen E. Lich and Dona B. Reeves, (Boston: Twayne, 1980), pp. 131–34.

peared in Galveston, the largest port in Texas and the western Gulf Coast. Paul Schumann (1876–1946), a native of Leipzig, came to America as a child and studied under Julius Stockfleth in Galveston during the late 1890s. Schumann became widely known for his renderings in oil and watercolor of the "true Gulf Coast," with scenes of the beach, waves, oyster boats, wharves, and fishermen. He exhibited widely in Texas and the United States before and after the turn of the century. His sea compositions were notable for his use of the palette knife in creating strong wave action.[12]

Julius Stockfleth (1857–1935), Schumann's teacher, arrived in Galveston from his native Wyk auf Föhr, in the North Frisian Islands, in 1885. Described in German art histories as a self-taught amateur, a house painter by trade, Stockfleth advertised himself as an artist or portrait painter throughout his stay in Galveston. The uneven quality of his work, ranging from naive treatments of shipping around the port to finely painted portraits of ships, testifies to an uncertain career, perhaps hampered by extreme poverty. Stockfleth's reputation rests primarily on his marine renderings of the port of Galveston and of the sailing and steam vessels that visited the city.[13]

The paintings of ships, harbors, and seascapes is a strict discipline, and Stockfleth faithfully portrayed the shape and rig of each vessel and the surrounding harbor. Of particular interest to Texans were his portraits of locally owned tug and pilot boats, including the *Mamie Higgins*, the *Charlotte M. Allen*, the *Charles Clarke*, and the *Texas*. Brigantines such as the *Kossak*, schooners, steamers, schooner-rigged barges, and smaller fishing boats that plied the waters of Galveston and surrounding bays were favorite subjects. From engraving and illustrations he also painted clippers, sailing yachts such as the *Volunteer* in the America's Cup Race off Newport, Rhode Island, and the U.S. Navy's Great White Fleet.[14]

Of particular historical interest are Stockfleth's paintings of Galveston during and after the great hurricane of September 8, 1900, which destroyed much of the island city and left more than six thou-

---

[12] Paul Schumann File, Institute of Texan Cultures; James Patrick McGuire, *Julius Stockfleth: Gulf Coast Marine and Landscape Painter* (San Antonio: Trinity University Press, 1976), p. 1.

[13] McGuire, *Stockfleth*, pp. 1–4.

[14] Ibid., pp. 18–79.

sand dead. Although the bachelor artist lost most of his relatives during this tragic event, he painted portraits of such ships as the S.S. *Pensacola* riding out the storm at sea and of the flooded and wind-devastated city, as *Tremont Street, Galveston, during Hurricane of Sept. 8th, 1900* and *East Broadway, Galveston, during Hurricane of Sept. 8th, 1900* (the latter now lost). Other scenes showed the destruction of such buildings as the Lucas Terrace apartments. The horror of the storm marked Stockfleth, causing him to pace the seawall restlessly when storms approached his native Wyk later in his life, after he had returned to Germany.[15]

Stockfleth's paintings also recorded the recovery of Texas' largest port following the hurricane. Scenes show people camping amid the ruins of their homes. Later the new seawall, the grade filling of the city behind the seawall, and the new causeway to the mainland were subjects of compositions. Many of his panoramic scenes of the rebuilt city were made into postcards for tourists, who were among his main customers.

Stockfleth returned to his native Wyk in 1907 and continued to paint for a living until his death in 1935. Although not great art, the body of his work provides an accurate record of Galveston and its shipping during the late nineteenth century, a time when steam vessels replaced sailing ships on the Gulf Coast. As such, it is unique.

Three German-born artists who were active in central Texas and its Hill Country from the mid- to late nineteenth century are of major historical and artistic importance. Carl G. von Iwonski (1830–1912), Richard Petri (1824–57), and Hermann Lungkwitz (1813–91) proved important figures in the history of art in Texas during that time. Iwonski flourished during midcentury and then returned to his native Germany. Petri survived only six years in the harsh frontier environment of the Hill Country, and Lungkwitz worked for four decades to establish landscape painting in central Texas.[16]

Carl G. von Iwonski was born in Hilbersdorf, Silesia, in 1830 and

[15] Ibid., pp. 8, 10, 54–59, 102–103, 110–13.

[16] James Patrick McGuire, *Hermann Lungkwitz: Romantic Landscapist on the Texas Frontier* (Austin: University of Texas Press, 1983), pp. 1–60; William W. Newcomb, Jr. and Mary S. Carnahan, *German Artist on the Texas Frontier: Friedrich Richard Petri* (Austin: University of Texas Press, 1978), pp. 3–159; Pinckney, *Painting in Texas*, pp. 122–37.

came to Texas as a youth of fifteen with his parents, who migrated with the Adelsverein to New Braunfels, the first German colony west of the Colorado River. Secondary sources point to early training in drawing at a school in Breslau, and circumstantial evidence indicates that he may have taken art lessons from Petri and Lungkwitz after they arrived in Texas in 1851. Iwonski had abundant talent and documented the German colonies of New Braunfels and San Antonio through his drawings, portraits, lithographs, and cartoons.[17]

New Braunfels, established in 1845 by Prince Carl of Solms-Braunfels, by 1850 had become the largest German town and the fourth-largest community in the state. The Iwonski family maintained a stage stop and saloon on the banks of the Guadalupe River, and Carl assisted with the family concerns, including farming, during his first years in Texas. His art career appears to have begun about 1855, when he completed portraits of local settlers and became associated with an amateur theatrical group in the town. Seventeen fine pencil-and-ink line drawings of the amateurs documented various comedies that were produced for local enjoyment and to benefit the town's school fund. These drawings, made between 1855 and 1857, pointed to his ability in drawing and caricature that culminated during Reconstruction in political cartoons beneficial to the new Republican party in San Antonio.[18]

By 1858, Iwonski had moved to San Antonio, where he became associated with William DeRyee in a photography business. San Antonio also provided a larger market for Iwonski's portrait commissions, though Civil War conditions forced him to teach drawing and painting in the German-English School.[19]

Landscapes such as *Log Cabin* and *Mission Concepción, San Antonio*, portraits of Indians (based on watercolors by Petri), one rare still life containing an 1851 Colt Navy revolver, and Civil War compositions point to Iwonski's versatility. *The Terry Rangers*, showing Sam Maverick and the Terry Rangers leaving San Antonio for the war front, is his only oil painting of a war subject. His pencil drawing *Camp Las Moras, C.S.A.* (1861), was the first war sketch engraved in *Harper's Weekly*, appearing in the issue of June 15, 1861. His best-known scene,

[17] James Patrick McGuire, *Iwonski in Texas: Painter and Citizen* (San Antonio: Museum Association, 1976), p. 11.
[18] Ibid., pp. 12–17.
[19] Ibid., pp. 17–22.

Mexican Camp. This drawing is attributed to Carl G. von Iwonski. Mrs. J. N. Terrell, copy courtesy University of Texas Institute of Texan Cultures, San Antonio.

a panorama of New Braunfels in the mid-1850s, was lithographed for sale to the public and has been subsequently used in many publications on the history of Texas.[20]

Following the war Iwonski, with Hermann Lungkwitz, opened a photography studio, which they operated jointly until 1870. Extant newspaper accounts point to Iwonski's curiosity about the camera, including mentions of his attempts to make "spiritual" photographs and to capture an eclipse of the sun. However, the mundane work of making portraits of customers, mainly of cartes-de-visite size, provided both men with the means to paint.[21]

Iwonski's art career in San Antonio was centered in the local German colony, which contained one-third of the population. For the German-English School and the Casino Club, a social organization habituated by the local "aristocrats," as they were described in postwar

[20] Ibid., pp. 37, 40, 42, 44, 56, 73, 78.
[21] Ibid., pp. 17–22.

Democratic newspapers, Iwonski painted a heroic-size group of the German general staff to mark the defeat of France, which was celebrated in the German colony in 1871. He also sculpted a bust of Baron Alexander von Humboldt for the Casino Club's celebration marking the centennial of that great German's birth.[22]

Reconstruction and the creation of the Republican party in Texas brought new opportunities to Iwonski and to his father, the latter serving as city tax collector and later as county treasurer. For the party Iwonski drew cartoons, called "caricatures" by the newspapers, to remind the Germans of their bitter experiences during the Civil War. *Answer of the Germans*, *Pas de Deux*, *Our Platform*, and others were intended to sway German voters during crucial elections, particularly in 1868, when Radical Republicans gained ascendancy in the Texas political arena. August Siemering, the German-born editor of the *San Antonio Express*, wrote about Iwonski in the February 12, 1868, issue that the "fertility of the artist's brain is equal to (Thomas) Nast, of *Harper's Weekly* celebrity, and we will hear of 'more richness' before the campaign is over."[23]

Although described as self-taught in contemporary San Antonio newspapers, Iwonski steadily improved his perspective, coloration, and composition. This is particularly evident in his portraits, mainly of German merchants and their wives. A year's training at the Academy of Art in Berlin in 1871 enhanced his ability in this genre. Unfortunately, in 1873, Iwonski chose to return permanently to his native Silesia with his widowed mother, thus ending a promising career in Texas.[24]

Iwonski can be characterized as both a dilettante and a professional artist. In the versatile range of subject matter that he chose, his work serves as a reminder of the cohesive and robust German colonies in Texas and their social, cultural, and political life. Although he, like others, tried to support himself through his art, he relied mostly on his earnings as a teacher, photographer, and like his father, for a time, as a public official. The social prominence of his wealthy parents undoubtedly proved helpful in his efforts to obtain portrait commissions from the German merchant princes of San Antonio.

Richard Petri, a native of Dresden, was not as fortunate as Iwonski

[22] Ibid., pp. 22–32.
[23] Ibid., pp. 24–26, 82–83.
[24] Ibid., pp. 32–33.

Richard Petri, *Plains Indian Family Emerging from the Woods*. Courtesy Texas Memorial Museum, University of Texas at Austin.

in obtaining commissions. Petri arrived in Texas in 1851 with his sister and brother-in-law, Hermann Lungkwitz, and other relatives, who immigrated to America following the failure of the revolution of May, 1849, in Saxony. And circumstances indicate that Petri, as well as Lungkwitz, gave Iwonski art lessons, first in New Braunfels and then in Fredericksburg, where the Lungkwitz-Petri family settled in 1852.[25]

In 1838, as a youth of fourteen, Petri entered the Royal Academy of Fine Arts in Dresden and continued classes there for over a decade. At the academy he attended the landscape classes of Ludwig Richter. But no doubt the greatest influence on Petri was his teacher Julius Hübner, who, in turn, had been a pupil of the "Nazarene" painter Wilhem von Schadow. The Nazarenes were a group of German artists working in Rome in the early nineteenth century. Among their interests were biblical and German folkloric themes, and Petri's surviving works indicate that he was extremely talented in such compositions.

[25] Mae Estelle Meyers, "The Lives and Works of Hermann Lungkwitz and Richard Petri" (Master's thesis, University of Texas at Austin, 1983), p. 1 and passim; Pinckney, *Painting in Texas*, pp. 74–86; McGuire, *Lungkwitz*, pp. 9–19.

He won six awards from the academy for his work. Family tradition reported that Petri was awarded a year's study in Rome but that ill health forced him to decline. He thus left Dresden for America at the beginning of a promising European career.[26]

Little is known of Petri's early life in Dresden and later in Texas. Most of what is preserved in the way of family stories by the descendants of his sister and brother-in-law indicates that ill health, most likely tuberculosis compounded by malaria (which affected many German pioneers in Texas), continued to plague him throughout his life. Family financial records show merely that Petri continued to purchase art supplies and sell portraits to German settlers in the Texas Hill Country.[27]

Living as they did on the edge of the western frontier in Texas, Petri and Lungkwitz were forced to farm for a living. Commissions were few, and the Lungkwitz family grew with the arrival of four children by 1857. The frontier, however, provided Petri with abundant new subjects—the southern Comanches, the Lipan Apaches, and remnants of the Delawares and Shawnees, who served as guides for troops at the nearby army post, Fort Martin Scott. Petri's pencil and watercolor sketches of these Indians are unique in Texas art, and their collection and classification by the Texas Memorial Museum on the campus of the University of Texas at Austin are of both artistic and ethnographic importance.[28]

Although few of his finished compositions have been identified, Petri was working on a painting of soldiers, Indians, and settlers at Fort Martin Scott at the time of his death by drowning in the Pedernales River near the family farm late in 1857. Family correspondence indicates that he and Lungkwitz sent drawings and paintings of Texas scenes to relatives in Germany and to dealers for the Dresden market, which might account for the survival of so few finished works in Texas. Furthermore, living on the frontier at the end of a very long ox-wagon supply line from the Texas coast, Petri and his relatives found imports, including art supplies, costly. Family stories reported that the artists experimented with local soils, plants, and minerals as pigment sub-

---

[26] McGuire, *Lungkwitz*, pp. 9–19.
[27] Ibid.
[28] Ibid.

Richard Petri, *Plains Indian with Hair-pipe Breastplate*. Courtesy
Texas Memorial Museum, University of Texas at Austin.

stitutes when their supplies ran low, and Petri sketched on any paper available, including the flyleaves of books.[29]

Of particular interest to Texas historians are Petri's sketches of pioneer life during the early 1850s at Fredericksburg. Scenes of farm life include threshing grain, shelling and bagging corn, hauling water, milking cows, and pursuing other agricultural occupations that the Dresden group had to learn as farmers. When Indians visited their farm, Petri set up his easel and invited them to watch him sketch. The few surviving pencil portraits of settlers indicate that Petri attempted to supplement family funds in this manner. The rest of Petri's portraits are of his family, including numerous sketches of his sister, Elise Petri Lungkwitz, and her children, Max and Martha.[30]

The great potential of Petri's contribution to the body of art in Texas ended with his death at the age of thirty-three. Such was not the case with his brother-in-law, Hermann Lungkwitz, who founded Texas landscape painting during his forty-year career in the state. The literature on both Dresden-trained artists has been intertwined, and exhibitions frequently presented examples of both men's work. Lungkwitz, unlike Petri or even Iwonski, was purely a landscapist.

Lungkwitz was a native of Halle, on the Saale, in Saxony. Like Petri a few years earlier, in 1840 he entered the Royal Academy of Fine Arts in Dresden and studied principally under Ludwig Richter, the late-Romantic master who during the last half of the century became famous for his illustrations for German folktales. Lungkwitz remained at the academy for only three years, taking the traditional academic courses in plaster-cast and live-model sketching as well as nature studies during student trips to local parks and along the Elbe River into the mountains dividing Saxony and Bohemia.[31]

Although few records of his early life in Europe survive, it is evident from his inscribed drawings that Lungkwitz made three late-summer sketching trips in the Austrian and Bavarian Alps between 1844 and 1846. As was traditional, he used his sketches to compose finished paintings in his studio during winter months in Dresden, where he settled after his student days. His fine pencil line renderings

[29] Ibid.
[30] Ibid.
[31] Ibid., pp. 1–8.

bear witness to his talent and excellent training under Richter. His studies of trees and vegetation, rocks and boulders and rushing water-falls in Saxony and in the Salzkammergut of Austria, along with oil paintings of castles, Gothic church ruins, and the Alps, were carefully packed and brought to America when Lungkwitz immigrated.[32]

Lungkwitz and Petri might be termed Forty-eighters. Family tra-dition said that in May, 1849, both young men fought with other stu-dents at the Dresden barricades against the troops of the Saxon and Prussian kings and that both chose to emigrate after the collapse of the insurrection. Although no factual information substantiates this story, it is evident, especially from Lungkwitz's later correspondence, that both men were attracted to the ideals of political freedom in America.[33]

Lungkwitz, Petri, and their relatives arrived in New York in Sep-tember, 1850, and spent the next winter in Wheeling, on the Ohio River. The next spring, after the ice melted, they traveled to New Braunfels, the new German colony in Texas, by way of the Ohio and Mississippi rivers, seeing much of the American South along the way. By the summer of 1852 they purchased a farm on the Pedernales River near Fredericksburg, the second German-colony village established in Texas by the Adelsverein. Perhaps the Dresden party chose Freder-icksburg because of the large German population in the area or for its dry climate, which they hoped might benefit Petri's health.[34]

Lungkwitz painted Hill Country landscapes for the remaining four decades of his life, establishing this genre first on the frontier line and then in growing cities, such as San Antonio and Austin. No other Ger-man-born artist was active for so many years. For the first twelve years Lungkwitz and his relatives struggled with farming. Petri's sketches make the struggle abundantly clear. Lungkwitz's own cattle brand, which was recorded in the local county courthouse, also offers an un-usual testimony for the Dresden-trained artist. While they were living on the farm, five children were born to the Lungkwitz family.[35]

Yet Lungkwitz also began to sketch and paint Texas scenes almost immediately upon arrival. Evidence from family financial accounts in-dicates that he sold paintings and gave lessons at Wheeling and New

[32] Ibid.
[33] Ibid.
[34] Ibid., pp. 9–19.
[35] Ibid.

Braunfels before moving to Fredericksburg. His earliest dated Texas sketch, that of 1853, was of an ancient cypress tree on the banks of the Guadalupe River at Sisterdale, a village of well-educated German immigrants that was often consequently called a "Latin colony." There Lungkwitz also drew scenes of Texas' first spa, a water-cure sanatorium run by Dr. Ernst Kapp, and a lithography to be used for an advertisement was produced in New York City from the sketches.[36]

The old Spanish colonial city of San Antonio also attracted Lungkwitz and Petri during their first years in Texas, and both made sketches of the missions. A handful of Lungkwitz's accurate sketches and finished oil paintings of the old missions and two panoramic scenes of the city have survived. In addition Lungkwitz sent his panoramic views of San Antonio and Fredericksburg to Dresden, where lithographs were prepared for the Texas market. In terms of historical accuracy his scenes are among the finest artistic records of pre–Civil War Texas.[37]

The family stayed on the Pedernales farm during much of the Civil War period, Lungkwitz being protected from conscription by his Prussian passport. During the war Lungkwitz, a Unionist who opposed secession, also supported the family of his sister-in-law Marie Petri Kuechler when her husband Jacob fled to Mexico. A leading Unionist of west Texas, Kuechler participated in the infamous Battle of Nueces, in which Germans fleeing to Mexico were slaughtered by the Texas militia in 1862. (In Mexico, Kuechler worked as a surveyor until 1867, when he returned to Texas and became a leading Radical Republican politician.)[38]

Sketches and paintings of the pristine Hill Country also date from the Fredericksburg period. Enchanted Rock, a one-square-mile dome-shaped outcropping of pink granite north of the town; the Pedernales Valley; Bear Mountain; and other promontories attracted his attention during those years, and his finished compositions accurately reflected his German training. His views of Enchanted Rock and the lithograph *Friedrichsburg* are imbued with the spirit of Romanticism, of idyllic nature in the wilderness. In many scenes tiny human and animal

[36] Ibid.
[37] Ibid., pp. 27–35, 121–22, 132.
[38] Ibid., pp. 20–35.

Hermann Lungkwitz, *Guenther's Mill on Live Oak Creek near Freder-icksburg*, 1855. Oil on academy board. Private Collection, copy cour-tesy University of Texas Institute of Texan Cultures, San Antonio.

figures, such as the shepherd boys and their sheep in *Friedrichsburg*, suggest happy people peacefully going about their daily tasks. As such they reflect the spirit of the Biedermeier school of art, which was becoming popular in Germany when Lungkwitz and his family emigrated.[39]

In 1864, as atrocities against Hill Country Germans who opposed slavery, secession, and the Confederacy increased, Lungkwitz was forced to abandon his farm for the safety of San Antonio. There he opened a photographic studio with his friend Iwonski. Experienced as they were from working with pioneer photographer William DeRyee in San Antonio just before the war, and with Lungkwitz's experience in a traveling magic-lantern show through Texas and up the Mississippi and Ohio rivers in the 1860s, the two artists used photography as a livelihood while pursuing their teaching and art in San Antonio during the first five years of the Reconstruction period.[40]

[39] Ibid., pp. 18, 120.
[40] Ibid., pp. 27–35.

Jacob Kuechler became commissioner of the General Land Office in Austin in 1870 as a political reward from the Republicans, and he hired Lungkwitz as the official photographer for the agency. Lungkwitz moved his family, now with six children, to Austin and worked at the land office for four years. Little painting was done during the decade that ended in 1874 with his dismissal as the Democrats returned to public office. Thereafter he was once again forced to rely for a livelihood on painting and on teaching drawing and painting in local German-English schools, especially the school of his son-in-law Jacob Bickler. The last fifteen years of his life were devoted primarily to painting.[41]

Austin remained Lungkwitz's home, though after his wife's death in 1880 he lived periodically with three married daughters in Galveston and on a sheep ranch near Johnson City. He used his bedroom as a studio and enjoyed sketching along streams and in the hills north and west of Austin, in the Pedernales Valley, and around Enchanted Rock in the region of Llano County that he called the "granite mountains." Freed from family responsibilities, Lungkwitz enjoyed leisure outdoor sketching trips during the late-summer months, often with fellow artists such as William H. Huddle, of Austin. Staying with ranchers and farmers near attractive scenery, Lungkwitz hiked many miles through untouched wilderness carrying twenty pounds of painting paraphernalia to a site where he drew and painted from dawn to dusk. His production during those years was considerable.[42]

Lungkwitz's correspondence with family and friends unfortunately reveals only a few insights into his views on art. When he was planning to move to Texas from Wheeling in 1851, for example, he commented tersely that "we are now entirely at ease regarding our existence in the United States, since we have learned that a person, so long as he remains in good health, can, if necessary, get by with his art, without humbug, and can with reasonable success or patronage, make a living."[43] Later in 1851 a friend from Wheeling could write to the Lungkwitzes in Texas much more expressively about the painter's abilities:

> I have been kept fully informed of your adventures since you left, and have wished that I could have been with you. I could have helped you

[41] Ibid.

[42] Ibid., pp. 36–50.

[43] Hermann Lungkwitz, Wheeling (Virginia, now West Virginia), to Adolph Lungkwitz, March 17, 1851, Jacob and Martha Bickler Family Papers, Courtesy Mrs. Ralph A. Bickler, Austin, Texas.

build your house, drive the oxen, chop wood, and all that kind of work while you, with me, could have viewed nature in the evening in all her loveliness and beauty, and you could have transferred to canvas those same beauties in a manner which would have surprised the natives.[44]

In response to a letter from his brother-in-law Kuechler in Mexico in 1865, Lungkwitz commented on the landscape of northern Mexico and revealed something of his own feelings: "I imagine everything great there among the trees, rich in colors. Perhaps I am mistaken. But that would be excusable because your lovely report of the mountain tour has led my phantasy astray and excited me terribly." Then, as if to bring himself down to earth again, he added, "Of course, your meeting with the Indians wasn't cozy."[45]

Late in life Lungkwitz evaluated one of his paintings according to its "natural freshness and accuracy" and described scenes near Enchanted Rock as "charming views" and as "wildly romantic." Like the Wheeling friend earlier, one of his old friends, the fellow artist W. C. A. Thielepape, also shed light on Lungkwitz's career when he observed in a letter in 1888: "I am particularly glad that the pursuit of your beautiful art is, for you, a source of the purest enjoyment which also enables you to fulfill the heavy duties as a teacher and to earn the means for your modest requirements."[46]

The last decade of Lungkwitz's life saw a final blossoming of his ability to capture the clear, rushing Hill Country rivers with their quiet pools of emerald water, the white limestone cliffs and red granite boulders of the dividing hills, and the twisted cedar and oaks of that region. Painting for the love of his art, he poured out his soul in the solitary wilderness of Texas, perhaps best expressing his own feelings toward the forces of nature and the Supreme Being through his interpretations of landscapes. In this manner he reconciled himself to nature, and his serenity and harmony with nature can be seen especially in the landscapes of his last years.

Realistic and technical accuracy in his drawing and paintings are,

[44] Henry B. Hubbard, Wheeling, to Dear Friends, December 15, 1851, Hubbard Family Papers, Courtesy the late Chester R. Hubbard, Wheeling.

[45] Hermann Lungkwitz, San Antonio, to My dear brother-in-law and friend [Jacob Kuechler], February 13, 1865, Kuechler-Wupperman Papers, Austin History Center, Austin, Texas.

[46] Wilhelm C. A. Thielepape, Chicago, to My dear, dear friend [Hermann Lungkwitz], May 20, 1888, Kuechler-Wupperman Papers, Austin History Center.

Hermann Lungkwitz, *Falls of the Colorado, Austin*, 1875. Oil on canvas. Private Collection, copy courtesy University of Texas Institute of Texan Cultures, San Antonio.

however, also evident. Many appear to have been captured at high noon in the bright Texas sunlight and thus lack the luminous effect of light at dawn or sunset upon clouds and mists. Most of his early Texas works, moreover, were imbued with strong lighting, almost as if the artist were attempting to introduce a supernatural essence or religious quality into his compositions. Later his postwar landscapes became more desolate, brooding panoramas, with infrequent use of luminous, radiant lighting. These landscapes strongly suggest, however, the power of nature and man's relationship to the supernatural. His later works show an increased tendency toward more monochromatic earth colors, with the choice of rocks, boulders, and cliffs as natural subjects.

The works of Lungkwitz, like those of Iwonski and Petri, provide compassionate, understanding, and sensitive perceptions of pioneer Texas. They communicate to us not only a point in time but also the spirit of the immigrants' experiences. As a body of art they show firm experiential roots in the overall process of the German immigration to Texas in the nineteenth century.

It has been suggested that all these artists faced a certain disillusionment in their American experiences, since they were forced to earn their livings through other means. It has also been said that they settled in the worst part of the most primitive state in America and felt a sense of loss because of the lack of a sufficiently stimulating intellectual environment. Their isolation from the mainstreams of art on the East Coast and in Europe and the general indifference of their fellow citizens, who mainly failed to patronize their work, may also have contributed to the sense of loss.

It is interesting to note, however, that, once settled in Texas, these artists did not travel far. Distances in Texas were great, and transportation was both expensive and primitive until the arrival of the railroad in the 1870s and 1880s. Their relative isolation, mainly in central Texas, tended to "ossify" their art. They continued to paint as they had in Germany, following their training in the late-Romantic and more popularized Biedermeier traditions. Their contributions to Texas, however, prove solid, providing for a pioneering region the foundation of a tradition in the fine arts.

It should also be said that these German immigrant artists in Texas formed a microcosm of the wider American scene, even if they were more limited in time, in number, and in the productivity and scope of their subjects and interpretations. In terms of their pioneer experience it is also noteworthy that they employed little of the usual iconography of America's westward expansion. Lacking almost entirely are those traditional symbols: the frontiersman, the pioneers, and their homesteads in the forests and on the plains; western wild animals; the cowboy and his cattle work; and the majestic scenery of the Rockies farther west. Instead, the legacy of Iwonski, Petri, and Lungkwitz is a more personal interpretation of Texas with its German colonies, landscapes, and social activities—an intimate insight into the artists' own experiences.

Tales of the Grandmothers: Women as Purveyors of German-Texan Culture

I

DONA REEVES-MARQUARDT

"ACH, nur noch ein paar Minuten—es ist zu herrlich so umher zu rennen in der freien Natur! Und bin ich erst wieder zu Hause, muss ich an der Nähmaschine sitzen, oder der Mutter beim Kochen helfen" ("Well—just for a few more minutes—it's so wonderful to wander about close to nature! When I get home, I'll have to sit down at the sewing machine again, or help Mother with the cooking"). This quietly emotional sigh, spoken by Trude, a German-Texan adolescent girl, in a short story, "Eine altmodische Liebesgeschichte" ("An Old-fashioned Love Story"), might not have been as easily written by a German-Texan man. He might well have found splendor in running about in free nature but likely would not have associated it with a woman's role, nor would he have favored the modal verb *muss* ("must") when describing the afternoon delights of the sewing machine or the kitchen. This short story was written by one of many literate and literary German-Texan grandmothers, Hedwig Schroeter, of San Antonio. It appeared in serial form in the *San Antonio Freie Presse für Texas* in 1936. Recently translated by her granddaughter, Helen Schroeter Sundstrom, it was published in 1984 in the English version in the *Newsletter* of the German Texas Heritage Society.

We are assured that women accompanied the German immigrants to Texas, for they are also recorded by the male chroniclers. Because men by and large have written the histories of Texas, including the histories of the Germans in Texas, we tend to believe them; they established the image of pioneer women as well. They recorded the "firsts": the first German woman was likely Louise Ernst Stöhr, wife of Friedrich Ernst, known as the father of German-Texan immigration. Oscar Haas records Margaretha Decker Ulrich and Betty Abbenthern Hole-kamp as the first two white women who crossed the Guadalupe.[1] Mrs. Ulrich's husband was the wagonmaster of the first train of settlers to New Braunfels, and Mrs. Holekamp rode horseback at the side of Prince Solms.

From the narrative and biographical material available on early pioneer women in Texas, folklorist Beverly Stoeltje defines three basic images: (1) the refined lady who could not adjust to the hardships of the frontier and died, went back to where she came from, or went mad; (2) the "backwoods belle," a helpmate for man "who could accomplish fantastic deeds involving strength and capability and [who] had the ability to establish informal elements of institutionalization, in particular the family"; and (3) the bad woman, found outside the boundaries of society and associated with sex and sin.[2] Of these three images our concept of the German-Texan pioneer woman generally falls within the parameters of the "backwoods belle" and helpmate. She exemplifies Barbara Welter's four cardinal virtues of "true womanhood": piety, purity, submissiveness, and domesticity.[3] For this reason, if for no other, Hedwig Schroeter's Trude becomes more interesting, because she breaks the image, so to speak, even if only to a modest degree. Through her we have cause to wonder about the validity of frontier images of women molded and nurtured by male writers.

Scholarly attention devoted to this in no way unique but nevertheless neglected aspect of German-American and German-Texan literature and culture has approximately paralleled the attention devoted to German-American studies in general: it has progressed from the slightly illegitimate through the back door of ethnic and sociolinguistic studies into a marginally acceptable area of our discipline. Certainly the celebration of the three-hundredth anniversary of the founding of the first German settlement on American soil has done much to raise scholarly as well as public awareness of meaningful and valid research

[1] Oscar Haas, *History of New Braunfels and Comal County, Texas, 1844–1946* (Austin: Hart Graphics, 1968), p. 23.

[2] Beverly J. Stoeltje, "'A Helpmate for Man Indeed': The Image of the Frontier Woman," in *Women and Folklore*, ed. Claire R. Farrer (Austin: University of Texas Press, 1975), pp. 33, 40.

[3] Ibid., p. 31.

terrain. However, *Auslandsdeutschtum* (German studies abroad) has
yet a peripheral ring in the Federal Republic of Germany. When I recently asked one of the editors of a new multivolume treatment of German literature whether German literature abroad might be included,
my question was met with outright disbelief and bemused demurral.
Few serious scholars can afford to waste their effort on the peripheral.
That, however, is the situation in Germany. We, on the other hand,
cannot afford to ignore an eventful, relevant, and noteworthy portion
of our own unique literary, linguistic, and cultural heritage, particularly when that portion is situated in our own back forty.

Publications such as the new format of the *Yearbook of German-
American Studies* and recent symposia do much to remove the stigma
of dilettantism and triviality. Other relatively new organizational structures also lend support to the exploration of this crosscultural or interdisciplinary topography, where we often find ourselves either alone or
in similarly questionable, but increasingly acceptable, company. The
Society for the Study of the Multi-Ethnic Literature of the United
States (MELUS) publishes a journal with refreshing new perspectives
and thematic concerns (one issue is devoted to ethnic women writers).
Women in German (WiG) promotes feminist scholarship in German literary and cultural studies. WiG lacks a scholarly publication but is host
to an effective annual conference.

Women in German brings us to a success story quite in contrast
to the slow ascendance of German-American studies: women's studies
have flourished in the United States during the past ten years. Since
1973, when 78 programs were first listed in the *Publications of the
Modern Language Association*, academic acceptance, based certainly
upon political expedience, advanced the number of women's-studies
programs in the United States to 334 in 1982 and 432 in 1983. Most of
these programs are interdisciplinary, but it is not clear to what degree
ethnic boundaries are considered in them.

To examine the immigrant experience not only through an idio-
syncratic national, that is, German, perspective but also through the
specific and divergent perspective of the immigrant woman or her descendant leads the researcher into what might at first glance seem to be
a poorly defined field of inquiry. Yet until such research is undertaken,
immigrant experience remains only half visible, an important constitu-
ent of the development of Texas remaining unexplored, nearly inac-

cessible. The tools of exploration are at hand; they are interdisciplinary and overlap the traditional areas of history, anthropology, folklore, sociology, literature, and language. What we propose, however, is a preliminary study, a kind of methodological experiment, rewarding as much for its perspective as for its findings.

A strong case can be made for approaching the subject of ethnic women through language, for it has been pointed out that language is the tip of an intersubjective iceberg, the husk of a living fruit, the most sensitive and efficient means of expressing and communicating thoughts and feelings among members of a human community.[4] Through language we learn of humanity, its products, and the symbols used and left behind. Virginia Woolf said, "If you consider any great figure of the past, . . . you will find that she is an inheritor as well as an originator."[5] A rendering of ourselves is transferred from one generation to another by means of language.[6] What women transfer from one generation differs in some degree from the associated cultural apparatus that denotes what we generally perceive as mainstream immigrant adjustment and assimilation processes. Does this cultural transfer lend itself to closer scrutiny?

It is our belief that such scrutiny from the salient focal point of the narratives of the women themselves may lead to fruitful insights and better understanding of the so-called "immigrant experience" and may shed light on both social and literary aspects of that experience:

> The growing body of studies on the language use of women in a variety of settings and cultural groups provides convincing evidence that differences will exist in the speech of men and women in every social group. From other perspectives, sociologists and anthropologists have observed that men and women have different roles and life experiences within their social groups all over the world, though these experiences and roles may differ from society to society. . . . We need now to formulate hypotheses about the connection between the kinds of life experiences available to women and the kinds of language use they will exhibit.[7]

---

[4]Victor Turner, Introduction to *Celebration: Studies in Festivity and Ritual*, ed. Victor Turner (Washington, D.C.: Smithsonian Institution Press, 1982), p. 19.

[5]Virginia Woolf, *A Room of One's Own* (New York: Harcourt Brace Jovanovich, 1929), p. 113.

[6]Turner, Introduction, p. 19.

[7]Patricia C. Nichols, "Women in Their Speech Communities," in *Women and Language in Literature and Society*, ed. Sally McConnel-Ginet, Ruth Borker, and Nelly Furman (New York: Praeger, 1980), p. 141.

Still, language and life experiences of immigrant women fall outside the usual boundaries of our attention. German-American scholars have continued to concentrate on the "forefathers" and mainstream themes, that is, historical, political, theological, literary, and sociological patterns, with an occasional excursion into a "significant" feminine figure, a Mathilde Franziska Anneke, a Molly Pitcher, a Maria Augusta von Trapp, or an Elisabet Ney, by means of a biography or critical interpretation. These are figures so legendary that they can scarcely be overlooked. Heinz Kloss, in his *Research Possibilities in the German-American Field*,[8] originally published in 1936–37, may not be faulted for overlooking the German-American woman in her speech community as a viable research area. More recent treatments, however, continue to overlook the gender-specific aspects of our topic. At least one study has unearthed (one has the impression quite by accident) complex language variations of German speakers in North America, with provisions for gender-specific variations. Kurt Rein, in his investigation of dialect use in the Hutterite colonies of the Dakotas and Manitoba, found that women and children speak what he designates as "Basic Hutterite" whereas men speak "Standard Hutterite" and may acquire "Preacher's Hutterite," depending on their activity in church and community.[9] Life experiences available to women connect with the kind of language they use. The fundamental choice is the object of inquiry. If Germanists are slow to respond to this challenging choice, scholars in related fields are inclined to welcome it.

The narratives of our grandmothers make up the history of daily life, an intimate view of community, familiar patterns, unfamiliar obstacles, small triumphs, defeats. Perhaps the best, certainly the most significant, recent work derived from authentic narrative sources is Joanna Stratton's *Pioneer Women*, published in 1981.[10] This work organizes and interprets a collection of memoirs of eight hundred Kan-

---

[8] Heinz Kloss, *Research Possibilities in the German-American Field*, ed. and trans. La Vern J. Rippley (Hamburg: Buske Verlag, 1980).

[9] Paul Schach, "Some Approaches to the Study of German Dialects in America," in *Occasional Papers of the Society for German-American Studies*, ed. La Vern J. Rippley and Steven M. Benjamin, no. 10, Papers from the Saint Olaf Symposium on German-Americans (Morgantown, W.Va: West Virginia University, 1980), pp. 101–102; Kurt Rein, "German Dialects in Anabaptist Colonies," in *Languages in Conflict*, ed. Paul Schach (Lincoln: University of Nebraska Press, 1980), pp. 107, 108.

[10] Joanna L. Stratton, *Pioneer Women* (New York: Simon and Schuster, 1981).

sas women gathered by Stratton's grandmother and later found in her attic. In Texas we have an abundance of biographies by women—memoirs, collections, letters, artifacts, narratives, stories, and supportive materials that provide ample raw material for review and analysis. Women's interests during the past decade or so have delivered at least three published accounts that include German-Texan women:

1. Annie Doom Pickrell's *Pioneer Women in Texas* is a 1970 reprint of a 1929 collection of biographies "compiled by descendants or friends, . . . a tribute to the feminine strength which supported the masculine determination to settle the West," containing essays on Rosa von Roeder and Elsie Petri.[11]

2. Ann Fears Crawford and Crystal Sasse Ragsdale's *Women in Texas: Their Lives, Their Experiences, Their Accomplishments* has a focus on success, offering the advantage of including not just pioneer women but today's leaders, e.g., Lorene Rogers, Liz Carpenter, and Lady Bird Johnson.[12] German-Texan women included are Louisa Ervendberg, Rosa von Roeder Kleberg, and Elisabet Ney. The introduction to Rosa von Roeder Kleberg illustrates the book's main concern: "She personified the work ethic inherent on the Texas frontier and proved a helpmate to her husband and an inspiration to her children and grandchildren, causing her husband to comment that marrying Rosa was the best act of his life."[13]

3. Crystal Sasse Ragsdale's *The Golden Free Land*, subtitled *The Reminiscences and Letters of Women on an American Frontier*, is the largest and, for us, one of the most important collections, since it deals entirely with Geman-Texan women of the mid-nineteenth century.[14] Some of these documents were originally published in German but appear here without exception in English through translations made by descendants and historians. Both complete and excerpted selections are preceded by an introductory paragraph giving biographical but little interpretative material.

[11]Annie Doom Pickrell, ed., *Pioneer Women in Texas* (Austin: Jenkins, 1970).
[12]Ann Fears Crawford and Crystal Sasse Ragsdale, *Women in Texas: Their Lives, Their Experiences, Their Accomplishments* (Burnet, Tex.: Eakin, 1982).
[13]Ibid., p. 75.
[14]Crystal Sasse Ragsdale, ed., *The Golden Free Land: The Reminiscences and Letters of Women on an American Frontier* (Austin: Landmark Press, 1976).

In addition to these anthologies we find additional resources in the production of German-Texan women writers. Indeed, the definitive critical work devoted to German-Texan literature was written by Selma Metzenthin-Raunick, a poet and creative writer herself, whose works were published in Germany and in the *Austin Wochenblatt*, the *Neu-Braunfelser Zeitung*, and the *Freie Presse für Texas*. Mrs. Raunick, whose two-volume work, *Deutsche Schriften in Texas*, published in 1934 and 1936, lists no less than nineteen women writers, with major contributions by Emma Murck Altgelt; Ottilie Fuchs Goeth; Louise Romberg Fuchs; Caroline Romberg Fuchs; Hedwig Schroeter; and the most significant, productive, and problematic, Clara Matthäi Palacios Reyes.[15] These women writers contributed in large measure to the evaluation by Robert Bishoff in his essay of 1983 on German-American literature:

> In the nineteenth century . . . at least two other significant bodies of German-American literature developed. Each had its origins in circumstances distinctly different from those of the early northeastern immigrant experience, and each produced a literature that at times diverged considerably from that of nineteenth-century English-American literature. For the sake of simplicity, we can label these two literary countertraditions Texas German-American literature and Midwestern German-American literature.[16]

Since 1936 the list of German-Texan women writers has grown and includes not only the descendants of the "grandmothers" mentioned by Raunick—Minetta Altgelt Goyne, Irma Goeth Guenther, Miriam York, Elizabeth Lehmann, Marjorie von Rosenberg, and Flora von Roeder—who, to be sure, write in English—but also a new contingent made up of postwar immigrants—Lisa Kahn, Christa Carvajal, and Elke Ditges—who write in German. The duality of ongoing language traditions presents yet another issue in considering the women as purveyors of German-Texan culture.

Intrinsic to any tradition that spans several generations, grandmothers to granddaughters, is a difficulty of identifying what a

---

[15] Selma Metzenthin-Raunick, *Deutsche Schriften in Texas*, 2 vols. (San Antonio: Freie Presse für Texas, 1934–36).

[16] Robert Bishoff, "German-American Literature," in *Ethnic Perspectives in American Literature*, ed. Robert J. Di Pietro and Edward Ifkovic (New York: Modern Language Association of America, 1983), p. 52.

German-Texan is, to say nothing of what a German-Texan woman is. We randomly and happily mingle descendants of prerevolution (Texas Revolution) immigrants, antebellum immigrants, late nineteenth-century arrivals, and more recent migrants, made up of, among others, Germans married to Americans, children of German-American marriages and Germans who have recently become Texan, for Texas is still an immigrant land. It is a triumph of continuity that world views, traditions, the cultural baggage brought along and cherished, except for language, are at least consonant, if not familiar and shared. The recently transplanted German, after an initial period of discovering the somewhat quaint vestiges of her homeland culture here, quite often becomes a leader in the preservation of not German but German-*Texan* culture. Several notable examples of this remarkable phenomenon come immediately to mind: Lisa Kahn, Ingrid Kuehne Kokinda, Anna Thompson, Liselotte Babin, Elke Ditges, and Ingeborg McCoy. Many more could be mentioned.

While we are fortunate to have so many memoirs, letters, and reports written by German-Texan women, we must also keep in mind that these documents are, as Kenneth Boulding calls them, "transcripts" of a culture,[17] communications independent of the communicator, conforming to tradition in the selection of messages. Each "transcript" reveals in some measure the environment in which it was produced. For German-Texan women this environment obtains in the move from Germany to Texas, for the most part to rural Texas at that, which before 1930 presented a more or less uniform, albeit demanding and semifrontier, image. Since that time, however, the culture can be expected to embroider the radical changes that have transformed Texas from a rural to an urban society, increasingly characterized by a looser family structure, a labor base supplied no longer by family but by machines, consolidated schools, modern communication, and rapid transportation—all forces that exert pressure to assimilate, to become more homogeneous and less distinct as a group. Even though the German language is no longer a unifying integer, the "German" search for self-validation or group validation differs from the search of other Texans in subtle but distinct ways. The peculiar conditions of the foundation

[17] Kenneth Boulding, *The Image* (Ann Arbor: University of Michigan Press, 1964), p. 54.

years for German-Texans (see Lich's chapter), their interactions with frontier hardships, a southern manner of living, lasting results of a civil war and two world wars, affirm the distinctive characteristics of the group. Often through a direct oral tradition, a recollection, or a legend, a collection of the world view held by members of the group brings each person to find meaning in a set of particular circumstances. This collective world view often breaks through its own layers as older people reminisce, as something past is made present, as something long disappeared reappears. Through the individual *homo narrans*, in this case perhaps better the *femina narrans*, humankind as storyteller, traditions which may span several generations are discovered; the stories provide a narrative view of the world, of a German-Texan world. Culture in general is, after all, the "stories," the literature, we tell about ourselves.

Incentive to pursue this project came from an experiment with the video camera as a research tool. In 1981 we set about recording authentic, natural, present-day German-Texan culture as it remains in the first German settlements in Texas, the area including Industry, Round Top, Cat Spring, Fayetteville, and New Ulm. The video program made us aware of the radical changes that are in process in the German-Texan communities. It was not directed specifically toward German-Texan women, but women became our principal informants, the *feminae narrantes* of their culture. We became absorbed with the stories we heard and found, to some extent, the rebirth of an ethnic culture, perhaps without the language, but fortified by enduring symbols and metaphors.

II

INGEBORG RUBERG MCCOY

For an introduction to my part of the chapter on the grandmothers' tales I offer a selection from the autobiography *Was Grossmutter Erzählt (What Grandmother Tells)*, by Ottilie Fuchs Goeth.[1] These lines convey both her style and the foregrounding of a metaphor central to

---

[1]Ottilie Fuchs Goeth, *Was Grossmutter Erzählt* (San Antonio: Passing Show Printing, 1915), p. 82–83.

the structural coherence of the text, a metaphor that has become instrumental for my study of the works of the German women in Texas in the nineteenth century:

> Die Zeit geht hin, die alten Sitten und Gebraüche haben sich verändert. Die alten holprigen Wege sind zu bequemen Fahrstrassen geworden, die "Schlitten" haben grossen Wagen Platz gemacht, die Buggies, die "Hacks," machten ihr Escheinen, und nun kommen die Söhre mit ihren lieben Familien aus Austin und San Antonio gar mit Automobilien, schon durch das Telephon im Hause angemeldet. Die Fahrgeschwindigkeit hat zugenommen, die Erde, einst so gross, wird immer kleiner, der Mensch versucht, ein Geisterreich sich zu erzwingen. Graf Zeppelin hat sein Luftschifft erbaut, den Erfolg kennt die Welt. Alles ist in Bewegung, keiner hat mehr das alte Sitzfleisch, auch die beliebten Quilt-Parties gehören fast schon zur Vergangenheit.
>
> Die waren einst unter den Frauen so beliebt. Da kam eine ganze Gesellschaft von Damen, um daran Teil zu nehmen. Männer wurden wenig zugelassen, sie durften allenfalls die Staffage herrichten, aber damit hatte es sein Bewenden. Erst gab es guten Kaffee und Kuchen, was nach dem Kriege ein fast neuer Luxus geworden. Dann setzten sich an der Seite jeder Decke vier oder fünf Damen und nun regten sich die flinken Hände, dass es eine Luft war:
>
> > "Wenn gute Reden sie begleiten,
> > Dann fliesst die Arbeit munter fort."
>
> Und dass es an Gesprächsstoff nicht gefehlt, brauche ich euch nicht zu versichern. Die Hauswirtschaft, der Garten, Kindererziehung, oder auch Litteratur und Kunst wurden besprochen. Die Schrecknisse des Bürgerkrieges, Indianergefahren gaben interessante Abwechslung. Wie die Ausgaben zu verkürzen, aber nicht den Brotkorb und die Bequemlichkeit. Wie gesunde und schmackhafte Gerichte zu bereiten. Waren wir doch aus aller Herren Ländern und versuchten wir Frauen, eine von der andern zu lernen. War ein Klavier zu Hause, so wurde derweil auch musiziert und gesungen. Da rückten die "Gegenparteien" in freundlichem Wetteifer sich einander rasch näher, ehe der Nachmittag zu Ende, war eine Steppdecke fertig geworden, und wir hatten nebenbei einen amüsanten Tag gehabt.—Abendgesellschaften gab es zu wenig, die Wege waren noch zu weit, und der kommende Tag brachte ja auch seinen Dienst und meistens schwerer als der vorhergehende. So brachen auch die "Quilt-Parties" frühzeitig auf, aber doch füllten sich die Koffer mit warmen Decken. Fast scheint es mir, als ob mit zunehmender Kultur auch die Kälte zugenommen. Wenn so ein "norther" durchs Land fegt, ruht es sich ganz behaglich unter Grossmutter und Mutters warmen Decken.

[Time passes, the old customs and practices have changed. The old bumpy paths have become comfortable roads, the "sleds" have given way to the larger wagons, the buggies, "hacks," have made their appearance, and now the sons even come with their dear families from Austin and San Antonio by automobile, their arrival already announced at home by phone. Speed of travel has quickened, the world, once so large, is growing ever smaller, man tries to carve out a realm of ideas. The Earl Zeppelin built his airship, the whole world knows of its success. Everything's in flux, no one still has the old *sitzfleisch*, even the popular quilt parties are now nearly a thing of the past.

They used to be so popular among women. An entire group of women would come to take part. Men were seldom permitted, at most they could help prepare the skeins, but that was all. First there was good coffee and cake, nearly a new luxury after the war. Then four or five women would sit down on each side of the quilt, and the hands would fly back and forth, you'd like to think the wind was blowing:

> "If pleasant talk can there be shared,
> Then work will pass without a care."

But that there was no lack of things to talk about, I need not assure you. Keeping house, the garden, rearing the children, or even literature and art were discussed. The horrors of the Civil War, danger from Indians made for an interesting change. How to cut expenses, but not skimp on food or comfort. How to prepare healthful and tasty dishes. We were, after all, from all corners of man's earth, and we women tried to learn from one another. If a piano was in the house, then we would make music and sing. Then, in a friendly competitive spirit, the two "teams" would quickly come closer together, before the afternoon was through, a quilt had been finished, and we'd had a pleasant day at the same time.—There were too few evening groups, distances were still too great, and, of course, the following day brought its chores, and most of the time more difficult than the day before. Thus the "quilt parties" would break up early, but still the suitcases became filled with warm covers. It almost seems to me that the more culture we get, the colder it gets too. When one of those "northers" sweeps through the land, it's nice and cozy under grandmother's and mother's warm covers.]

Since exhibits, museum installations, and catalogs of German Americana always contain quilts as part of the material culture, we have come to accept this textile as such a commonplace artifact that we tend to forget the degree to which the ritual of quilting ordered the experience of quilters such as those whom Ottilie Fuchs Goeth so beautifully describes in this passage. The metaphor of the quilt as physical and emotional warmth, protecting against the blustering cold of an increasingly technological society, pronounces the value of traditional cultural performances and artifacts and, as "text-ile," equates the ordering of old and new bits of cloth into an artistic pattern with the quilters' ability to function as *bricoleuses*, who collect and retain elements and signs of traditional culture to recombine them with newly encountered cultural facets, thus constantly fashioning their own order of cultural experience. The true *bricoleur*, Claude Levi-Strauss explains,[2] speaks not only with things but also through the medium of things, just as Goeth relates to us the meaning of her tale through the metaphor of the quilt. The textile-textual interstices of this passage and of the other tales of the grandmothers suggest that the women in the German settlements in Texas in the nineteenth century were the true purveyors of German culture.

Since this statement flies in the face of the long-held and cherished view that men were the bearers of German culture—even to the extent that the schoolteachers were generally men—I wish to broaden the perspective of this belief by briefly describing the current status of scholarship regarding the texts, exploring the value of the symbolic form in folk culture, explaining the formulaic nature of the tales, and, finally, delineating the women's role as cultural *bricoleuses*.

Mary Daly recently commented that women, commonly accepted as spinners and weavers, have traditionally been associated with textiles in the etymologically original sense of the Latin word *texere*, meaning "to weave," but that women have seldom been connected with *texts*, a word which also derives from the Latin verb.[3] Hence we regard with pride the unusual collection of texts—letters, interviews, memoirs, autobiographies—originated by German women in Texas during or about the time of the early settlements, texts which are readily available thanks to the love and labor expended on the originals by descendant women, in particular Irma Goeth Guenther, who in 1982 published her second, enlarged translation and edition of Goeth's autobiography,[4] and Crystal Sasse Ragsdale, who is well known for her col-

---

[2] Claude Levi-Strauss, *The Savage Mind* (Chicago: University of Chicago Press, 1968), p. 21.

[3] Mary Daly, *Gyn/Ecology: The Metaethics of Radical Feminism* (Boston: Beacon Press, 1978), p. 4.

[4] Ottilie Fuchs Goeth, *Memoirs of a Texas Pioneer Grandmother*, trans. Irma Goeth Guenther (Burnet, Tex.: Eakin Press, 1982).

lection of translated texts entitled *The Golden Free Land*, published in 1976.[5] Although the original works, Goeth's memoirs, for example, were accessible as early as 1915, no comprehensive study of them has ever been undertaken. And so, to this day the tales of the German grandmothers in Texas remain testimony to the forgotten half of the German immigration. Unquestionably these texts have literary value, if for no other reason than that autobiographical and epistolary genres represent traditional literary forms. But the tales are even more important in the context of folkloric modes, akin to oral histories.

Mary Douglas cites the conspicuous lack of scholarly commitment to the understanding and study of such symbols and, in fact, worries about the general absence of commitment to common symbols. She considers this situation symptomatic of the practice in our contemporary culture of rejecting the implications of ritual and its accompanying symbols, despite the fact that "symbols are the only means of communication. They are the only means of expressing value; the main instruments of thought; the only regulators of experience."[6] Her study relates the initial attempt to understand and interpret the symbolic codes of the texts. The metaphor of the quilt parties, described by Goeth, forms the type of cultural symbol which, according to Victor Turner, implies the crystallization of large-scale processes going on for a long time in a society.[7] The women's ritual of quilting delivers a message about continuity in addition to its other symbolic messages.[8] Because of its rich symbolic value Goeth's passage provides keys to the message of the tales of the grandmothers. These texts, like the society from which they sprang and like the lives of their authors, contain their own interpretations: one has only to learn how to gain access to them.

For reading the symbols in passages like the one from Goeth's memoirs, I apply two types of analysis, linguistic and structural, a strategy developed in exemplary fashion by Susan Wittig in *Stylistic and Narrative Structures in the Middle English Romances*.[9] Not only has

---

[5] Crystal Sasse Ragsdale, *The Golden Free Land* (Austin: Landmark Press, 1976).

[6] Mary Douglas, *Natural Symbols* (New York: Vintage Books, 1973), pp. 19, 68.

[7] Victor Turner, "Comments, and Conclusions," in *The Reversible World: Symbolic Inversion in Art and Society*, ed. Barbara A. Babcock (Ithaca, N.Y.: Cornell University Press, 1978), p. 288.

[8] Barbara Meyerhoff, *Number Our Days* (New York: Simon and Schuster, 1978), p. 86.

[9] Susan Wittig, *Stylistic and Narrative Structures in the Middle English Romances* (Austin: University of Texas Press, 1978).

this formidable work furnished a highly applicable model for our own interpretative endeavors, but Susan Wittig has personally generated a number of spiritual breakthroughs—epiphanies, that is,—for me without which this study would not have progressed. Thus, I would like to express my deep gratitude to Wittig at this point.

The grandmothers' tales—I am referring generally to Goeth's autobiography and the texts in Ragsdale's book—are characterized by a pervasive, thematically formulaic structure that may have helped contribute to the neglect of these documents by literary scholars. This stylistic-thematic feature of redundancy is so stereotyped that it suggests consultation and collaboration among the various authors; yet I am quite convinced that such is not the case. Rather, the repeated themes appear to fit the definition of formula works proposed by Milman Parry,[10] employed successfully in the study of oral formulaic works, particularly in recent years in folklore,[11] and applied and extended by Wittig to the written formulaic narratives of the Middle English romances. The formula is a composite structural unit which can appear in small-scale textual as well as large-scale thematic forms. As a further extension of Wittig's model for the purpose of this argument and to convey the formulaic nature of the tales, I will list the redundant themes only as they were derived inductively from the texts themselves, an approach that finds increasing use for interpreting folkloric expressive modes.[12] I do not enumerate the themes as they might occur sequentially in the tales; in fact, the authors arrange them quite arbitrarily. Also, some of the longer texts incorporate additional, but again redundant, themes. The following themes appear to be the prescribed code, so to speak, for most of the tales:

1. The chronicle of the journey by boat or ship—the awesome and frequently awful voyage across the Atlantic.

---

[10] Milman Parry, "Studies in the Epic Technique of Oral Verse-making," *Harvard Studies in Classical Philology* 41 (1930): 73–197.

[11] Albert Lord, *The Singer of Tales* (Cambridge, Mass.: Harvard University Press, 1960).

[12] Alan Dundes, "From Etic to Emic Units in the Structural Study of Folktales," *Journal of American Folklore* 75 (1966): 95–105; Joe Graham, "The *Caso*: An Emic Genre of Folk Narrative," in *And Other Neighborly Names*, ed. Richard Bauman and Roger D. Abrahams (Austin: University of Texas Press, 1981), pp. 11–43.

2. The description of the port of Galveston—the dismal reality of the envisioned magical West.

3. The report about the land—its incredible vastness and emptiness—and the joy about the smallest bit of vegetation, not to mention trees.

4. The version of the wagon trek—the cursing teamsters, the knee-deep mud, and the icy northers breaking into the dream of a climate like southern Italy.

5. The narrative about the one-room house—the shack with neither floor nor ceiling.

6. The complaint about the primitive housekeeping—the strange foods, the outcry about the lack or the poor quality of milk and butter to accompany the corn bread baked in pots.

7. The account of the kitchen garden—the incredible toil and the amazing crops.

8. The horror story about the war against Mexico or the Civil War—the flight, the losses, the deaths.

9. The yarn about appearances or attacks by the Indians—the encounters with indigenous owners of the land.

Longer texts extend the formulaic plots by adding genealogies as well as descriptions of reasons and preparations for the emigration, or enlarge the core by adding yarns about childrens' marriages, grandchildren, and relatives, thus supplying another strand of descent. Goeth's text, incidentally, is the most inclusive of all such themes: Grandmother Ottilie embeds herself firmly in the thick crown of the ancestral tree of a traditional, cultured German family.

Immediately upon discovering the formulaic thematics of the tales, one must raise the question, What underlying deep structure has generated such redundancies? Wittig concludes her long investigation into the value system that underlies formulaic styles, from the heroic epics to the lyrics of popular songs, by remarking that formulaic language—be it small, syntactical elements or larger thematic cores—is psychologically a highly efficient means of conveying a message as opposed to imparting a large amount of diverse information. Such a message is communicated on a level below conscious attention and as a "powerful social source supports, reinforces, and perpetuates the social beliefs and customs held by the culture." Moreover, such a message contains an "implicit faith in the already established workings of the world on the social, the political, and the natural levels, an unquestioning assumption of regularity and stability and unfailing order in life but at the same time reduces the opportunity for innovation and change."[13]

To claim that the deep-structural message of texts written by German immigrant women about the immigration experience projects— albeit on an unconscious level—a firm grip on sociocultural traditions appears to fly in the face of the seemingly inherent cause for emigrating, that is, to bring about change. And, indeed, male German settlers, as exemplified by Friedrich Ernst, the first permanent German settler in Texas, arrived with a new, modernizing, change-oriented, instrumental world view. Ernst, immediately after his arrival, began a cottage industry in cigar making, marketing the product to various places, including Houston.[14] Shortly thereafter he founded a town named Industry for which he advertised, like an astute real-estate businessman, the availability of fine city lots.[15] Dona Reeves-Marquardt and I were able to document a contemporary view about the change-oriented mind of the cofounder of the first settlement, Charles Fordtran. His granddaughter, Fairy Wittner, of Industry, answered the question how, in her opinion, her grandfather would have liked all the changes occurring in Industry these days: "Oh, he would like it. He really would. Our daddies, they liked change, they were for new stuff. Have you ever heard of a Crit? Well, we had the first new Crit in town."

Contrary to this instrumental, change-affecting world view of the men, the German women were tradition-bound. We also need to remember at this juncture that the women generally did not make decisions about emigration but rather came along with their fathers or husbands. And Ottilie Goeth, of course, leaves no doubt in our minds what she thought of the kind of technological changes which she called "increasing culture" and which, in her mind, increased the cold. A close reading in the interstices of her memoirs, in effect, makes it abundantly clear that her tale has one major didactic function: to persuade her descendants to continue the traditions of the German culture, including the use of the German language, and to realize that such continuity of *Deutschtum* evolves from the continued existence of

---

[13] Wittig, *Stylistic and Narrative Structures*, p. 45.

[14] Detlev Dunt, *Reise nach Texas* (Bremen: n.p., 1834), p. 13.

[15] Friedrich Ernst, "Ausruf" (MS, Barker History Center, Austin).

a close family. Clearly Goeth's representative tale confirms Wittig's conclusion that texts characterized by formulaic stylistics convey the values of traditional belief systems.

Wittig further contends that any formula that contains such codes
of values will itself be preserved by the community, often past the
point when it ceases to hold importance for the whole group.[16] In this
respect it becomes significant that in several oral histories collected
from contemporary German Texan women a few of the formulaic themes
enumerated above reemerge: the lineages of descent, the descriptions
of gardens, the stories that their grandmothers or great-aunts told
about the voyage, the small cabins, the lack of milk and butter. It was
as if these women, who are living in a rest home, had read the grandmothers' tales; yet they had not and did not even know of the existence
of these texts. As we continue to collect and study such oral histories,
we will probably substantiate the thesis of the formula characteristic of
the women's tales and the inherent deep-structural, traditional sociocultural value system.

The syntagmatic study of the formulaic strategies of the grandmothers' tales needs now to proceed by use of a paradigmatic coordi-
nate; that is, we must go beyond the linearity of the surface order to
a deeper structural examination in which the infrastructure of formal
oppositions is revealed in synchronic organization. This applies the
model established by Claude Levi-Strauss for the exploration of mythic
tales. I propose, by employing this method, that the major substructural
binary pattern underlying the tales, which is particularly noticeable in
Goeth's text, is that of nature and culture; that, as a remarkable configu-
ration of vitality, this pattern is present in countless surface homologies
throughout the texts under study; that the women emerge as the mediators between the poles of nature and culture; and, finally, that in
this mediating role they are true *bricoleuses* whose creative objects
and texts represent the nonverbal as well as verbal orderings of German cultural experience.

The conflict between nature and culture constitutes the central
theme of the work of Levi-Strauss,[17] who has acknowledged his debt for
this conceptual foundation of his studies to Rousseau, who was a master of the passage from nature to culture, from affectivity to intellectu-

---

[16] Wittig, *Stylistic and Narrative Structures*, p. 45.
[17] See Gisela Steinwachs, *Mythologie des Surrealismus oder die Rückverwandlung von Kultur in Natur* (Neuwied: Luchterhand, 1971).

ality. Perhaps the fact that Ottilie Fuchs grew up in an educational climate based on the traditional classical-romantic themes of Rousseauism and German nature idealism can account for the abundant textual configurations in her work that focus on the nature-culture binary poles and the mediation between them.[18]

The first example demonstrating this functional interrelationship of nature and culture occurs on the first page of Goeth's memoirs, where she juxtaposes the description of the family's garden in Germany and its delicious varieties of fruit with an account of the family's sparse first Christmas in Texas. From this passage we obtain the following Levi-Strauss–type formula to account for the interrelationship of nature and culture and the various homologies for each pole: garden = fruit = nature > Christmas = ceremony = lights = cookies = culture. Goeth even puts emphasis on the kinds of cookies baked by the women, the mediators of nature and culture, cookies that were of "braunem Molassenteigh" (brown molasses dough), not even dough made with refined—that is, more cultured—sugar.

The nature-culture infrastructure appears in an amazing number of surface homologies throughout Goeth's as well as the other texts. One example, which has haunted my imagination ever since I read the lines for the first time, is related by Friedrich Ernst's wife, Louise Ernst Stöhr, who came from a very cultured family.[19] She relates in her narrative: "Da sassen wir nun am Rand der Zivilisation, gerade westlich wohnten die Indianer. So lebten wir ganz allein in der Wildnis, es schien sogar einsam zu sein für die Indianer. Diese brachten oft unsere weggelaufenen Pferde und Kühe zurück für ein bisschen Milch und Butter" ("There we sat, at the edge of civilization; just to the west lived the Indians. And so we lived all alone in the wilderness; it even seemed lonely for the Indians. They would bring back horses and cows that strayed away, in exchange for milk and butter").[20]

Imagine Mrs. Ernst holding out to an Indian, who surely represented to her the epitome of nature and wilderness, that important

[18] Ingeborg McCoy, "Was Grossmutter Erzählt: Memoirs of a German Woman Settler in Texas" (Paper read at the Annual Meeting of the Southern Conference of the Modern Language Association, October, 1983).

[19] Personal communication from Miriam York, Giddings, Tex., October, 1982.

[20] Louise Ernst Stöhr, "Die erste deutsche Frau in Texas," in Der Deutsche Pioneer (Galveston, Tex., 1884).

vestige of culture on the frontier, the precious butter that had been processed from its raw, natural state with much labor. How courageous this woman appears in her role as mediator of nature and culture: a true heroine of the frontier experience. Her gift of butter signifies her as homology of the culture pole; her act brings the cultural elements into a functional relationship with the elements of the nature pole of which the Indian is the respective homology.

Time and again the tales contain the textual configurations of how the women structured the similarities and differences in both the natural and the cultural realms, respectively, how they established connections between these two orders, and how this ordering happened by means of objects that, according to Levi-Strauss, are not just objects but, in effect, messages.[21] This kind of ordering of experiences into new arrangements is characteristic of *bricoleurs*: through the medium of objects that equated message the women were the mediators between nature and culture.[22]

Levi-Strauss maintains that there are analogies between mythical thought on the theoretical and *bricolage* on the practical plane and that artistic creation lies midway between science and these two forms of activity.[23] The artistic creation of the *bricoleuses* as displayed in the symbolic passage from Goeth's text is, of course, the quilt, Goeth's multifaceted message about the increasing imbalance between the warmth of mediated nature and the increasing cold of unmediated technological culture. It is significant for our topic that the German women were mediator *bricoleuses* not only by way of their objects but also by way of their texts, through not only nonverbal but also verbal messages. This important fact differentiates our group of women from those Jewish women whom Barbara Meyerhoff, in her study of the elderly members of the Aliyah Center, identified as culture bearers also, but in the manner of a domestic religion and culture—Yiddishkeit, in fact—or Robert Redfield's Little Tradition.[24]

[21] Peter Worsley, "Groote Eylandt Totemism and Le Totémisme aujourd'hui," in *The Structural Study of Myth and Totemism*, ed. Edmund Leach (London: Tavistock, 1967), pp. 141–60.

[22] I am deeply appreciative of Susan Wittig's comments regarding the parallel between the mediator and the *bricoleur*.

[23] Levi-Strauss, *The Savage Mind*, p. 30.

[24] Meyerhoff, *Number Our Days*, p. 256; Robert Redfield, *Peasant Society and Culture* (Chicago: University of Chicago Press, 1965), p. 42.

We have come full circle, all the pieces of the argument in place; but just in case we are still not convinced of the *bricoleuses* having been the true culture purveyors, I would like to relate the following thought-provoking episode from the time of the early German settlements in Texas: the commune called Bettina, founded by a famous group of highly literate, highly cultured Forty-eighters. This communistic settlement did not allow women as members; it lasted less than a year. The entire incident has never been satisfactorily explored and explained; a new and different perspective is needed to accomplish this. I quote from Ottilie Fuchs again, who does not in these lines refer directly to the Bettina episode but indirectly does address the phenomenon of the high-culture German male on the frontier in Texas as she describes her father, the famous Pastor Fuchs, in his attempts at cultivating on the edge of the *Urwald* ("primal forest"):

> Es war im Frühling, 1846, als wir nach Cat Spring gekommen, und da hiess es denn nun auch gleich, Hand ans Werk zu legen. Ein bescheidener Pflug, von einem Joch Ochsen, gezogen war zur Hand, wie denn die Farm schon vorher besiedelt. Wie mochte dem Gelehrten hinterm Pfluge zu Mute sein, wie ungeschick und schwerfällig ihm alles von der Hand ging, die wohl den Violinbogen und die leichtere Gartenschere zu handhaben gewusst. Aber diese Ochsen, dieser Pflug! Was nützte alle Geometrie, sechs Sprachen und Logarithmen, es ging nicht.

> [It was in the spring, 1846, when we arrived at Cat Spring, and then the first order of the day was to get to work. A modest plow, pulled by a team of oxen, was there, since the farm had been lived on before. How must the scholar have felt behind this plow, how awkward and difficult everything was for him, who otherwise could manage the violin bow and the lighter garden shears. But these oxen, this plow! What good was geometry, six languages, and logarithms? It was no use.]

In conclusion, we have argued that the life-sustaining force of the German culture in Texas in the nineteenth century, the purveyors of German life-style and cultural values, were, in fact, the German women.

JOSEPH WILSON

Texas German and Other American Immigrant Languages: Problems and Prospects

"ER managet die Show, er ordert die Tickets, er chartert einen Jet"—Texas German?[1] No, modern standard German, as found in the magazine *Stern*, but in such common usage as to need no citation of place found. In the use of English words there is no difference in principle between standard German and Texas German; both use English words, and in much the same way. The only difference is that Texas German often uses different English words from those used in standard German; the "German Germans" hear English words where they would not use them, and so they are tempted to deride Texas German, conveniently forgetting that they themselves in other situations also use many English words (or even French words—one can imagine a Texas German saying "Meine Subscription ist abgelaufen," whereupon the German laughs and says, "Don't you know the German word is not *Subscription* but *Abonnement*?).

The crucial problem of the Texas-German language and of Texas-German language research has always been the lack of appreciation and esteem. Since most Germanists deal with great literature written in standard German, such an attitude is easy to understand. Let us, however, consider two parallels that may help us appreciate the necessity of collecting even the seemingly most trivial information about Texas German.

The Gothic language is extremely important for our knowledge of the history of German and English. We have a Gothic New Testament from about A.D. 500, and thus we know Gothic from that early period

[1] "Texas German" is used here to mean the spoken language and the written language of the general language population. The language of the pulpit, of books, and of newspapers is grammatically correct, avoids anglicisms, and so is scarcely distinguishable from standard German.

fairly well. We know almost nothing about Gothic of later periods, though there are indications that isolated groups in the Crimea spoke the language until the seventeenth century. In 1560, more than a thousand years after the heyday of the Goths, the Flemish ambassador at Constantinople found two men who still spoke Gothic, though only poorly. He asked them to say various things in Gothic and put together a list of about a hundred words and a few phrases. No one was very much interested at the time, but that list is now known as one of the most precious documents ever written. It is all we have to show that the Gothic language survived more than a thousand years in the Crimea, and it shows how the language changed in the course of that thousand years. Fifty years from now there will be no speakers of Texas German left, and monolingual Texans will find it hard to believe that German was a living language in Texas, spoken by hundreds of thousands for two hundred years. Every sample of Texas German that we can collect now, while Texas German is still alive, will be precious in the future.

The second parallel concerns the Wendish-Germans of east-central Texas, who have been among the most persistent in continuing the use of the German language. The Wends had a unique linguistic situation, which makes the study of their German and Wendish exceptionally interesting. They were an old Slavic minority group in Germany that had been undergoing assimilation into the German majority for hundreds of years. When they came to Texas in 1854, they were bilingual in Wendish, which they used mostly as a home and church language, and German, which they used for most writing and for documents and other more "official" purposes. In the same way that German in Texas has been surrounded by English, and naturally has adopted many English words, Wendish—though basically Slavic and thus very different from German—had for centuries been surrounded by German and similarly adopted many German words. "To console" was *troschtowacz*, from German *trösten*; "to punish" was *schtrafowacz*, from *strafen*; "freedom" was *frejota*; "citizenship" was *birgarstwo*, and so on. In Texas, Wendish continued to be surrounded by German as the Wends maintained their bilingual existence and their intermingling with Germans. Their use of Wendish continued to wane, and their Germanization proceeded until about 1920, after which they spoke German almost exclusively and naturally no longer considered themselves Wends or Wendish-Germans but simply Germans.

The linguistic situation of this group in the years before 1920, when Wendish was still actively spoken alongside German, was consequently unique and interesting. How we now wish that we could turn back the clock to that era when there were still regular Wendish sermons and hundreds of people bilingual in Wendish and German, and many trilingual, as English was added. There would be a wealth of linguistic information to be learned, as well as folklore, superstitions, feelings of nationality, linguistic allegiance, and so on. Unfortunately, almost no one saved any Wendish letters or other examples of ordinary "trivial" language, and today we have almost no materials to show how the common people spoke or wrote Wendish. Of course, we cannot turn back the clock to listen to a Wendish sermon or hear Wendish in community usage. But the clock is still running for German, even though it is the eleventh hour. Texas German is still spoken today, in much the situation of Wendish in 1920: spoken mostly by older people but still in use, with regular church services in German. For now, we can still experience Texas German in a way that in the future we will be able only wistfully to yearn for.

In evaluating Texas German, let us also remember that "good German" and "bad German" are relative terms based on subjective judgment. Even when we are listening to capable and fluent speakers of Texas German, if we expect to hear the German of a person from Berlin, and if we focus our attention not on how much "good" German is being spoken but rather on how many English words are being used or what simplifications of German grammar have been introduced, we may indeed call it "bad German." If, on the other hand, we listen with a positive attitude and realize that the Texas Germans have been away from Germany for more than a hundred years, we can appreciate how large their German vocabulary is and how relatively correct their German grammar.

Refreshingly, many Germans do appreciate these things and do compliment Texas Germans on their German; unfortunately, however, many others do not. With native Germans often ridiculing Texas Germans' speech and their teachers and parents sometimes scolding them, Texas Germans have naturally suffered from lack of appreciation. It is easy to understand why most Texas Germans think that their German is poor and why many people abandoned their home language for English as the simplest expedient. Our educational task is to teach the appreciation of Texas German both to the Texas Germans themselves and to others. In Texas as elsewhere we talk Texas English, not British English or even Boston English. No one expects us to say "cahn't" or "tomahto." We ought to view Texas German similarly and proudly say, "Yes, we know they say *schön* in Germany, but here we say *scheen*."

On the positive side of the ledger we should note (and Texas Germans need to be told) that Texas German is not a dialect but a form of standard German. We need not get into a linguistic dispute about the definition of dialect versus language, but in the common terms of description of types of German, we say, for instance, that Swiss German is a dialect or Bavarian German is a dialect. "Dialect" means a rather radically different form of the language, usually unintelligible to the speaker of the standard language.[2] Texas German is quite intelligible to the speaker of standard German and is not a dialect like Swiss German, Bavarian, or Low German. There are actually three basic types of speech in Germany At one end is standard German, without regional coloration. At the other end is the dialect—Swiss, Bavarian, Low German, and so on. In the middle is what many Germans speak: standard German with regional coloration. Thus Swiss Germans and Bavarians talking together will speak not their dialects but this middle form: modified standard German. Small differences of pronunciation and vocabulary remain, and we can readily identify the one as Swiss and the other as Bavarian, but there is practically no problem of mutual intelligibility. If we compare this with American English regional variants, for example, southern versus northern speech, we note that, by European standards, these regional variants of American English are not dialects but modifications of the standard language: we can hear the regional variations, but there is no serious question of intelligibility. Or, to put it another way, there is no regional form of American English that differs from standard American English as Bavarian dialect differs from standard German. By this generally accepted terminology Texas

[2]Cf. Oskar Bandle, "Soziolinguistische Strukturen in den nordischen Sprachen: Zum Verhältnis von Standard, Regionalsprache und Dialekt," in *Standard und Dialekt, Festschrift für Heinz Rupp*, ed. Heinrich Löffler et al. (Bern: Francke, 1979), p. 218.

German is not a dialect like Bavarian but a modified standard German, that is, standard German with regional coloration.

Texas German thus differs radically from Pennsylvania German, which is basically a German dialect, *Pfälzisch* (Palatinate German), in which even many common household words are different from standard German in a way that is not the case with Texas German.

Texas German starts with a huge stock of everyday German words: *Mann* and *Frau*, *Haus* and *Kind*, *Junge* and *Mädchen*, *Bibel* and *Kirche*, and so on. Its major deviations from standard German can be quickly summarized. First, there is the "unrounding of the umlauts," that is, the pronunciation of *ö* and *ü* as if written *e* and *ie*, respectively, as in *schön* and *müde*. This modification is not due to the influence of English but is a German regionalism (this is the chief "dialectlike" trait of Texas German). In the "eastern focus" of the Texas Germans, that is, in the large German colonies east of Austin, near Giddings and La Grange (which include the Wends), the German *w* is pronounced very similarly to the American *w* (another German regionalism). In all areas of Texas German the dative and genitive cases are understood but not actively used, so that one hears "er geht mit seine Frau" and "sie ist gut zu die Kinder." These modifications, and the use of a considerable number of anglicisms, characterize Texas German. When we consider that practically all other features of German grammar and pronunciation are perfectly maintained—for example, the pronunciation of *ach* and *ich*, the entire system of categorizing the things of the world as *der/die/das*, the verb system, and so on—these few modifications seem very small, which is to say that Texas German seems, to the sympathetic listener, remarkably good.

Aside from Pennsylvania German, which is a special case because of its dialect base, most forms of American German are strikingly alike. Thus the German of Texas is very similar to that of Missouri and Wisconsin. The other forms of American German also unround the umlauts, do not use the dative or genitive, and employ essentially the same anglicisms. As a matter of fact, one of the research problems of Texas German is to determine the differences between the varieties of Texas German and between Texas German and other forms of American German. We must even ask whether we are justified in talking about Texas Geman at all or should simply call it American German.

In regard to the varieties of Texas German, in talking with different Texas German speakers, we again run into the problem of subjective impressions, on the one hand, and the fact, on the other hand, that certain speakers' Texas German may be in isolated instances the product more of their individual home language than of their area of Texas; that is, their speech may show more dialect items because their parents came from a certain German area, than is typical of the area of Texas in which they happen to live. Because of these factors we may hear such diametrically opposed statements (from informants as well as nonlinguist scholars of German) as "Texas German is all the same; there are no area differences" and "They all talk differently, every family has its peculiarities." And both of these differing judgments are partly true: All Texas Germans talk much the same, but there are also minor differences. The problem for the researcher is to sift out the similarities and the differences. The situation is similar in describing American English. We might well say that all Americans talk alike, especially if we are contrasting their speech with that of the British, but we know, of course, that there are general regional differences and sometimes even differences from family to family.

Let us now briefly consider the anglicisms of Texas German. Some of the most widely used are *die Fenz, die Road, die Penne (Schweinepenne, Kuhpenne), der Crop, das Korn, der Paster* ("pasture"), *der Bucket, das Supper, sure (das ist sure wahr), fixen, plenty (wir haben plenty Arbeit), mufen* ("move"). Naturally there are "hybrid compounds," like *Pecanbaum, Storehalter,* and *Butchermesser.* Most of these words were taken up in the first few years in Texas; they represent the categories of new things (mosquitos, pecans), "place-names" in a wide sense (Rabb's Creek, Johnson's Store, and then *creek* and *store* in general), and other words used in contacts with the Anglos. To the uninitiated it may seem that Texas Germans speak a hodgepodge of German and English or that English words are mixed in indiscriminately. This is not at all the case; the use of English words proceeds through a multitude of subconscious rules. A number of different types of anglicisms are used, and there are different uses of anglicisms at the different levels of speech (written language having fewer levels than spoken language, for example). There are older and younger anglicisms, some more Germanized than others, some more accepted than others, some even being taken up as part of the standard language. Words like *Farm, Farmer, Gentleman, Lady,* and *Whiskey* had already entered the German language in Germany before the immigration to Texas. The English words naturally had to be adapted to German grammar: nouns had to have gender (*der/die/das*); adjectives and verbs normally had to have German inflection (*ein pinkes Kleid*; *sie hat Supper gefixt*. English, of course, does the same thing with foreign words; consider *consuls, vetoed, rendezvoused*). Sometimes (*pecans* again) the speaker may not know the German word to use, but often the German word is known: the two may be interchangeable (*Supper/Abenbrot*; *painten/anstreichen*), or the German word may be considered a "book word" or a "better word," while the English word is used in everyday speech (*Fenz [fence]/Zaun, Bucket/Eimer, Creek/Bach*). We must be cautious about labeling any given usage an anglicism; the usage may look English but may turn out to be standard German (*Acker/acre*), German dialect (*Mutt/mud, schmoken/smoke*), French, and so on. Each word demands its own study.

One of the most prevalent mechanisms is the merging of German and English features—in regard to anglicisms the merging of German and English words. If, for a new English word, for example, *mile* or *car*, a similar German word is known, for example, *Meile* (in Germany an old unit of approximately five English miles) or *Karre* (*cart*, sometimes deprecatingly for *car* or *carriage*), the German word will usually take on the English meaning. This process gives rise to yet another category of anglicisms that is much less noticeable than the overt use of English words: the use of standard German words whose meanings have changed. In some of these usages, for example, *Meile*, only the German form is used; in others, such as *Karre/car*, the German form apparently facilitated the understanding and adoption of the English word, and the words have become interchangeable.

When the Texas German says *sie hat ihr ganzes Geld gespent* (*gespendet*), he is not simply using the English word *spend/spent*, but the German word *spenden/gespendet*, meaning "to donate," which has taken on the different but closely related meaning "to spend." In this case *spenden* has become so commonly used in the new sense, "to spend," that it can no longer be used in its less common original sense, "to donate"; consequently, there is no way to say "donate" except by the use of the English word: *sie hat es gedonatet* (or possibly, less directly, *geschenkt* or *gegeben*). The situation is similar with the German word *ringen*, except that here the correspondence between the German and the English words is only that of sound and form (*ring/rang/ rung*; *ringen/rang/gerungen*), not of meaning: the German word means "wrestle" or "struggle." Although the German word *läuten* is still in active use, *ringen* has become so common in the sense of "ring" that it is no longer understood in its original sense of "wrestle," and for this, again, the English word fills the gap.

If a person switches back and forth constantly between two languages, this merging of similar words is only too natural. It is very difficult to remember that *Rente* is different from *rent*, and even German professors use *Klasse* in the various senses of "class" (*ich habe zu viele Klassen*). Texas Germans are nearly always conscious of which words are English in their German, but there naturally are confusing cases where they are not sure or are mistaken. Since *fish/Fisch* are "the same" in German and English, some people think that *shrimp* is German as well as English. In a few instances a word like *Fenz*, plural *Fenzen*, has been so thoroughly Germanized, with German pronunciation, spelling, and plural, that the uninitiated could hardly be expected to know that it is an anglicism. As a matter of fact, technically it is not a "foreign word" any longer but a "(Texas) German word of foreign origin" (in regard to the two types, compare *détente* and *kindergarten* in English). Nevertheless, the basic fact remains that most English words used in Texas German (*Creek, Supper, Store*) are still recognized as such by the speaker.

To have such an insight into the speaker's linguistic thought processes is very important. In interviews we can ask our informants whether they consider a certain word to be German or English. In analyzing old documents, such as letters or diaries, we cannot consult with the writer, but often the alternation between "German" and "Latin" handwriting is used for the same distinction: words felt to be German are written in the standard Old German hand, while words considered to be foreign (which in Texas usually means English) are put into Latin characters much like English handwriting. Unfortunately, many printed materials (books and newspapers) did not make the distinction (though some did), but in handwriting the distinction was often made, even by people like farmers, who did not normally use much writing in their business. Thus, for instance, letters in my possession show that *Stor[e]*, in spite of its adaptation to German spelling, is still considered to be English, as demonstrated by the use of Latin handwriting for it, whereas *gemuft* ("moved"), whose spelling and inflection show full adaptation to German, is written in German handwriting, blending completely into its German context.

Merging of similarities also occurs in pronunciation. Really different sounds, like *ach* and *ich*, are not affected by English, but similar sounds, such as English *r* and German *r* and English *l* and German *l*, are usually not kept separate in an individual's speech. People whose German is stronger than their English will use the German *r* and *l* in both German and English (they speak "with a German accent"), while those whose dominant language has become English will use the English *r* and *l* also in their German.

It should be noted, in contrast to the common mergings of words and sounds, that German word order has remained almost totally unaffected by English. No Texas German would ever say *er hat gespent sein Geld* in English order, nor is there any loss of the German ability to start with other elements than the subject (*mein Geld hab ich verloren*).

Differences in cultures naturally cause problems for transplanted languages. The major problem of this kind for Texas German was in the German pronoun of address, *du* versus *Sie*. The German language makes social distinctions that American society, especially in frontier Texas, did not make. We have a hint of this problem in English in the use of first name versus last name, but the situation in German, though degenerating somewhat in recent years, is much more rigid—indeed, potentially socially catastrophic if the wrong pronoun is used. The German does not casually call an acquaintance by the first name or say *du* to the person. In English in any situation we say *you* to the other person. When one is speaking German in Texas, the distinctions of the pronouns clash with the informality of social life. My father-in-law once said, "If I see somebody in town that I don't know very well, I don't know whether to say *du* or *Sie* to them, so I often just talk English to them."

There is yet a third alternative of address. I was amazed the first time a man addressed me as *Ihr*. I had thought that this usage of *Ihr* as the polite form for one person had died out before the immigration to Texas, but it is still very much alive in Texas. In the "western focus" (as in New Braunfels) it is the normal formal pronoun, replacing *Sie* (or at least seriously competing with it). In the "eastern focus" it serves as a kind of middle ground between the intimacy of *du* and the formality of *Sie*. It is commonly used to address older people. (By the way, it seems natural in the German-speaking areas to talk German to elderly persons. I remember that at the community picnics the younger people might be talking English, but when my father-in-law walked up to them, they would instinctively address him in German and with the pronoun *Ihr*: "Wie geht's, Mr. Herbrich, ich hab Euch lange nicht mehr gesehn"—some people of Texas-German extraction must be surprised when they move to the big cities and find that not all people over sixty speak German.) The use of *Ihr* is, of course, older standard German and evidently not at all unusual for mid-nineteenth-century German; Sealsfield, for instance, used it as the common pronoun of respect between German-speaking cowboys in his famous *Das Kajütenbuch* (*The Cabin Book*).

With respect to the adoption of English words and the simplification of German grammar (as in the loss of cases), it is only natural to surmise that these tendencies progressively increased with time. Although this is undeniably true to a certain extent, I find an amazing stability of German grammar (even in the nonstandard usages) and vocabulary, and certainly no precipitous decline. One might think that the Texas-Germans used more and more English words in German until gradually it was more English than German, but such was not at all the case. I have estimated that Texas German never falls below 90 percent pure German; that is, the embedded English words never form more than one word in ten—in a count of more than one isolated sentence, of course.[3] The switch from German to English by an individual speaker is abrupt and conscious. Thus it is also for the linguistic community: German of relatively constant purity is passed from generation to generation, but finally bilingual parents raise monolingual English-speaking children. The transition is abrupt.

As a specific instance of the problems of possible linguistic decline, consider the lack of the dative case in the "popular level" of spoken and written Texas German. This is usually considered to be a loss that the German language suffered in Texas, hastened by the lack

[3] My estimate is only a rough guess; Jan Bender, "The Impact of English on a Low German Dialect in Nebraska," in *Languages in Conflict*, ed. Paul Schach (Lincoln: University of Nebraska Press, 1980), p. 84, makes a similar estimate on the basis of word counts.

of cases in English.[4] However, many old letters I have seen that were written by the ordinary people would indicate that the dative case had been lost by the common people long before the immigration to Texas. Only the publication of a great body of everyday Texas-German documents will allow an accurate answer to this and other such questions.

To heighten our appreciation of Texas German, we need to call attention to the former great strength of the German language in Texas. Most Texans are now unaware that many thousands of Texans, several generations of them, lived their entire lives as Germans, using German for almost all purposes. German was extensively used even for many "official" purposes. The churches, the communities, the schools, the social clubs operated in German; all correspondence was in German; all documents and periodicals were in German. Histories of the churches (of individual congregations as well as of the church bodies), such as those published on anniversary occasions, were in German— not as German translations or parallel versions but as the only forms. This exclusive use of German for such purposes continued into the 1930s and sometimes even later. Such "official" documents as certificates of baptism (the equivalent of birth certificates) and marriage, and the churches' death records were in German. Even today these documents are accepted by state offices as proof of birth, marriage, or death. The oil drilling activity in the Giddings area a few years ago caused a rash of inquiries into the churches' old German record books to clarify inheritance and landownership questions. The beautiful old ceritificates now frequently adorn the walls of the homes of descendants. The most eloquent and visible documents, however, are the stately gravestones, with their often lengthy inscriptions, including hymn verses and Bible passages. At least thirty-five Texas towns had a German-language newspaper, and some had several.[5] Four German newspapers lasted through World War II and several years beyond, until about 1950. Some state documents, such as the proclamation of secession, reportedly were published by the state in German as well as

---

[4] For a discussion of varying opinions, see Glenn Gilbert, "Dative and Accusative in the German Dialects of Central Texas," *Zeitschrift für Mundartforschung* 32 (1965): 288–96.

[5] See the listings for Texas, which span pp. 614–35, in Karl Arndt and May Olson, *German-American Newspapers and Periodicals, 1732–1955*, 2nd ed. (New York: Johnson Reprint, 1965).

in English. The congregational meetings of the Wendish-Germans at Serbin were held in German until 1966, and then bilingually in German and English until 1969. The Wends were so accustomed to using German as the language of government that when they applied as a group for citizenship they made up the necessary statement in German (on this occasion they did not come up against the right clerk at Bastrop—they were told to go home and get their request translated into English). Apparently some Czechoslovakian groups, or at least some individuals, also used German at times; for example, Joseph Ernst (Arnošt) Bergmann, called the father of Czech immigration to Texas, wrote his short autobiography in German, in the form of the typical German *Lebenslauf.*[6]

To illustrate the "generations" of Texas German, consider a typical family (one line of the ancestors of my wife, Adele Herbrich/Herbrig) of Wendish-Germans. The first generation is represented by a person who came from Germany as a teenager in 1854; he spoke German (and possibly Wendish) and never learned English. His children, the second generation, were born in Texas about 1865; they spoke only German and never learned English. The third generation (that of my wife's parents), born about 1885, learned English, some poorly, some quite fluently, but German remained their primary language all their lives. Some of these people are now in their nineties. Members of the fourth generation, born about 1920 to 1930, were reared in German homes and community settings, they were confirmed in German, and some were even married in German; they were exposed to a considerable amount of English even in their early years, and their school language was more English than German. After their childhood years English became the language of the world around them, and they themselves have become more comfortable in English, though they can still speak German fluently and normally speak German to their parents. Their children, the fifth generation, born about 1940 to 1960—that is, the current generation of younger adults—were reared almost completely in English, with almost no contact with German church services or other environmental exposure to German. They may know a considerable number of German words and phrases, but for all practical purposes they must be considered monolingual English-speakers.

[6] Manuscript copy made available to me by Albert Blaha, Houston.

This sketch is typical for the more German-oriented of the Wends and for the non-Wendish Germans of the area. With modifications to show the stronger use of Wendish in the first two or three generations, the same patterns hold true for those Wends who were more Wendish-oriented. The early generations were bilingual in Wendish and German, but usually by the third generation a monolingual German generation had arisen that was completely merged with non-Wendish Germans. Since ethnic identification primarily follows language usage, from that point on the people considered themselves simply German.

One noteworthy and probably obvious fact emerges from such generational studies: in this kind of natural language transition everyone in the group or family is always able to understand everyone else. German-speaking grandparents can talk to their bilingual grandchildren. Only after the monolingual German generation has passed away does there arise a monolingual English generation.

The effect on Texas German of the two wars with Germany and of other manifestations of anti-German and anti-foreign language sentiments has not been resurrected. Frederick Luebke's excellent "Legal Restrictions on Foreign Languages in the Great Plains States, 1917–1923" touches only briefly on Texas.[7] Luebke writes that Texas was among at least seven states which even in the pre–World War I years passed laws obliging teachers to use English exclusively in their instruction. He states that the Texas law was passed in 1905. This law clearly had little effect on the use of German in the German Lutheran schools and probably in most other German schools (in 1905 one might just as well have passed a law ordering leopards not to be spotted). Luebke reports an instance of the beating of a pastor for preaching in German in Nueces County (in the western focus), and we could research the newspapers to learn the prevalence of such incidents. My impression is that the English-speaking people in the eastern focus were more understanding toward their German neighbors.

I have not studied the newspapers, but I have searched the minutes of the congregational meetings of Serbin for the World War I years and found only one brief mention, after the United States' entry into the war, to the effect that the state officials had requested that the Ser-

---

[7] Frederick Luebke, "Legal Restrictions on Foreign Languages in the Great Plains States, 1917–1923," in *Languages in Conflict*, pp. 1–19.

bin people try to conduct their school in English. There is no mention of any objection to the public use of German in the churches or in the congregational meetings or church records, and this use continued unimpeded. I have also searched in the Serbin cemetery and found the uninterrupted, nearly exclusive use of German-language inscriptions in 1917 and 1918. There is even one gravestone of a young soldier, showing a porcelain picture of him in his doughboy uniform, with the tragic and ironic inscription "geboren in Serbin, gestorben in Frankreich" ("born in Serbin, died in France"). There are even German inscriptions from the World War II years, and the latest German inscription I have found is from 1964, 109 years after the immigration. The Wends and other Germans of these areas saw no problem with being German and patriotic Americans at the same time. Many German groups in the United States did not fare as well, of course. Luebke reports that more than 1,500 German Mennonites left the German Plains states in 1918 and resettled in Canada, where they found the freedom denied them in the United States.[8]

As mentioned, Texas German is very similar to other forms of American German, including, to a great extent, the use of the same anglicisms.[9] Even more remarkable, however, are the great similarities to other American immigrant languages. This is especially striking in the anglicisms: in American Norwegian, for instance, we find *boss, ranch, gallon, all right, supper, country, corn, crop, fence,* and *gate;*[10] in American Swedish: *fence, store, porch, lika* ("to like," similar to Texas German *gleichen*);[11] in American Danish: *car, road, fence, fix, creek.*[12] Naturally there are also some differences in the various languages in their use of anglicisms, in part because of the presence or absence of similarities of native words in those languages to English

[8] Ibid., p. 10.
[9] Cf. Lester Seifert, "The Problem of Speech-Mixture in the German Spoken in Northwestern Dane County, Wisconsin," in *Transactions of the Wisconsin Academy of Sciences, Art, and Letters* 39 (1949): 127–39.
[10] Einar Haugen, "Frontier Norwegian in South Dakota," in *Languages in Conflict,* p. 23; Kjell Johansen, "Some Observations on Norwegian in Bosque County, Texas," in *Texas Studies in Bilingualism,* ed. Glenn Gilbert (Berlin: de Gruyter, 1970), p. 175.
[11] Folke Hedblom, "Swedish Dialects in the Midwest: Notes from Field Research," in *Languages in Conflict,* pp. 37, 45.
[12] Donald Watkins, "Danes and Danish on the Great Plains: Some Sociolinguistic Aspects," in ibid., p. 61.

words. But the striking fact remains that a central core of English words was adopted into every immigrant language.

The lack of linguistic appreciation by others and by the people themselves also seems to be shared by all American immigrant groups. The use of anglicisms is similarly castigated. Hasselmo, for example, maintains: "It is rather strange that the Swedes in America are considered to be lacking in culture because . . . they mix a little English into their Swedish, when in Sweden it is actually regarded as a sign of culture to be able to use as many English words as possible," and he decries the opinion of some who believe that "when the beautiful Swedish and the not so beautiful English language form a union, a misshapen monster is born."[13] Swedish-Americans commonly said, "We don't talk fine Swedish."[14] As with the above-mentioned periodic abandonment of German because of its *du/Sie/Ihr* distinctions, Swedes felt liberated by English from old social classes: "When we talk English, . . . we are more equal."[15] Texas German was in a better situation than American Swedish and some other immigrant languages, because among the German immigrants in Texas there were no serious dialect differences from one community to another. The Swedes, on the other hand, often clustered as dialect groups, speaking their home dialect rather than the more unified standard language. This caused additional problems for the American Swedes. First, their use of dialect contributed greatly to the lowering of their own linguistic self-esteem and the respect of outsiders: "In English they speak as well as anyone else; if they open their mouths for Swedish, they talk peasant language, of which they are ashamed."[16] Second, the various dialect groups sometimes ridiculed each other, and again English provided a convenient escape.[17]

Texas German also offers a number of comparisons with Texas Spanish that could be most instructive for the speakers of Texas Spanish and also for the English-speaking majority. Texas Spanish is alive today in the way that Texas German was at its peak, at the turn of the

[13] Nils Hasselmo, "The Linguistic Norm and the Language Shift in Swedish America," in ibid., pp. 50–51.

[14] Hedblom, "Swedish Dialects in the Midwest," p. 36.

[15] Hasselmo, "The Linguistic Norm," p. 54.

[16] Ibid.

[17] Hedblom, "Swedish Dialects in the Midwest," p. 41.

century, with new monolingual speakers entering the state every day.
Like all other immigrant languages, there is a lack of appreciation of
Texas Spanish, both by speakers and by nonspeakers. From my own
experience and from the studies I have seen, I believe that the quality
of Texas Spanish and Texas German is much the same and that the sympathetic observer will conclude that Texas Spanish is pretty good Spanish. In a study by Janet Sawyer, an educated Mexican-Texan is described as follows:

> She was highly critical of the "Tex Mex" that her San Antonian friends
> spoke, disapproving particularly of the way they "threw English words"
> into Spanish sentences. However, study of her interview materials re-
> vealed little or no differences between her Spanish and that of the other
> Latins in basic phonological structure and grammar. What did become
> clear was the fact that the other Latin informants, who knew only infor-
> mal, oral Spanish, supplemented their communications with English
> words and, as a result, felt ashamed of their Spanish as well as their En-
> glish. This linguistic embarrassment was felt by all of the Latin informants
> with the exception of this lady. . . . During years of contact with Spanish-
> speaking students from Central and South America at the University of
> Texas, the author [Sawyer] observed a sharp difference between the pride
> and confidence that the foreign student[s] felt for their language and cul-
> ture and the insecure embarrassment which the Texas speakers of Spanish
> exhibited. The Texans avoided contact with the foreign students.[18]

In regard to other informants Sawyer again mentions their "reluctance
to speak Spanish to non-Texans, that is, to natives of other Spanish-
speaking countries."[19]

To speakers of Texas Spanish who wish to preserve their Spanish
language, I would give the advice to learn some lessons from Texas
German: Teach each other and your children to appreciate Texas Spanish; teach your children as much standard Spanish as possible, but not
that they should give up their Texas Spanish for standard Spanish—
that is impossible anyway. Do not ridicule them for their anglicisms.
Let them read their Spanish with the same pronunciation they use at
home. Remember that we do not try to make Texas Anglo children read
English with a British accent. Surely Texas German would have sur-

---

[18] Janet Sawyer, "Spanish-English Bilingualism in San Antonio, Texas," in *Texas Studies in Bilingualism*, p. 24.
[19] Ibid., p. 25.

vived longer in many places if there had not been frequent carping by parents and teachers about what poor German the children spoke.

The experiences of Texas German can also help the English speaker have more understanding for the linguistic situation of the Texas Spanish. From the Texas-Germans we can understand how immigrants can preserve a love for their old country and for their native language and still be patriotic Americans. We often read and hear, "Let these people learn English, as my grandparents did"; however, it should be remembered that many of our grandparents had no intention of learning English. They formed their German colonies for the express purpose of continuing their lives in the German language. We also hear, "English is the language of this country"; again, our foreparents knew that English was the language of government and of the majority, but the people of the country spoke all kinds of languages, and the freedom to speak one's own language was a basic American right. In 1923, after many repressive laws against German and other languages had been passed during and after World War I, the U.S. Supreme Court reversed many of them, stating that the liberty to use immigrant languages, especially in schools, was "a right long freely enjoyed."[20]

As for our grandparents learning English as a model for the Texas Spanish today, we might consider that if the Hispanic Texans follow the example of the Texas-Germans, today's Spanish-speaking immigrants will never learn English, nor will their yet unborn children; their grandchildren will learn English but will still be primarily Spanish-speaking. Their great-grandchildren, about a hundred years from now, will still be bilingual, but stronger in English, and their great-great-grandchildren finally will be monolingual in English. Following the model of the Texas-Germans, Spanish will be the language of their churches, weddings, and newspapers until approximately the year 2070.

Looking toward the future of Texas-German studies, there is reason for optimism. About five years ago a new wave of public interest in Texas German began, and we are still riding the crest of this wave. Several elements contributed to this new interest: World War II was finally being put into historical perspective, and people were again proud of

[20] Luebke, "Legal Restrictions," p. 15.

their German heritage. Contributing to this pride was and is the position that West Germany has again emerged as an economic and moral leader among the nations of the world. The "roots" phenomenon is part of it too, even though, unfortunately, the "roots" phenomenon itself is basically a demonstration of the general law that cultural manifestations are taken for granted while they are alive and appreciated only when they are dead or dying.

About five years ago the German-Texan Heritage Society and the Texas Wendish Heritage Society were formed. Today these societies are prospering, with hundreds of members; the Wendish Society has a thriving museum, and the German-Texan Society has a two-day annual meeting and a splendid popular journal, its *Newsletter*, which appears several times a year. Each issue of the journal brings articles on language, folklore, history, genealogy, and so on. How refreshing it is to know that there is actually a public eager to read what we have to say, instead of feeling, as in the past, that our research is read—if at all— only by a few university professors.

This surge of public interest has yielded a spate of research by enthusiastic nonprofessionals. They translate old documents, compile family histories, and write and review books. Obviously the quality of this research varies, but all of it is extremely important. Clearly what is necessary is close cooperation between these lay researchers and academic people, so that we can help each other reach and maintain good-quality research. (It is unfortunate and embarrassing to have to note that too frequently, books in English about the German heritage make glaring mistakes in German words and names cited).

We need new journals. There should be a journal of high-level research studies, similar to the *Yearbook of German-American Studies*, but exclusively for Texas German. The *Newsletter* of the German-Texan Heritage Society is doing a splendid job on the popular level, but too few libraries subscribe to it because it is incorrectly seen to be more of a newsletter than a permanent reference work. There should also be an archival journal devoted to the publication of source materials—old documents, letters, diaries, anything we can find—in the original German, and transcriptions of recorded interviews. Most of these source materials seem as trivial today as that scrap of Crimean Gothic did in 1560. To understand the Texas-German language and its history, its rise and decline, the lessons it offers to other languages and to future generations, we need thousands of accessible pages of the old letters and documents and hundreds of interviews. And such apparently trivial materials also contain a wealth of information on customs, attitudes, and many other aspects not just of Texas-German life but of Texas and American life. At present much excellent work is being done in the way of English translations, but for research work we also need access to the original German documents. Ideally these documents should be published both in photocopy of the handwritten form and in transliterated German print, on facing pages. With the photocopying methods available today and the ability of research workers to typeset their own works on office computers, this kind of low-quantity publication is no longer impossible. The photocopy of the original handwriting is the indispensable source for serious study, because even the best transliterated German form may contain errors where the transcriber has misinterpreted the manuscript, and, as mentioned, the handwriting itself (German versus Latin) may offer valuable information. But the transcription into normal print can be a valuable tool; anyone who works with the old German script knows that there are great variations in handwriting, and one must often laboriously work oneself into each different hand. An accurate transcription, made by someone who has become expert in the particular hand and studied the document, is a helpful parallel to the photocopy of the original.

The newspapers and other printed works we already have are excellent source materials, but they represent a different level; they do not show us the German that was spoken in the homes. Even the "letters to the editor," we must assume, were corrected to what the editor considered better German.

We need a concentrated campaign of recording interviews with people who still speak Texas German. An admirable example was set by the Institute of Dialect and Folklore Research of Uppsala, which in the 1960s sent professional teams to investigate American Swedish, recording "over five hundred voices . . . with a combined recording time of almost three hundred hours."[21] Such interviews can preserve a wealth not only of linguistic information but also of folklore, oral history, and so on.

Only a considerable quantity of such published basic source mate-

[21] Hasselmo, "The Linguistic Norm," p. 33.

rials will allow us to answer such questions as the following: What is the size of the normal person's German vocabulary? What are the regional differences? What anglicisms are used? Do the German grammar and vocabulary show a steady decline of correctness and a steady increase in English words used?

The recent interest in Texas-German affairs has also yielded fruit in the schools and universities. Texas-German studies are gaining in prestige, more students and professors are becoming interested, and more courses are being offered. These courses are frequently given in English; they are meant to be studies of the Texas-Germans and their culture, rather than of the German language. This is good; lack of knowledge of German should not deter such studies. Nevertheless, we should encourage the pursuit of German as a "heritage study" for those of German extraction and for anyone else interested in the Texas-Germans. We could have intermediate or even elementary courses in German based on Texas-German writings. As mentioned, these writings are in standard German, with few of the anglicisms or other idiosyncrasies of the spoken language that have been under discussion here. They appropriately could form the basis of instruction in standard German, not that many students would become fluent in German, but they would at least know the basics of their ancestors' language.

Those with German heritage will see the language in many places. It is sad to think that many German descendants cannot read their grandparents' gravestones or their parents' certificates and letters, and that many Lutheran ministerial students cannot read quotations from Luther or the historical records of their church. One need not be fluent in German to be able to work with it, using a dictionary, in these situations. It is also sad to hear that schools in German communities sometimes offer Spanish but not German (it would be just as sad if it were the other way around—if a school in a Spanish community offered German but not Spanish). There are various reasons for learning foreign languages; surely learning the language of our grandparents should be high among our priorities.

Contributors

HANS GALINSKY earned his Ph.D. at the University of Breslau and was professor of Anglistics at the University of Mainz until his retirement in 1977. He still serves on examination boards for doctoral candidates at the University of Mainz. He has taught at several American universities and is the recipient of a number of awards, including the Distinguished Senior Scholar Award of the German Fulbright Commission and the prize of the Schiller Society in Breslau. He is the author of many articles and books, including *Amerikanisch–deutsche Sprach–und Literaturbeziehungen: Systematische Übersicht und Forschungsbericht, 1945–1970.*

THEODORE GISH is professor of German at the University of Houston, where he has taught a course on the Texas-Germans for several years. He has published several articles on Texas-German literary and historical topics, a monograph, *Germans in Houston*, and a critical edition and translation of the only Texas-German musical in existence, *Texas Fahrten (Travel in Texas)*, by the pioneer and cultural and civic leader, Hermann Seele.

ANNELIESE HARDING is art historian at the Goethe Institute, Boston. Born and educated in Germany, she earned her Ph.D. in art history at the Charles University of Prague and in 1977 was awarded an honorary degree from Suffolk University, Boston. She is the author of *German Sculptures in New England Museums, America through the Eyes of the German Immigrant Painters*, and essays on German architecture. She regularly lectures at the Busch-Reisinger Museum at Harvard University and occasionally at other New England universities and museums. In 1981 she was awarded the Cross of Merit of the Federal Republic of Germany.

HUBERT P. HEINEN earned his Ph.D. in 1964 from the University of Texas, where he has been associate professor since 1969. He has conducted extensive research on the German-Texan cultural heritage, and his publications include "The Function of the German Literary Heritage," "German in Texas Schools, 1849–1939," and articles and translations of poetry (including *Paths to*

German Poetry, edited with Lore B. Foltin) in addition to reviews in many journals. He is a member of the German-Texan Heritage Society and the Society for German-American Studies.

GILBERT JORDAN is a native Texan. He received his B.A. from Southwestern University, his M.A. from the University of Texas, and his Ph.D. from Ohio State University. He was professor of German at Southern Methodist University and Sam Houston State University for many years and wrote many English and German articles, essays, and books on German language and literature, such as a verse translation of Schiller's *Wilhelm Tell.* He now lives in Dallas, where he does private research, writing, and publishing. His recent books include *Yesterday in the Texas Hill Country* and *German Texana.*

GLEN E. LICH is the author of *The German Texans*, which received an award from the Texas Historical Commission in 1982. He was a consultant of the University of Texas Institute of Texan Cultures in San Antonio and since 1980 has been a professor at Schreiner College in Kerrville. He travels extensively in this country and in Europe, and writes and lectures frequently on folklife and literature of the Southwest, on visual aspects of history, and on German-American cultural exchanges.

INGEBORG RUBERG MCCOY was born and educated in Germany, and in 1972 she earned a Ph.D. from the University of Texas. She is associate professor at Southwest Texas State University. Her publications include articles on second-language acquisition, psycholinguistics, and German-Texan subjects as well as translations of German literary works. She is a member of the German-Texan Heritage Society, the South Central Modern Language Association, and the American Association of Teachers of German.

JAMES PATRICK MCGUIRE joined the University of Texas Institute of Texan Cultures upon its founding in 1967. For several years he was director of program management, and he is now research associate. A native of Austin, McGuire was educated at the University of Texas at Austin, St. Mary's University in San Antonio, and the University of London. He has written several articles on German-American painters in Texas and is also the author of *Iwonski in Texas: Painter and Citizen, Julius Stockfleth: Gulf Coast Marine and Landscape Painter*, and *Hermann Lungkwitz: German Romantic Landscapist on the Texas Frontier.*

GÜNTER MOLTMANN is professor of medieval and modern history (with special reference to overseas history) at the University of Hamburg. He was a student at the universities of Hamburg and Marburg and received his Ph.D. in 1956. In addition to teaching at the *Gymnasium* level, Moltmann has also taught at the University of Bielefeld and was a visiting professor at Indiana University. He has published numerous books and articles on German-American relations and German immigration to the United States. He was also the editor of the official collection of essays published by the Federal Republic for the tricentennial observation: *Germans to America: Three Hundred Years of Immigration, 1683–1983.*

DONA REEVES-MARQUARDT, professor of German at Southwest Texas State University in San Marcos, completed her Ph.D. in German at the University of Texas at Austin and did postgraduate work at the University of California, Berkeley, and at the University of Mainz. Her publications include books, articles, and translations in the fields of German Renaissance drama, foreign-language teaching, ethnicity, and multicultural studies. She has served as president of the Texas Foreign Language Association, was cofounder of the German-Texan Heritage Society, and was elected to serve on the National Executive Board of Directors of the American Historical Society of Germans from Russia. In 1981 she was named Texas Language Teacher of the Year by the Texas Foreign Language Association, and she received the Presidential Award for Excellence in Teaching at Southwest Texas State University in 1983.

LUTZ RÖHRICH received his Ph.D. from the University of Tübingen and did postdoctoral research at the University of Mainz. Since 1967 he has been professor at the University of Freiburg, where he now serves as director of the Folklore Department and of the German Archives of Folksongs. He has written many articles on folklore and is particularly interested in saga, fairy tales, and folk music. He is the author of *Handbuch des Volksliedes, Deutsche Volkslieder: Texte und Melodien*, and *Handbuch des deutschen Spruches.*

RICHARD SPULER is assistant professor of German at the University of Houston. His teaching interests include a course entitled "The German-American Experience." He has written a number of articles on German-American intellectual history, and he is also the author of *"Germanistik" in America: The Reception of German Classicism, 1870–1905.*

RICHARD THOMA has been associated with the German cultural and language organization, the Goethe Institute, for more than twenty-five years. In addition to serving in the United States, Dr. Thoma has served with the Institute in India, Nigeria, Pakistan, and Hong Kong. He is now on assignment at the Institute's headquarters in Munich.

JOSEPH WILSON, associate professor of German at Rice University in Houston, was educated at Rice University, the University of Stockholm, and Stanford University. Most of his publications have been concerned with the Texas-Germans, in particular the Wendish-Germans in Lee County; others have dealt with Old Germanic, computerized lexicography, and Texas archeology. He has spent research leaves at the universities of Kiel and Marburg with the aid of grants from the Humboldt Foundation. The Peter Foundation of Texas is currently giving grant support for his work on the Wendish-Germans.

Index